Sean Smith is the UK's leading celebrity biographer whose bestselling books have been translated throughout the world. His subjects include J.K. Rowling, Robbie Williams, Kylie Minogue, Justin Timberlake, Britney Spears and Jennifer Aniston. Described by the *Independent* as a 'fearless chronicler', he specializes in meticulous research, leaving his West London home to go 'on the road' to find the real person behind the star image.

Also by Sean Smith

Kylie: The Biography
Robbie: The Biography
Justin: The Biography
Britney: The Biography
J.K. Rowling: A Biography
Jennifer: The Unauthorized Biography
Royal Racing
The Union Game
Sophie's Kiss
Stone Me! (with Dale Lawrence)

Victoria
The Biography

SEAN SMITH

POCKET
BOOKS

LONDON • SYDNEY • NEW YORK • TORONTO

First published in Great Britain by Simon & Schuster UK Ltd, 2008
This edition first published by Pocket Books, 2009
An imprint of Simon & Schuster UK Ltd
A CBS COMPANY

1 3 5 7 9 10 8 6 4 2

Simon & Schuster UK Ltd
1st Floor
222 Gray's Inn Road
London WC1X 8HB

www.simonandschuster.co.uk

Simon & Schuster Australia
Sydney

A CIP catalogue record for this book
is available from the British Library

ISBN: 978-1-84739-316-6

Typeset in Baskerville by M Rules
Printed by CPI Cox & Wyman, Reading, Berkshire RG1 8EX

For Mum and Dad, much loved and missed.

Contents

Introduction

Spicing Up My Life: The Spice Girls in concert at the O2 Centre, London, Friday, 11 January 2008

The girl next to me leaned across excitedly. 'Look,' she said, pointing towards the front row. 'It's Brooklyn and his granddad.' She had come well equipped for this large arena – a pair of binoculars seemingly glued to her face. I followed her line of sight and, sure enough, a boy dressed in blue was standing up beside a casually dressed, silver-haired man. They may or may not have been Master Beckham and Mister Adams but, frustratingly, were a yard or two too far away to see clearly with the naked eye. I wasn't too sure I could identify them even with the Hubble telescope. My chatty informant, however, was, I thought, just the sort of person who sent in celebrity sightings to the 'spotted' columns of glossy magazines and tabloid newspapers. She continued, 'Now, is that Cruz or Romeo? I think it's Cruz in white and Romeo in blue.'

By now I was eager for a closer look at the most famous show business/sporting family in Britain today. Come to think of it, they are probably the most famous family of any kind. Having borrowed – snatched – the now communal binoculars, I could see that it was indeed Brooklyn and Victoria's father, Tony. And there was Nan Jackie, looking very glamorous. Victoria's younger sister, Louise, was dressed in red, chatting to a pretty little girl with a short dark bob whom I guessed was her daughter, Liberty. I thought it a splendid turn-out to support their daughter/sister/ mother/aunt Victoria. After all, it was not even the first night of the Spice Girls' tour. At least three burly minders patrolled in front of the stage, gazing impassively back towards the audience but Victoria's family seemed completely unaffected by the bodyguards just feet away as they chatted and laughed and kissed newcomers on the cheek.

The Spice Girls had no support act on this tour so this episode of 'The Beckhams' filled the time divertingly. The Beckhams remind me of *The Waltons*, the cornball television series of the seventies. At the end of each episode, the whole Walton family could be heard wishing each other goodnight. It must be like that in Goff's Oak when David, Victoria and the boys are staying with her parents. The Adams' family compound now comprises three luxury homes: one for the parents, one for Louise and one for younger brother Christian. Between them the siblings have six children. If everyone had to say goodnight individually, it would take until morning. The key difference, of course, is that *The Waltons* was set in the Blue Ridge Mountains of Virginia during the Great Depression of the 1930s, a million miles away from an affluent area of Hertfordshire where Victoria's father drove a Rolls-Royce years before she made her millions.

Even before the girls took to the stage, there was a tangible feeling of cheerfulness. This was an evening when the great British public were determined to enjoy themselves; from small children to elderly grannies they radiated expectation with a smile on its face. My thoughts drifted towards an evening at the circus or the pantomime – an anticipation that this was going to be fun. I couldn't see any of the nerdy grey men who come out of the woodwork when some ageing rock band takes to the stage again after a twenty- or thirty-year gap. Instead, a huge cheer went round the arena when a group of swarthy young men took their seats wearing their version of the Union Jack mini dress, made so famous by Geri Halliwell in her Ginger Spice heyday. This promised not to be a concert but an occasion.

The Spice Girls did not disappoint. From the first song, inevitably 'Spice Up Your Life', the famous five maintained a level of excitement that never flagged. The show was all bright lights, big city entertainment for the whole ninety minutes. It was unapologetically Las Vegas. They bombarded us with their hits: 'Who Do You Think You Are', 'Stop' and 'Say You'll Be There' followed each other in quick succession. Not only did I discover that I knew the melodies to all these songs but I knew all the words as well.

This was instant nostalgia and that, to my mind, is no bad thing. Nostalgia has become strangely contemporary, if that is not a non-sensical paradox. Like Take That, the other hugely successful revivalists, the Spice Girls seem just a blink in the past. It's little more than ten years since they burst on to the pop stage with 'Wannabe', which sold more than one and a quarter million copies in the UK alone. 'Holler', their last number one, was as recent as November 2000. That may seem far too early for a nostalgic reunion but my own rule of thumb for music is that a generation lasts five years. Lasting longer than one generation is a tall order for any act for a number of reasons; divisions within the group or between artist and record company are obvious ones but, perhaps more signif-icantly, fans grow up and change. There's a huge difference between a thirteen-year-old and an eighteen-year-old. Take That originally lasted five years, Boyzone and Wham also five years, Kylie's first incarnation with Stock, Aitken and Waterman was five years. The Spice Girls were top of the charts for four years and four months.

I quickly discarded my homespun analysis of the sentimental appeal of recent favourites because, as the concert began, there were some serious outfits to appraise. Victoria began the evening wearing a silver spray-on catsuit. She is probably not tall enough to be a catwalk model but she looks like a slender willow among shrubs when she stands alongside Geri Halliwell and Emma Bunton. Victoria is not much above 5ft 4in but Geri and Emma are petite at 5ft 2in, if that. Victoria moves likes a model, a study in ele-gant poise. Goodness knows how she manages it in those heels. The most extraordinary thing happened when Victoria had the rare opportunity to sing a solo line in a song. The volume of noise from the audience rose emphatically in the sort of crescendo that might greet a pinpoint pass from Beckham that puts Rooney clean through on goal. Throughout the night, every time that Victoria had the spotlight, the roar of the crowd left me in no doubt what-soever that her popularity somehow had far outstripped her four sidekicks'. The cheering quite obviously reflected a genuine affec-tion. Here is a key question I must answer in my search for the real Victoria Beckham: Why is she so popular? She seemed by far the weakest vocally. Fortunately, it mattered little, because the arena was filled with a wall of noise that made the voices sound eerily the same, except for Melanie C, who stood out in the bunch of mediocrity as much as she always did.

Emma Bunton was probably the second best singer. She wore some lovely, flowy designs that disguised the fact that she had recently had her first baby, a boy called Beau. Mel B, too, gave birth in 2007 and looked fantastic, fit and assertive – still quite Scary Spice. She had a sense of fun about her. Geri Halliwell was perhaps a tad too thin, although she looked very fit. She remains energetic. Melanie C, besides having the best voice, was also the most athletic, even if her costumes were the least flattering.

Superficially, one might think Victoria was the weakest. She never throws herself into the dancing, perhaps for fear that it would upset her poise and elegance to do so. She has an amazing strut but every pose comes from the catwalk manual of poses on the runway. Each of the girls did a solo number – Geri, for instance, belted out her number one 'It's Raining Men'. Victoria, however, just pranced up the stage as if taking part in a faux fashion show. I thought it was pretty stupid but no one seemed to care. It did give her the opportunity to smile close up at her children. I suddenly realized that David Beckham had sneaked in and was standing next to Cruz. How did I miss that?

Victoria obviously saw him, declaring, 'I love you David' and 'I love you boys' as she pranced about, striking a series of sexy poses. I wonder if that's part of her secret – being a sex bomb superstar as well as being mumsy. One could never describe Madonna, for instance, as 'mumsy'. I think it's an almost impossible combination to master and present believably to the general public. I can think of only one woman who managed it successfully prior to Victoria: Princess Diana. This might be a comparison to bear in mind as I explore Victoria's story. Diana, for all too short a period of time, was the most famous woman in the land. She had little discernible intellect or talent but something about her touched people. She was one of us, even though she was the daughter of an earl and a millionairess. I always recall the famous photograph of Diana and her young children on the water slide at Thorpe Park. I can imagine Victoria doing exactly the same thing, provided there were no photographers lurking. If there were, she would have to make sure she was appropriately styled.

The Spice Girls now have seven children between them – only Melanie C is not a mum – so the schmaltzy sequence of 'maternal' numbers was not as achingly cheesy as it might have been. Just before Christmas 2007, they had their kids up on stage during the performance of the number one 'Mama'. Victoria is on the record as saying that she is doing the reunion tour for her boys so they will know that their mother really was a pop star once upon a time. That's a motive very much in keeping with her public image, although the slightly cynical side of me might point out that the tour will also remind potential audiences in the US who Mrs Beckham, new resident of Los Angeles, California, is at a time when she wants promotion there.

The encore was a joyous affair, beginning with 'If You Can't Dance', an ironic title considering that dancing is one accomplishment all of the Spice Girls share. They are undoubtedly better dancers than singers. And then came 'Wannabe', the song that started it all. Victoria was the only one of the five not to get a solo line in the song, which I always thought a shame. They finished with a reprise of 'Spice Up Your Life' to spirited and enthusiastic applause. The old cliché 'good time had by all' rang true on this occasion. I noticed David Beckham slipping out with a bodyguard and his two youngest boys, one on each shoulder. He managed to beat the scrum. The rest of us, in exuberant mood and clutching our £15 ($30) programmes, wended our way back to the Underground station.

Thinking about things on the way home, I was struck by how approachable Victoria's stage persona was. When someone threw some Y-fronts on to the stage in front of her, she good-naturedly picked them up and said, 'I hope these are clean! I will give them to David and we'll re-use them . . . even if it's a shower cap! It's good to recycle.' It may not have been a quip worthy of Oscar Wilde but it displayed an easy natural quality that the catwalk posturing can sometimes obscure.

So, finally, I was left thinking three questions on the way home. What motivates her? What talents does she actually have? Why is she so popular?

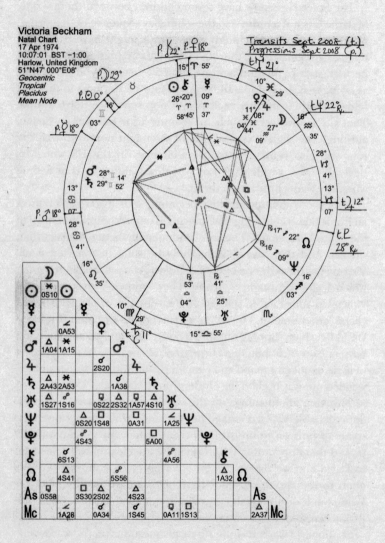

Victoria Beckham
Natal Chart
17 Apr 1974
10:07:01 BST −1:00
Harlow, United Kingdom
51°N47' 000°E08'
Geocentric
Tropical
Placidus
Mean Node

The Victoria Beckham Birth Chart

To arrive at an early understanding of how one would like to spend one's life is a fortunate thing. This is the birth chart of one such person – a woman with a sure and focused awareness of where she wants to go, delightfully determined about her goals, certain and cheerful about the great journey.

Victoria Beckham's birth chart is dominated by an intriguing, though not uncommon, pattern of lines which resemble a kite. The lines which make up this formation are links between many of the major astrological planets – the Sun, Moon, Saturn, Mars and Uranus. The Sun, the planet symbolizing the future, where we want to go and the person we are trying to be, sits at the pinnacle of this grand kite, in the fiery sign of Aries. It provides Victoria with a keen competitive instinct, whilst a neat little aspect to Saturn, the planet of endurance, means she will have the discipline to stay in the game. Victoria likes to lead, seems keen to be first and possesses apparent singleness of purpose.

The chart also reveals someone who has the capacity to be original but often isn't. Frequently, she will see this trait as belonging to someone else – her Sun sits opposite Uranus, the planet of individuality, and it is one of her lifetime tasks to develop this ability within herself. Those with the Sun sign Aries can be brilliant at picking up ideas without a second thought and running with them. As a rule, self-reflection isn't a major part of Aries make-up; where they are at any given time is good enough – a fine place to look forward to the next new project.

Paradoxically, the Uranus opposite Victoria's Sun, together with a few more difficult links to other planets, is actually of ultimate benefit to her. Part of the kite pattern in Victoria's chart is a triangle shape, a grand trine. These are aspects associated with luck.

Things come easily to such individuals, so easily there can be an inclination to just go with the flow. This may lead to a certain passivity and this is where more tricky aspects can provide weight and substance to the individual. Battles aren't bad; some conflict in a lifetime provides experience, growth and the opportunity to learn more about yourself.

Victoria's weak spots do revolve around her identity and individuality, something already suggested by the Sun–Uranus opposition. There is unquestionably a strong wilful element to her character which is determined to be different, although this instinct will sometimes conflict with a need to conform; so far, a standard Sun–Uranus tune. Additionally, that Sun sits next to Chiron, the planet known as the 'wounded healer'. Chiron the centaur, half man, half horse, was the son of a god and rejected by both parents. While this is doubtless not the case with Victoria, it is possible that at a young age she may have perceived herself as not being the centre of her parents' lives. It is possible they were young and coping with the vital practical demands of establishing the family unit. It could be just such a simple thing which contributes to the wound around identity, which those who have Sun–Chiron together in their chart generally feel.

One consequence of this might be that Victoria learnt to delight and please others in order to gain attention. A further typical behaviour would be the adoption of many different personas as one searches for a sense of validity, a search which is doomed, no matter what eminence is achieved. Additionally, the Sun symbolizes the masculine principle and energy within every person, the more assertive, extrovert, proactive side to one's character. As the Sun is compromised, we can expect a lack of confidence in these qualities within her and a likely preoccupation with finding a man who overtly embodies them. Such a partnership will enhance Victoria's sense of who she is, providing her with a sense of wholeness and purpose, albeit in a transitory way.

Chiron was brought up by Apollo, god of music, poetry and medicine, becoming a healer and teacher himself. However, the most central aspect of the centaur's story revolves around his inadvertent wounding, a terrible injury which would never mend and which he could not escape through death, as he was immortal. He was a creature who could heal others, but never himself – thus the wounded healer. The closeness of this planet, and all it symbolizes, to Victoria's Sun suggests that, like the mythic wounded healer, Victoria can help others with such problems but will never ease her own vulnerability.

This vulnerability does not just revolve around her individuality but also encompasses the way she looks. The awkward link between the Sun, a symbol of the ideal, and Venus, the planet of beauty and femininity, makes it likely that Victoria will never feel quite attractive enough. Of course, this is not unusual for women. These are standard-issue twenty-first century vulnerabilities. But Victoria is fated to explore the issues on behalf of all of us. The links between the Sun and Venus to the outer planets, suggest her involvement in generational concerns – one of these clearly being our attempts to halt the effects of time or even genetics on human appearance. In Victoria's chart, Saturn, planet of discipline, restriction and Mars (a symbol of cutting and surgery) sit together and link to the Moon, associated with the public. Even if Victoria has not pursued the plastic surgery route, her followers and fans will view her as the ideal end product of the surgical process.

Victoria's persona is dependent upon the hugely disciplined and inspirational presentation of her appearance, generating enormous praise, adulation and success, buttressing the sense of who she is. Getting lost in the dressing-up cupboard must have been a most glorious experience. However, as the chart suggests, this could be a double-edged sword, raising certain questions such as whether Victoria will be able to stop spending her life pleasing others. Is she born to serve through pleasing – or to find herself in rebelling, perhaps against what some of her public might see as society's definitions of beauty? It is a beauty which comes at a heavy price. That her wonderful sense of style and beauty is uplifting and joyous, bringing great pleasure to those who value fashion for the fun and creativity it brings to mundane lives, is clear from the delightful conjunction of Venus and Jupiter in her chart, a link which is also associated with commerce and wealth. Ultimately, this woman, who mirrors back what a generation has done to itself, but who has a superb sense of timing (identified by the Saturn/Mars links to the Sun), and awareness of the public mood, will move on; the chart gives manifold indications of this as I detail further on.

Victoria's chart suggests she benefited from a stable parental relationship. Whilst each parent played a very different role in her life, they both shared particular character traits; for example, a certain unpredictability and quickness in terms of their emotional response to things. One would expect a volatile home but one with united parental goals and beliefs and plenty of spontaneous fun. It is likely that mother was kind-hearted, sympathetic and keen to help, a protective influence, although with an element of detachment to her nature. Probably she found it easier to relate to Victoria as she reached adolescence and adulthood. Almost certainly, to Victoria, she was busy, her interests spread widely. Perhaps Victoria needed to grow up quickly, becoming self-sufficient emotionally at an early age, not always getting a strong sense of her own personal importance. This might be an effect of the arrival of younger family members. A link between the Moon and Saturn is common in the charts of those who are sensitive to their mother's needs, who consequently seek to please. As an adult, Victoria will remain in need of others' approval, an element of vulnerability in terms of emotional confidence being a deeply rooted part of her personality, which will see her turning again and again for validation to her public. It is pleasing that a benign link between Mars and the Moon indicates that whatever issues create annoyance or anger between Victoria and her mother will be easy enough to confront and resolve. Similarly, Victoria's public will be supportive of any firm handling of crisis she may experience in her personal life – firm is what they expect and what she has the courage and honesty to deliver.

To Victoria, her father appeared unpredictable. Alongside this sometimes disconcerting trait, Victoria would have appreciated his highly individual personality. He is a man with a competitive streak, the courage to match his ambitions and authoritative firmness. There are strong links between the two planets, the Sun and Saturn, which represent father in the chart, with this latter forming a difficult link to Pluto, an astrological symbol of power. Part of the picture which emerges is one of high parental expectations of Victoria and indeed, challenges, which at some level she is still attempting to meet. This is the birth chart of a young person, given many gifts by the gods, who has used them with courage and intelligence, travelling very far in a short space of time.

Victoria has recently been through an extraordinarily advantageous period; her aims in life and the development of her identity supported by a lengthy transit from heavyweight Pluto. The energy to transform and deepen her life would have been felt intensely around February 2006, progressing to a culmination in August 2007, with any projects initiated earlier manifesting successfully. At this time, Saturn, planet of ambition and recognition, together with Pluto, formed the most beneficial aspects to her Sun. In terms of Victoria achieving many aspects of her worldly quest, this was an optimal, never-to-be-repeated period.

In September 2008, Victoria will find herself ready for a new project; one involving, initially, the gathering of information and the forging of links with new social groups. There follows, in November, a potential clash with authority figures and the likelihood of important changes to her circumstances. In the sky, Pluto moves opposite Victoria's Saturn, prompting the possible surrender or loss of things she holds dear. The best response to the energy of this period is to let go of whatever she no longer needs; resistance will be fruitless. Victoria will find those she needs to help her through this period, without having to search.

The glorious grand trine – in the kite – in Victoria's birth chart will always come to her aid in times of turmoil, providing her with an inner balance, so that she can deal with pressure. This will stand her in good stead as the opening months leading up to her birthday in 2009 may be somewhat bumpy. On 17 April to the day, the progressed Venus, joining Chiron, indicates that Victoria will experience something very healing – or conversely a physical injury may force her to re-assess her health, leading to the beginning of a significant change of attitude. Essentially, life should remain exciting and dramatic, yet manageable, until approximately February 2010.

Here, Victoria enters a period of fairly major change, likely to bring endings and closure to aspects of her life. This change is brought about by something termed the Pluto Square, a tough transit, normally as comforting as a scalding bath. The effects of this will last, on and off, until October 2011. Everyone experiences this transit, it is part of a package that brings mid-life trials which challenges any sense of control we may feel we have established. Victoria is likely to experience power struggles, resulting in the death of obsolete aspects of her life. The influence of Pluto is non-negotiable, the more one fights, the greater the strife. One must retain integrity and accept we cannot determine everything and that certain forces and circumstances have a way of forcing humility upon us. Pluto is known as the planet of regeneration – before new growth can occur, there must be a dying off of things no longer needed for the future. Victoria will experience this at quite an early age – but it is a feature of her chart that she seems to arrive faster than most at important goals and turning points. Given her courage, natural sense of adventure and fortitude, one would expect Victoria to enter her forties with flair and real woman power, leaving behind that keen-to-please girl who so entranced generations with her stage talents in the 90s.

Madeleine Moore
June 2008

PART ONE

VICTORIA ADAMS

Victoria

The Biography

1

A Grand Design

Edmonton, a cough and a sneeze off London's North Circular Road, is a depressing area, just as it was when Victoria's father was growing up there in the fifties and sixties. Mind you, there was a sense of community then. The spirit of wartime still prevailed when Tony Adams was born in 1946. His house at number 97 Chiswick Road had no bathroom, an outside toilet and just two bedrooms, one for his parents, Bill and Winnie, and one for him and his elder sister Sheila. There was no heating.

Half a mile away was Edmonton Green Market, one of the great old markets of London. The house next door to the Adams's home was double-fronted, one of several in the neighbourhood specially designed for the marketers to bring home their stall and barrows and store them safely overnight in the front of the house. The market thrived post-war, as did the stately old pubs of Middlesex, several of which were near Chiswick Road – the Railway Tavern, the Cross Keys and the King William IV, known to the regulars as 'The William'.

Money was rationed in this working-class area of North London just as much as food had been during the war. These were austere times in Britain but you knew the name of your neighbours and chatted to them amiably in the street. The local factories were the lifeblood of the community. Factory workers would cram on to trains, using the 'Workers' Line' as it was called, to take them up to Enfield or south to Tottenham. In the evening, after tea, it would be down the pub – no computer games, no games consuls and, for the most part, no televisions.

In 1957, Prime Minister Harold Macmillan famously said, 'most of our people have never had it so good', which was small consolation for young Tony Adams, hanging around outside the pub waiting for his father to finish his pint. Sometimes he would be pressed into collecting cigarette butts from the overflowing ashtrays for his dad to smoke. Truly, Edmonton was a place to aspire to leave in order to make something of yourself in the world.

Families here pulled together and survived together. Tony might have had a Spartan upbringing but he developed a strong sense of family that has never left him. Local residents displayed pride in their modest surroundings. One neighbour never went on holiday, preferring to spend two weeks each summer painting the outside of his house. On the corner was a sweet shop, a favourite of the kids, and, a few paces further on, the grown-ups frequented the tobacconist's – all gone now. Unsurprisingly, Chiswick Road was one of thousands of streets that held parties to celebrate the Queen's Silver Jubilee in 1977 – perhaps the last time an overwhelming sense of innocent national fervour permeated through the country. Twenty-five years later, the Golden Jubilee, by contrast, was a strangely muted affair diluted by health and safety regulations, political correctness and national apathy.

Victoria's grandfather's name was William but everyone called him 'Bill'. He was a quiet, unassuming man who liked his pint, unlike his no-nonsense wife, Winnie, who was not one for drinking. When son Tony was born, Bill listed his occupation as 'rubber compound mixer, cable making', a job that would have stumped the panel on one of those old game shows like *What's My Line*. He actually worked in a local rubber factory, making different coloured rubber – an occupation a good deal more hazardous to his health than he realized at the time. In later life, he went down with the lung complaint emphysema, which eventually led to his death in his late seventies.

By the time Tony was in long trousers, the family had moved to the other side of Edmonton Green to a house in Lyndhurst Road. It was a distinct improvement, as it had a bathroom and an inside toilet. Bill had changed jobs, and was a capstan operator, responsible for shifting heavy loads in the factory. As a schoolboy, Tony earned some extra money with a newspaper round, the starting point of many a successful business career. Around him, the sixties ruined old Edmonton by bulldozing tradition and building tower blocks. The old market square was replaced with a large underground shopping centre, which these days resembles an oversized public convenience.

Tony, meanwhile, dreamed of becoming a pop star but left school to train as an electrician. North London had a thriving live music scene in the sixties, when the large pubs made excellent venues for smoky nights of rock 'n' roll and Beatles' covers. The most popular local band was The Migil Five, who had a top ten hit with 'Mockingbird Hill' in 1964, when Tony was an ambitious eighteen-year-old. They were well known around Edmonton and Enfield as the backing group for another local celebrity, the blind pianist Lennie Peters, who would later find fame as one half of Peters and Lee, winners of *Opportunity Knocks* and responsible for the tedious number one 'Welcome Home'. Rolling Stones fans will know that Peters, who died in 1992, was the uncle of Charlie Watts.

Tony's quest for musical fame would be very useful thirty years later when his daughter stood on the brink of success. He shone as the lead singer in two groups, first in the Calettos and then in the Soniks, which was mainly a covers band. They played local pubs, including the Golden Fleece, which was just a hundred yards from his home. The biggest gig they ever had was performing at the Lyceum, the famous ballroom off the Strand. Tony caught the attention of the legendary impresario and manager Joe Meek, the man responsible for one of the biggest hits of the sixties, 'Telstar' by the Tornados, which has the distinction of being the first US number one by a British group. That was in November 1962, more than a year before the Beatles conquered the States. Meek signed Tony to a contract but, unknown to many in the music business, Meek's life was falling apart because of money problems and allegations of blackmail about his homosexuality. In February 1967, he murdered his landlady, Violet Shenton, before killing himself with a shotgun. Theories abound about what really happened that

fateful day, which have inevitably added to the mystery and noto-
riety of it all. The problem for Tony Adams was that he was under
contract to Meek at the time of the latter's death and legal red tape
prevented him from recording for five years.

The disappointment must have been huge. Victoria revealed in
her autobiography, *Learning to Fly*, that her father had just finished
his first demo, a song called 'Redder On You', and was working on
the B-side when Meek died. The saga resulted in Tony Adams
always being extremely careful when it came to business and contracts – a trait inherited by his daughter.

Thwarted in his pop ambition, Tony turned to what he knew.
He was an electrician by trade, so he began working as a rep for an
electrical company. He had a plan, however, to start his own business as an electrical wholesaler. By now, he had even more of a
purpose to his life. He had fallen in love with a girl from
Tottenham, Jackie Cannon, whom he met at a party. Stanmore
Road was a better class of neighbourhood than Edmonton. Jackie,
an only child, grew up in a substantial Victorian semi directly
across the road from the local church. Jackie was a very popular
and good-looking young woman with long brown hair and a sultry
expression not unlike her daughter's teenage look. She was training to be a hairdresser when she started going out with Tony but
gave it up to work for an insurance company in Central London.

Jackie's father, George, was a stevedore, working in the docks
loading and unloading ships. He worked all hours to do his best to
improve his family's life, a work ethic that was very much followed
over the years by Tony and Jackie. Her mother, Dorothy, known to
all as 'Doll', was the musical one of the family, and played the
piano and the accordion. A neighbour recalls, 'He was more serious but she was very jolly.' Doll had a great ear for music and could
pick out the melody of a popular song after hearing it only a time
or two. Victoria loved all her grandparents but speaks with great
affection about her maternal grandfather. She described her
granddad as always being a gentleman, and she loved to visit the
house in Stanmore Road. She probably wouldn't recognize it now;
it has been converted into flats and is close to the kebab mecca of
West Green Road and Turnpike Lane.

Tony and Jackie married on 25 July 1970. The bride walked twenty yards across the road from her front door to the church, a beautiful building that is now also a block of flats. The newlyweds decided to start their married life away from London and bought a small house in Caxton Road, Hoddesdon, on the border of Hertfordshire and Essex and half an hour by car from Edmonton and Tottenham. It was a newbuild on an estate attracting first-time buyers and commuters with its proximity to the A10, London and work. The house was clean and tidy with a small garden at the back. The area is a little soulless but it was a good place for a young couple wanting to start a family. Victoria Caroline Adams was born on 17 April 1974 in the Princess Alexandra Hospital in Harlow, which technically makes her an Essex girl. When he got married, Tony described his occupation as a sales representative. When Victoria was born, he had upgraded to sales manager. He would soon be director of his own family-run business.

In 1977, when Victoria was three, Tony bought The Old School House, a few miles down the road in Goff's Oak. It needed a lot of work but had a large garage, which he foresaw being the hub of his new electrical supplies business. Tony was always one of those men who like to do things rather than just talk about them. He set about transforming the Victorian property into a mock-Georgian dream home, enlisting the help of Jackie's father, George, and friends he had made working as an electrician in the building trade. He was determined to plough every spare penny into his business, so saved money by doing the work himself, a labour of love.

Goff's Oak was still a farming area when Tony and Jackie moved there. The village gained its name from the local squires, the Goff family, and from a famous gnarled old oak tree that blew down during the hurricane of 1987. The Old School House was surrounded by fields. A pub, the Prince of Wales, was at the end of the street. The local St James's Church, always vying with the pub to be the focal point of the village, was across the road. Traditionally, this was as much of a working-class area as Edmonton to the south. Instead of the factories of North London, this corner of rural Hertfordshire had farms, and Goff's Oak was home to the legions of labourers who worked on them. The first proper school in the village was a church primary, opened in 1873, and early records reveal the children were 'all very backward'. When a new school was built in 1960, the original Victorian building became a private residence and one Tony and Jackie instantly fell in love with, even if Tony completely gutted the inside.

In the centre of Goff's Oak, as in so many towns and villages in Britain, stands a war memorial dedicated to the thirty-two local young men who lost their lives in the First World War. During the Second World War, a V1 doodlebug landed on Goff's Lane, destroying a line of cottages and killing five people.

Goff's Oak did have a small connection to the pop world that Tony had aspired to join in the sixties. One of the original members of Unit Four plus Two, Buster Meikle, came from the village. The band's number one hit 'Concrete and Clay' was one of the most popular songs of the mid-sixties. Tony, however, was much more of a Beatles man, and Victoria's childhood soundtrack consisted of Lennon and McCartney and her father's other great favourite, Stevie Wonder. Tony would dance his little girl around the house to the sound of the great Motown star's hit 'Sir Duke', an experience Jackie once said gave her daughter a love of performing. Tony never forgot those happy times and years later asked DJ Ed Stewart to play the track on his Radio 2 show as Victoria and David Beckham drove to the airport on the way to their wedding in Ireland. Jackie preferred Barry Manilow and Cliff Richard. Cliff spent his teenage years on the Bury Green Estate in Cheshunt and was the biggest name in pop associated with this part of Hertfordshire.

These days all the little villages and towns in the area seem to merge into one large commuter belt. Going up the A10 from Enfield towards Hertford and Ware is one continuous mash of traffic lights and roundabouts. Cheshunt merges into Broxbourne, which merges into Hoddesdon. Goff's Oak might still like to call itself a village but it is really a suburb. One commodity that Goff's Oak does have, however, is money. One ex-teacher at the local primary school observes witheringly, 'The inhabitants of this part of Hertfordshire are nouveau riche, affluent, materialistic and more than a little ignorant. Wait outside the school gates on any given day and you'd wish you had shares in a fake tan company and one making leather trousers. They are women with too much time on their hands. They have nothing better to do than shop and get their hair and nails done.' The area is almost exclusively white and none of the 200 plus children at the school when Victoria was there was black.

By the time Tony had finished his 'Grand Design', The Old School House was just about the nicest house in the village and the only one with a swimming pool in the garden. Over the years, the house has been joined by other lovely million-pound homes, as the old fields and nurseries have been built on and built up. The Old School House no longer stands out, although the family, who still live there, now have more land to the back. They have built two more houses, and live in close proximity to one another, rather like J. R. Ewing's family in the hit television saga *Dallas*.

The new school, built about three miles away in Millcrest Road, was where Victoria started her formal education. She was now the eldest of three children. Her sister Louise was born in November 1977; baby brother Christian followed in August 1979. Victoria was the first to don the brown and buttercup uniform, described by one classmate as 'rather grim' and another as 'rank'. She was driven to school in her father's old Hillman, which also doubled as his new company's delivery van. Throughout her schooldays, Victoria was pretty undistinguished. She was a quiet little girl who was a million miles away from the outspoken woman with the ready remark she would later become. She did not respond well to old-fashioned teaching methods, maintaining that her lack of confidence in reading was a result of harsh treatment by a teacher. An early humiliation in class over her reading might even have been responsible for a general lack of confidence that has plagued her ever since. She responded much better to Mrs Jane Hardy, her class teacher when she was six. One member of the class, Ruth Moor, recalls, 'She was a wonderful teacher and everyone loved her.' Another, Greg Stewart, says, 'Mrs Hardy was everyone's favourite. She drank cups of hot water, which at the time we thought was a bit wacky. She was very creative and loved to give us art projects.' One day Mrs Hardy brought in a little lamb that they named Lottie. Victoria joined the other children in looking after the animal. Lottie the Lamb was with them for several weeks.

With Mrs Hardy's encouragement, Victoria began to blossom, displaying an early talent for dancing and, more significantly, enjoying performing in front of the class. She recalled, 'No one did any work after lunch because she'd get me to do a dance on the carpet, with everyone sitting there watching me.' Academically, she was not the brightest. One former teacher recalls that she took extra lessons in reading, comprehension and spelling: 'She was poor at English, middle of the range at Maths but good at singing, drama and dance. She was not sporty.'

Every Christmas the school would put on a show and Victoria nearly always bagged a main part. One teacher, Sue Bailey, recalls, 'She always loved acting and enjoyed our drama lessons. We would improvise and do role play. She liked to sing and dance. She shone one year as Frosty the Snowman. She was a very sweet girl.' Sue did not realize that the 'very sweet girl' told the teachers she had the costume so that she would get the part and then went home and pleaded with Jackie to make it. Her long-suffering mother was up all night sewing.

Victoria's parents always did their best to be part of what was going on at the school, especially plays and fetes and harvest festival events. Sue Bailey observes, 'Her family were very supportive and her mother very helpful. Her mum and dad were very generous to the other children. All the children used to go down and have swims in their pool. They were great friends to everybody.'

Victoria was soon joined at the school by Louise. The two could not have been less alike. Where Victoria was shy and quiet, Louise was bubbly, bouncy and sociable – she even had a boyfriend at primary school. Louise summed it up, 'I liked being naughty. She was a teacher's pet.' The two sisters grew up, as siblings often do, in a permanent state of friendly hostility. They did not look much like sisters. Louise was freckly, small and ginger. Victoria was taller, skinny and brunette. They used to share a bedroom, the first of the rooms at The Old School House to be properly finished. Eventually, Victoria had her own room, primarily pink, which she described as 'very girlie'. The wallpaper was white with pink stripes, the bedcover was white and pink, and the carpet was completely pink. As she grew up, the posters of her favourite pop stars (Matt Goss) and footballers (Ryan Giggs) took their places on the walls. In these days before home makeovers, Tony and Jackie favoured neutral browns and comfortable sofas with big floral prints. They could not be too precious about furniture with three young children and three Yorkshire terriers – Bambi, Lucy and Truffle – causing havoc around the place.

Victoria did not give her parents a huge amount of concern growing up. She did cause a panic once when they thought she had meningitis but, fortunately, it turned out to be a severe bout of flu. On another occasion she had to be rushed to hospital when she accidentally swigged a cup of bleach. She recalls, 'I ran out to the garden where my mum was. "Stop being so rude, I'm talking to the gardener," she said as I was gasping away. She thought I was joking. Then she realized and the gardener held me up by my feet and shook me up and down to make me throw up, which is actually the worst thing to do, because it just brings the burning sensation back up. Finally Mum took me to the hospital and it turned out OK.'

The fact that the Adams family now had a gardener is further proof of how quickly the family's fortunes were transformed by the success of Tony's business. From a very early age, Victoria could see that hard work and prudence equalled success. She would never know the hardships that her father had endured growing up but she could appreciate the efforts he had made to change his life and his family's. She may not have seen as much of him as she might have liked because he was always working but she enjoyed a beautiful home and holidays abroad as a result of his labour. Neither Victoria nor her family was ever posh. Their roots are firmly working class but money gave the Adamses a more privileged and refined lifestyle. Success in this primarily white part of the Hertfordshire commuter belt is judged by material wealth – the size of the house, the burglar alarm on the front gates, the swimming pool in the back garden, the number of sports cars in the driveway. No wonder that the first thing Tony

Adams did when he made a few bob was to go out and buy a Rolls-Royce and stick a personalized number plate, '51 AWA', on the front. It was his pride and joy, although Victoria maintained she always hated it.

> **'My Dad's self-made. He worked very hard for everything he's got.'**

2

The First Rung

Victoria is not the first nor the last major star to have been inspired by the film *Fame*. So much youthful exuberance and optimism run through Alan Parker's classic 1980 movie that children all over the world dreamed of attending the High School for the Performing Arts in New York. Jennifer Aniston, for one, set her heart on going to the Manhattan school. Her life changed forever when she finally won a place there. Victoria, likewise, was determined to go to New York but in the end had to settle for something nearer home.

Fame followed the adventures of an assorted bunch of teenagers auditioning and then studying at the school. In approach it was old-fashioned, harking back to the Judy Garland and Mickey Rooney putting-on-a-show movies, although Parker did sprinkle it with a little teenage sexploitation, racial prejudice, drugs and violence. All in all, though, it was pretty tame and perfect for an impressionable girl in Hertfordshire. Jackie took her to see it when she was eight. Victoria wanted to be Coco, the multi-talented black girl played so memorably by Irene Cara. The Oscar-nominated theme tune 'Fame', which she sang, made such an impact on Victoria that she would call her autobiography *Learning to Fly*. The lyrics contain the words 'I'm gonna live for ever. I'm gonna learn how to fly. High!' Victoria bought Cara's number one record, stuck a poster of Leroy (Gene Anthony Ray) on her wall and tuned in every week to watch the TV spin-off. She even persuaded Jackie to take her to see The Kids From *Fame* on tour. Looking back, the

Spice Girls would have fitted into the film of *Fame* perfectly. They could have danced on the desks and sung in the streets with the rest of the students.

Victoria started to badger Jackie about going to a '*Fame* school'. The nearest thing her mother could find was a couple of miles down the road in Broxbourne. She came across the Jason Theatre School purely by chance when the family went to see a local pantomime and discovered that it was run by the school. Fortunately, one of Victoria's closest friends at the time, Emma Comolli, was keen to go as well, which meant Victoria did not have to face it alone. Emma's father used to be in a band with Tony and the families lived just a couple of miles apart, so, naturally, the children became friends. Emma also loved the TV series of *Fame* but only Victoria taped every one so that she could learn all the dance routines and songs by heart. That hard work paid off when Victoria performed a dance from *Fame* as the opening number of her junior school play. Another favourite was *Grease*. 'We must have watched the video twenty times,' recalls Emma. 'When we performed, Victoria would always have to be Olivia Newton-John, even though she was the dark one and I was blonde.'

The Jason Theatre School was founded in Enfield in 1951 by respected dance teacher Joy Spriggs. She chose Jason as the name of her school because it included her initials, J. A. S. In the late seventies, she opened a branch in Broxbourne. Elegant and poised, Joy Spriggs was going strong when Victoria first attended in 1982 and is still at the helm a further twenty-six years later. One of her students when Victoria was there, Kelly Fordham, observes, 'Joy was very vibrant with a strong personality. She was a force to be reckoned with!' Victoria and Emma had to audition in front of the principal and then, having been accepted, Jackie paid the registration fee of £2.50 ($5). The fees of about £300 ($600) per term were paid in advance.

Right from the first class, Joy Spriggs identified Victoria as one of most eager students: 'Victoria was really keen on The Kids from *Fame*. At the time, all the children wanted to do jazz dancing. Street dance and hip hop is all the thing now but then it was jazz, with the ankle warmers and the leotards and the colourful catsuits.

There was Hot Gossip on television and they wanted to copy that. It was the style of the time.'

Eight may seem very young to start dance training but, in fact, Victoria was well behind her contemporaries, most of whom had joined Jason when they were three. Joy recalls, 'She was quite a late starter and had to work really hard to catch up.'

Joy Spriggs has no time for the *X Factor* generation, the hordes of young wannabes who believe that reality shows are a shortcut to becoming famous. Victoria took no shortcuts. She worked her tap shoes off to improve. 'She did live for her dancing and her drama. Now, the ambition is just to become famous. But Victoria wanted to be a performer, to be on the stage, to be in films, to be on television. She just had this yen to do it.'

In the pre-reality TV days, the best way for youngsters to get on television was to write to shows. Emma recalls that they wrote to *Jim'll Fix It* to ask if Jimmy Savile would arrange for them to meet Toyah, who, although a regular on *Top of the Pops* at the time, was a strangely unexciting 'fix', which unsurprisingly did not register a response from the programme. They also wrote to a ghastly programme called *Mini Tots* in which kids performed as their favourite pop stars. Victoria worked out a routine for her and Emma based on the famous Eurovision Song Contest routine of Buck's Fizz, in which the guys ripped the skirts off the two girls. Again, they had no luck. Victoria was a fan of Buck's Fizz and would practise the routine at home with Louise. She even persuaded Jackie to make her a skirt like the ones worn by Cheryl Baker and Jay Aston. She wore it to school and performed the dance in the playground. At the appropriate moment, Louise whipped off the skirt.

To begin with, Victoria and Emma would go once or twice a week to the Jason Theatre School. The classes were held at various unglamorous-sounding settings around the area, like the scout headquarters in Wormley, the local sports club or, further afield, the Gentleman's Row Church Hall in Enfield. They started with one class lasting about forty minutes but this built up until Victoria was taking as many as three classes a night. Emma's enthusiasm started to flag as she became older but Victoria never lost her desire, even when her contemporaries became more interested in boys. She stayed with the Jason Theatre School until she was seventeen and by the end she was taking classes practically every night. She received a special medal that Joy gave to her longest serving pupils.

Over the years, Joy Spriggs has often been misquoted on the thorny subject of Victoria's talent – or lack of it. Sometimes the media decide they want to quote her saying she knew that Victoria was talented from the first time she saw her. At other times they want her to say that Victoria had no talent. She explains, 'These people phone up and they say, "Was she the most talented person you ever had?" I can't answer questions like that. I'm not going to say she is or she isn't because whatever I say is going to upset somebody. She had a certain natural ability and we just channelled it in the right way. Victoria would shine because she was a very pretty little girl with big, dark brown eyes and long, dark curly hair but she was a little bit self-conscious to start with. She was very vivacious but equally she was shy. She didn't hold back but she wasn't quite as outward going, not quite as confident as some of the others. We had to build confidence with her.'

Reading between the lines, Victoria may not have been the most talented dancer to ever grace the Jason Theatre School but she did have a natural ability that made it possible for her to make dramatic improvement through hard work, determination and old-fashioned practice. Quite simply, the harder Victoria worked, the better she became.

Victoria's first teacher at the Jason School was called Christine Shakespeare. She managed to motivate her young charge, and Victoria won the inaugural Shakespeare Shield in 1989, when she was fifteen, for 'dedication and good work'. Miss Christine, as the girls called her, did not hold back from warning Victoria at the outset that she would have to work hard in order to get anywhere. She echoed the philosophy of her employer: 'We don't blow people up and say you're going to be able to do this, you're going to be able to do that, because you don't know. We're just the grounding really, the first rung of the ladder.' Victoria freely admits that Christine was one of the most inspirational figures in her show business life. She took Victoria to the West End to see the most popular musicals of the time – *Cats, Miss Saigon, Les Miserables* and *Starlight Express*. These outings helped convince the young Victoria that she belonged on stage.

Jackie and Tony were not pushy parents. They were very proud of their children but there is no indication that they coerced Victoria in any way to work so hard at her dancing. The motivation for the traditional domineering mother dragging her child to talent contests and beauty pageants is a desire to change her own circumstances and to use her offspring as a means to achieve that. Jackie already had a life to envy – plenty of money, a beautiful home, a pool, a Rolls-Royce, three happy children, holidays abroad and, eventually, their own place in Spain. How different it might have all been if Tony had remained an electrician in Edmonton.

Instead of pushing Victoria, Jackie allowed Victoria to push her. Both she and Tony indulged their children. If Victoria had not loved her dancing so much, she could have left the Jason School, as her sister Louise did. Victoria was unusual for a child whose parents were well-off in that she chose to concentrate on one thing. Joy Spriggs explains, 'It's quite a wealthy area and the children do everything. They do dancing, they do horse riding, they do swimming, they do netball. Just trying to get them in for an extra class or rehearsal is so difficult. The parents say they want them to have all these opportunities and they dabble in lots of things and maybe they don't have the same motivation to go for one particular thing, like Victoria did. Her be-all and end-all was to come and do her dancing or her drama. She wanted to be on the stage.' For Jackie and Tony, it was enough to see their daughter thrive and perform. 'It's a wonderful experience to see your child on the stage,' says Joy. 'I don't care who it is, people love to see their children performing.'

Victoria had plenty of opportunity to perform, especially when the Jason School linked up with the local amateur dramatic society in the school's productions. She appeared in *Hello Dolly, Sleeping Beauty* and made a memorable munchkin in *The Wizard of Oz*. She also took part in the annual pantomime. Every couple of years the school held their big spectacular involving all the pupils and always called *Let Us Entertain You*. Almost all the productions were held at the Broxbourne Civic Hall, which may sound unpromising but was a serious, large and very professionally run theatre. Victoria found it daunting and exciting at the same time. Joy acted as compère, introducing all the numbers, whether they were the tiniest tot pretending to be a bee or the older girls displaying their prowess at ballet or dancing to the latest hits. Jackie and Tony would be in the audience, cheering with the other parents.

Often Victoria would be paired with a girl called Sally Brown because she was very blonde and Joy thought it made a nice contrast with dark-haired Victoria. The pair won a trophy together for their performance of Hans Christian Andersen. Sally performed 'The Red Shoes', while Victoria sang 'The King's New Clothes'. Joy recalls, 'Her personality really came through.'

Week after week, the Jason Theatre School proved a welcome escape from real school for Victoria. A proper academic education had not seemed so bad at Goff's Oak junior, where she had something in common with other children. A classmate explained, 'Most children had parents who were quite well off. I never really thought of Victoria as having money.' That all changed when her parents decided to send her to St Mary's High School, a working-class school where she stood out like a beacon. One parent observes, 'Goodness knows why they let her come here. Perhaps it was different thinking then. These days she would have been packed off to Roedean.'

Tony and Jackie Adams had plenty of money but their daughter went to the Cheshunt equivalent of Grange Hill. Perhaps education was not something they believed you should spend money on. They were happy to pick up the bill for her to attend a private dancing school. Nobody would have looked twice at a Rolls-Royce dropping off a smartly dressed young girl at a Home Counties public school but at St Mary's it immediately marginalized their daughter. A classmate observes, 'It was working class, predominantly white and probably reflected Cheshunt at that time.'

Victoria has always used her father's Rolls-Royce as a starting point to illustrate how she was isolated and ultimately victimized and bullied at senior school. It does pose the question why, if she had really wanted to, she didn't catch the school bus like many of her classmates. She has claimed that she hated the Rolls-Royce, never wanted to go in it and was thoroughly embarrassed by it. She has maintained that the car was brown and not gold – it may well have been more brown than gold – as if that made it less of a Roller somehow. The simple fact is that being faced with this sort of privilege probably did aggravate a few of her classmates but not in a major way. Ruth Moor, who also went to St Mary's, says the Rolls-Royce was not much of an issue. She recalls, 'To be honest there were very few occasions she got dropped off in her dad's gold Rolls. Her mum drove an ordinary Renault Espace and then changed to a sporty Mazda. I suppose a few eyebrows were raised when her dad did pick her up but it happened so rarely it was no big deal really.'

It might, however, have alienated a million potential Spice Girls' fans to hear of Daddy dropping her off in the Rolls-Royce, whatever colour it was. There is a world of difference between earning the money yourself and being presented with it on a plate – there is nothing whatsoever Girl Power in having rich parents. Victoria has always been very careful not to describe any memorable days beginning with a ride in the Roller and ending with a dip in the pool.

Her careful, self-deprecating approach also involved calling herself a 'right idiot' for wearing the proper school uniform on her very first day at school. She looked shiny and smart in a blue blazer with the school crest, red tie, white socks, black shoes and grey and black kilt. She also had a brand-new school bag. In short, she looked like any eleven-year-old girl being sent off to school by very proud parents. They even took a picture of her smiling in the garden before she set off. She did look as if a well-aimed custard pie might have improved things.

Emma Comolli recalls that, unwisely, Victoria would talk about how rich her family was and how she was going to be famous one day. It amounts to little more than naïveté from a well-protected girl. 'The other children would turn on her and call her names,' says Emma. Another girl says simply, 'Victoria was considered snooty.' Many of her classmates blossomed at St Mary's under the splendidly eccentric stewardship of headmaster Tony Rowan-Wickes. One of

Victoria's contemporaries, Steve Chapman, recalls, 'He was a tall guy with a grey beard and long, grey, flowing shoulder-length hair. He smoked but never in front of the kids.' Mr Rowan-Wickes was very popular with the boy pupils because he allowed them to grow their hair long and scruffy in the style schoolboys prefer. His clearest recollection of Victoria is that she was 'very quiet' and never joined the naughty queue outside his study. He recalls, 'She was just a very sweet girl.'

There are always two sides to everything and many thrived at St Mary's, embracing the strong music department, sport and field trips. The school also put on lavish dramatic productions. Victoria danced in two of them, *Les Miserables* and *Jesus Christ Superstar.* Ruth Moor recalls, 'They were good shows and she was good in them.' Another big budget show, called *The Dracula Spectacular,* had smoke machines, radio mics and other special effects. Victoria was not in it; she preferred to concentrate on the Jason School events. The first boy she ever dated played the lead. He was an American boy, memorably called Franco McCurio, who came to the school when his father was appointed the minister at the St Mary's Church that was right by the school entrance in Christchurch. Throughout her school career Victoria had to go to a church service once a week.

Franco was a breath of fresh air at St Mary's. Steve Chapman recalls, 'He was quite a novelty to everyone. At the age of eleven to fifteen, American accents are very cool. I remember he had quite a solid build, not fat but muscular. He wore glasses with black rims.' Franco looked older than the other boys at school, which gave him a head start where the girls were concerned. He was the sort of boy whose personality would be described as larger than life. Ruth Moor confirms, 'Franco was a lovely guy and quite popular.' He took 'Vic' to see a movie in Waltham Cross. The rather comic thing about the date was that it was the first time Victoria, aged fifteen, had ever been on a bus. It may well be the only time. The date was not helped by Franco's dress sense – baggy jeans, white socks and a tucked-in T-shirt. Rather unkindly, she later referred to him as a 'dweeb'. They had only one date.

Bullying is very much in the eye of the beholder. What one child might laugh off, another might find a nightmare. Ruth Moor recalls that there was the usual amount of bullying in a school with a few bitchy girls, but adds, 'When I hear what goes on in schools now, it was a breeze back then.' The full extent of Victoria's victimization at St Mary's is a bit of a grey area but her isolation and upset as a result of her treatment is much more black and white. Cynics may note that celebrities invariably reveal that they were bullied. Both Geri Halliwell and Melanie Chisholm were beaten up at school, while Victoria had to get teachers to walk her to the Rolls-Royce so that the girls waiting for her at the gate could not get their hands on her. One of the catalysts for aggression towards Victoria was a temporary crush she had on a boy called Glen. Apparently his girlfriend and her cronies took great exception to this and were determined to let her know it.

Ironically, it was left to kid sister Louise to stick up for Victoria, although she tellingly recalls, 'I don't think she was bullied that badly. She got a bit of verbal abuse, but it wasn't anything major.' Victoria does not remember it like that, claiming she used to dread going back to school after the holidays. Louise never had any problems at school. She had plenty of friends, including boyfriends, was well adjusted and apparently had a normal time.

The relationship between the two sisters has ebbed and flowed over the years. They were both totally different growing up. Louise fitted in, whether it was having a smoke behind the bike sheds or going out clubbing or chatting up boys. They used to have big arguments at home and, with disarming honesty, Louise admits that she took no notice when Victoria would twitter on about wanting to be a dancer on the telly.

The different personalities of the two sisters highlight why Victoria had a tough time at school. Simply, Victoria was never one of the girls, whereas Louise was. Victoria had a natural shyness that could be exploited by her peers. Beneath her apparent vulnerability, however, was a girl who was thoroughly determined and as tough as old boots. Her motto might be: 'I'll show you!' One of the first times the star of the future was captured on film was at the Jason School, dressed in top hat and tails, dancing to the classic 'If They Could See Me Now'.

Away from the perimeters of St Mary's, Victoria continued to flourish at the Jason School, spending more and more time there, especially in the holidays. Many of the good friends she had as a girl went to Jason with her: Louise Pickering, whose mother ran the Flash Dance shop in Hoddesdon, where the young dancers would all be kitted out with shoes; Lorraine Weatherhogg, whose parents were great friends with Tony and Jackie and who would later go to Victoria's wedding; and Lynsey Britton, who is now patron of the school and a West End star.

Victoria saw her dancing as a means of escape. She had no escape, however, from a problem that began to plague her as a teenager and has stayed with her – she had terrible spots. She had the worst skin of anyone she knew at school. She later confessed, 'I was bullied at school because I had bad skin, so I wasn't confident about the way I looked back then.' In the same way as a child with spectacles is always called 'Four-eyes' by the other kids, Victoria had to suffer all manner of name-calling, from 'Acne-features' to 'Crater-face'. Joy Spriggs is very pragmatic about it: 'They all go through that, don't they? I think some of the press have been quite beastly to her about that really. They seem to delight in showing horrible photographs of her. I wasn't aware of her spots any more than the other girls. It didn't occur to me, you just get on with what you're doing.'

Spots, bullying and isolation have led Victoria to be very harsh on St Mary's. Not everyone struggled along and, as her classmates pointed out, if it was so bad Tony and Jackie would not have sent Louise and Christian there. Victoria's passion for dancing was a double-edged sword. It gave her a sense of escape but it also meant she seldom socialized with her contemporaries at secondary school. As one friend put it, 'It's just one of those things that if your face doesn't fit, then there is nothing you can do about it.'

'I think children are really mean.'

3

Mark

Victoria was sixteen and had never had a proper kiss, let alone a real boyfriend. Instead, on the wall of her bedroom, she had a giant poster of Matt Goss, lead singer of Bros, the premier teeny heart-throb band of the late eighties. His dyed platinum blond hair, orange complexion and dazzlingly white smile were the ultimate in sex appeal for teenagers everywhere. Victoria was no exception. She dressed like him and screamed her head off when she went to see the group play live. She would later explain his appeal to *The Face*: 'With his spiky hair, he looked like a duck that had just broken out of its egg.'

The hunk she bumped into in her parents' kitchen was nothing like a duck. He was proof that 'tall, dark and handsome' did exist outside the pages of a Jane Austen novel. Mark Wood also had an infectious, toothy grin that dazzled Victoria right from the start. This particular 'Mister Darcy' was a nineteen-year-old from Harlow who was at The Old School House that afternoon fitting a burglar alarm. Mark had ambitions to be a model and an actor but was making do helping out at his father's security firm, Telmark. He was nothing like the 'dweebs and dorks' at school who seemed so young at the time. When you are sixteen, a nineteen-year-old seems the height of maturity, especially when he's 6ft 2ins.

Victoria might have been an innocent teenager, plagued with spots and puppy fat, but she was still quite a catch for the local male population. Mark had a girlfriend at the time but she was swiftly elbowed into touch when he had the prospect of asking out the daughter of Tony Adams. He would take the opportunity to pop back whenever he was in the area to check if the alarm was working properly. Really, he was hoping to chat again to the eldest daughter of the house. 'I thought she was gorgeous,' he admits. 'She was a cute and giggly kind of girl and quite shy.' Fortunately, the attraction was mutual. Victoria thought he resembled the actor Ralph Macchio, who had a legion of female fans in the eighties from his portrayal of the Karate Kid in a series of films. She enjoyed the feeling of fancying someone and looked forward to seeing him again. Nothing, however, would interfere with her dancing classes, and she never stayed in hoping to see Mark. Sometimes she pretended she was out. 'Sometimes she was there but didn't want to see me because she wasn't dressed up,' says Mark.

Eventually, he rang her up and suggested they go out for a drink. Victoria readily agreed. She had never been out for a drink before and was technically too young to be served alcohol but that has never stopped a teenager from going on a date. The important thing was that Mark had a set of wheels, so there would be no repeat of the ghastly trip on the bus with Franco. Instead, he picked her up in his dad's white van and took the ladders off the roof for the occasion. They went to a wine bar closer to London. Their recollections of their first evening differ. Mark recalls that Victoria asked for a Bacardi and Coke and downed it before he had finished paying for the round. Victoria says it was a vodka and tonic but they both agree on one thing: she quickly became drunk. Mark recalls, 'She knocked them back and by the end of the night she just sat opposite me smiling and giggling.'

To his credit, Mark did not try to take advantage of his young date's inexperience. They settled first for going steady. Jackie thought he was lovely, which meant he was always welcome at the house. Perhaps naturally, because of the age difference, they tended to do what he wanted to do and, certainly at first, she was thrilled at having a real 'boyfriend' at last. Sex could wait. Her views were strong: 'Too many people think because all their friends are doing it, they should too. But everybody should make up their own minds about it.'

Victoria, or 'Toria' as Mark called her, waited seven months before making love to her boyfriend – at least that's what he later told the *Sun* newspaper. She has never talked of it, although they were in a long-term, loving relationship for five years. He would later be all but airbrushed out of her life, but he was a constant presence while she set about becoming famous. He claimed they had sex for the first time in her bedroom, which would not be the worst place in the world and definitely beat the back of his dad's van.

Losing her virginity was not necessarily the most important event in Victoria's life that year. She was determined to leave St Mary's to further her chances of a career in show business. She set her heart on being accepted at a stage school. She still regretted not going to a '*Fame* school' like the famous Sylvia Young Theatre School or the Italia Conti Academy.

With the encouragement of Christine Shakespeare and Joy Spriggs, Victoria did a tour of the leading 'finishing' schools in and around London – Laine Theatre Arts in Epsom, the Doreen Bird College of Performing Arts in Sidcup, Kent, and the Stella Mann Dance School in Hampstead. She saw their summer shows and made up her mind that Laine Theatre Arts, run by the famed and formidable Betty Laine, was the one for her. Joy Spriggs was in total agreement. 'Laine is the crème de la crème really. Everybody aims to get there. It is the foremost theatre school – people come from all over the world to train there.'

Victoria auditioned for Laine, which was an ordeal in itself and a good grounding for more nerve-racking battles later on. Auditions were held in the assembly hall at the college with Miss Laine presiding. She might have been small in stature but she had a fiery disposition. One fellow student from Victoria's year recalls, 'I was impressed with the authority she projected. You wouldn't want to cross her! There wasn't really a spoken interview and not much communication at all, really, but Miss Laine and the teachers present managed to convey a sort of good cop–bad cop aura. Betty was quite remote and didn't display much in either censure or appreciation. She was the bad cop!'

At the end of the audition, none of the applicants had any idea if she or he had made a good impression. Victoria was thrilled and so were her mentors at the Jason School when she was accepted. She was one of three that year who were considered promising enough to win grants from the local education authority. Joy observes, 'I know her parents would have paid for her to go there but she deserved her place. She'd worked hard for it and it is so competitive. For the school to get three in with scholarships was quite something. They were a talented bunch and I think they used to spark off one another.'

Once again Victoria's successful application demolishes the opinion that she has no talent or that she was in some way lucky to achieve any success. Only serious, dedicated and talented young professionals were accepted by Laine Theatre Arts, which had a Premier League reputation to maintain. The other two accepted from Victoria's year were her friend Lynsey Britton and Danny Teeson, one of the relatively few male students. In the world of dance, there are probably ten female dancers to every male. Danny has since carved out a considerable reputation working as a choreographer with Kylie Minogue and Geri Halliwell and on the Robbie Williams stage show at Knebworth in 2003. He has also been a regular on *Queer Eye for a Straight Gal* on US television. Lynsey, meanwhile, has played Miss Adelaide in *Guys and Dolls*, taking over the West End role from Claire Sweeney. She has also been in *Cats* and *Beauty and the Beast*. Keeping such company is a tribute to Victoria's abilities.

Leaving the Jason Theatre School was quite a wrench. It had been part of her life for nine years and she left it with a trayful of trophies. She never forgot how much it meant to her and, in 2001, went back to present the prizes when the school celebrated its fiftieth anniversary. Joy presented her with the Jason Anniversary Award, which is the school's equivalent of a lifetime achievement award or a fellowship. She told the girls, 'I want to come to the school to give back something that they've given me.'

Victoria was not quite so sorry to leave St Mary's, although she had managed five GCSE passes and won a cookery prize. She used to cook a lot for Mark, especially pasta. In many ways, she was a now a sixteen-year-old girl in a relationship in which she and Mark were like an old married couple.

Laine Theatre Arts is in the town of Epsom, just south of London and more famously home to the Derby horse race each June, when thousands of enthusiasts pack the commuter trains for a day out on the Downs. It was too far to travel there from home, so Victoria had to find a place to stay. Tony drove her and her large suitcase down to some lodgings in Epsom. Goff's Oak to Epsom was quite a trek by train, so, to begin with, Victoria felt isolated and homesick as she tried to settle in. Victoria was quite young for her age and this was the first time she had left home. One friend from Goff's Oak observes, 'She was quite naive when she went to college, not very streetwise at all.' She made sure she went home every weekend.

Victoria has given every impression of not enjoying her time at Laine's, putting the school more in the category that included St Mary's High School rather than the one that included the Jason Theatre School. The principal gripe appears to have been her weight. Victoria was very upset to be told she was carrying too many pounds. Mark Wood recalls that she rang him in tears: 'The teachers told her she was too fat. She had put on a few pounds after going on the pill. She said the other girls were awful and she wanted to come home.'

The brutal fact is that Victoria was not being singled out when she was told to lose weight. She was no longer a child being treated in a kindly fashion. She was very close to beginning a professional career as a dancer. Joy Spriggs puts it into perspective, 'It didn't occur to me that Victoria was overweight or underweight. But most of the colleges would say, "You've got to lose weight if you want to get work." They would say that to everybody. They put them on a diet and you have to get on with it. And I'm afraid that's the way it is. They just want the girls to be slim, particularly if they are doing lift work. The boys won't want to lift them if they're over-weight, will they?'

That pragmatic approach did not mean that Victoria was not genuinely affected by what she perceived to be very personal criticism. She was a healthy and fit teenage girl, ten stone (140 pounds) and size twelve. By no stretch of the imagination was she fat – but, in dancing terms, she was not one of those bony visions that glide about in tutus. She liked a McDonald's when she was out – there was a convenient branch right in Epsom High Street – and her mum's cooking when she was home. And she loved chocolate. A fellow student explains, 'It was generally accepted that if you put on a little too much weight in the holidays, then Betty would have no qualms in telling you that you were too fat and needed to sort it out ASAP. We were constantly fretting about this possibility.' Like many of her peers, Victoria started to smoke cigarettes to help her eat less. She has had the habit ever since, although, like her fellow Spice Girls, she has always been very careful not to be photographed with a fag between her fingers.

Betty Laine's presence pervaded every corridor of the building. She was not highly visible to Victoria and the other students as they began their eight-hour intensive days of dancing but the stories about her were legendary. One of the favourites was that none of the girls, Victoria included, was allowed to prepare 'I Don't Know How to Love Him' as an audition piece. That memorable song from the Tim Rice/Andrew Lloyd Webber musical *Jesus Christ Superstar* was apparently frowned upon by Miss Laine because it contained the line: 'I've had so many men before, in very many ways . . .', which was not considered quite suitable for the young girls from Laine's.

On another occasion, Victoria joined other students crammed into the school hall for an assembly talk about AIDS and HIV: transmission and prevention. The speaker was a homosexual in his thirties, who was a little too graphic in his descriptions of various sexual acts and their level of risk. Suddenly, Betty Laine jumped up and proclaimed, 'I think that's quite enough, thank you,' and ushered the bemused man out.

The relentless regime of hard work at Laine's would be of great benefit to Victoria later on when she was training to be a pop star. A typical day would be: 8.30 a.m., a warm-up in one of the studios in East Street, Epsom; 9.15 a.m., a double session of ballet, lasting ninety minutes; 11 a.m., a double session of jazz dance. Lunch would then be an hour. After lunch, at 2 p.m., it would be back to the studio for a class of singing or drama; 2.45 p.m., a national dance class; 3.30 p.m., a final dance class of either ballet or jazz. By the time that was over, Victoria had been dancing pretty much for eight hours. Her day was not over, however, because then there were rehearsals for one of the college productions or students would be encouraged to practise on an area of particular weakness. It might have been a few years later than she had hoped but Victoria really was at a Fame Academy.

Competition at Laine's was very high and Victoria did not stand out in a year of many fine dancers. An insider at the college explains that they tend to favour the students whom they consider to be the best and therefore have most chance of being successful: 'They tend to home in on the ones they feel are going to make their way into the higher echelons and a lot of the others are just paying the rent. They didn't spot Victoria.'

Victoria did, however, excel at one of the courses at Laine's. She was the star pupil in image classes. Betty Laine explains, 'She was always very conscious of image, which is, of course, paramount to success. She trained in dance, singing and acting but, in the business, if they are going into the pop world, image is very important. She took this extremely seriously. She was always first or second in our image classes.'

Victoria did learn something invaluable at Laine's, after all. Subsequently, she may not have shouted it from the rooftops but she had a flair for image and completely understood its importance. She was also nurturing plans for a pop career well before the Spice Girls came along.

Her parents gave Victoria a second-hand Fiat Uno and a course of driving lessons for her seventeenth birthday. That same year they also bought her a flat in Epsom, which she shared with four girls from the college, so life became easier even if she was still struggling to make an impact at Laine's. Victoria liked having the flat because it meant her family could come and see her and, if Mark came down, she would pull out the sofa bed in the lounge and they would sleep there. One of her flatmates, Tamsin Sessions, had no idea Victoria was interested in pop until her mother sat next to Jackie at a parents' evening at Laine's: 'I remember Jackie telling her that her daughter was going to be a pop star. She had not mentioned it to me and I was taken aback. Most of us had absolutely no idea what we were going to do.'

Just after the New Year, 1992, Victoria started to plot a professional career more seriously. The first thing she did when she returned to Laine's was set about organizing some photographs. Almost all of the students at the school used a local photographer called Geoff Marchant, who charged them £25 ($50) for what was, in effect, their first modelling session. Every young professional needs a portfolio ready for agents and job applications. Victoria arranged to go with Tamsin. Geoff picked them up from the school and took them to the studio in Smallfield near Horley. Victoria knew exactly what she did not want – she did not want to be photographed smiling. Already the image that later would become her trademark look was taking shape.

Geoff recalls, 'She wanted "moody" photographs. It was unusual. Most of the girls who came along would say, "I haven't got a clue what to do. I'll leave it to you." I don't think she had too much of a clue what to do but she did know what she didn't want. She didn't want to make herself girly and she didn't want to make herself pretty-pretty. She wanted this moody sort of expression even though it meant that there was a lot of shadow, which didn't help her skin at all. It would have been better with softer lighting. But it was unusual for a girl of her age to have in her mind the look she wanted.'

Eventually, Geoff managed to persuade Victoria that it might be a good idea to smile occasionally. He explains, 'I told her that somewhere down the line an agent was going to say, "I hope you've got some shots smiling." I said I would have to do a couple and she said, "All right, but only a couple."'

Victoria had taken along a large bag of clothes to wear for the shoot. Almost all of them were black with a few white things for contrast. She scraped her hair right back in the South American fashion she has favoured many times in recent years. 'She was quite an image-seeker, even then,' says Geoff. Victoria very much saw the session as business and she took it very seriously. Her demeanour was in total contrast to her friend Tamsin's.

Geoff observes, 'She was very, very quiet. Tamsin was so bubbly and yap, yap, yap the whole time but Victoria didn't say an awful lot. My first impression was that she was a nice kid but that was about it. Looking back, I think my view of her has changed – then I thought she was very cold but I think it may well have been a mixture of shyness and determination.'

To be totally honest, Geoff did not spot Victoria as an obvious star of the future. He did think she had an 'unusual face'. He took many pictures of the college students and sometimes felt he could spot potential. He felt it, for instance, when a young Ruthie Henshall bounced into his studio in the mid-eighties. She had a natural vivacity. In many ways, Ruthie is the archetypal Laine success story – a West End star performer.

Victoria liked the finished pictures from these sessions and later in the year persuaded Mark that they should go together. It was September and the young couple had spent their summer holiday at Tony and Jackie's villa in southern Spain. Victoria had a new look with a new hairstyle and she wanted to show it off. Geoff was a little dismayed to see how tanned Victoria was because that look never photographs very well. Victoria, however, was in a great mood. 'I'm sure it was her that wanted him to come along,' he says. 'I think Victoria was in charge.' Geoff recalls one other intriguing thing: 'She was all over him.'

He managed to persuade them to do some shots together before the end of the session. Victoria is scarcely recognizable as the young girl, happy in the arms of the man she loves. They posed in a number of fully clothed yet intimate, entwined shots. For once it did not seem to be about the image. Geoff thought Mark was good-looking and relaxed but possibly lacked that extra something to be a male model. In both sessions, Victoria appears naturally photogenic. In the first, she is severe and posed. In the second, she is more natural and happier.

By this time, Mark had begun living full time at The Old School House. Mark says he moved in after Victoria had a row with his mother. Victoria says he had a big row with his parents that did not involve her and he had nowhere else to go. Her sister Louise confirms her version of events and admits that she did not like Mark.

Clearly, their relationship at the time was flourishing enough for her parents to agree to him becoming part of the furniture, which is quite a big step when dealing with a teenage daughter.

For her eighteenth birthday, Tony and Jackie arranged for the two of them to go by Eurostar to stay in Paris. For his twenty-first, Victoria organized a surprise dinner at an Italian restaurant in the West End for the two of them and his closest friends. He also went skiing with Victoria and her parents in Austria – all in addition to the romantic breaks at the villa in Riviera Del Sol. Was it too soon to think about getting engaged?

'I was convinced I was going to marry Matt Goss.'

4

Bertie

During the last year at Laine's, students started to audition for professional shows. You had to ask Betty Laine's permission to go for an audition, which was never something Victoria enjoyed. She did, however, receive encouragement from her two favourite teachers, Maureen and Gwyn Hughes, who urged her to audition for *Starlight Express*. She did not get it, nor did she really expect to, but at least she was putting herself out there. One of Victoria's classmates describes Maureen and Gwyn: 'They were sweet. They were very "musical theatre" and their classes were a mixture of singing and performance-related exercises.' When not teaching, the couple worked on their own big musical, called *Bernadette*, which sadly did not make it to the West End although it has been performed in public.

Under their guidance, Victoria developed her love of musicals and became more determined that her future would be on the stage. She decided on the classic 'Mein Herr' from *Cabaret* as her principal audition piece, a choice that was to work very well for her in the future. The other great source of inspiration was her father, Tony, whose philosophy of life was, broadly, 'Don't let the buggers get you down.' He had pulled himself up by his bootlaces and he was determined to make sure his children shared his strength of character. He succeeded admirably where Victoria was concerned. She even managed to survive the big end of year Summer Show at the Epsom Playhouse that Laine's used as a showcase for agents and producers to view the talent the school had to offer that year.

The production featured a medley showcasing the different styles of dance. The female star was a petite, freckle-faced brunette called Zoë Smith who, on leaving college, won a part in a touring production of *Cats*. She has been in several West End productions since then, although she has yet to be a headliner like other ex-Lainees, like Ruthie Henshall or Victoria's friend Lynsey Britton. Her latest role was playing Stephanie Mangano in a revival of *Saturday Night Fever*. The leading man was Christian Horsfell, who had caught Victoria's eye when she first went to college. He was athletic with thick brown hair that he wore in a ponytail. He, too, went on to the West End but was the envy of other college students for his success in commercials. The highlight of the show was when Zoë joined him for a stunning pas de deux that Victoria could only watch from the wings.

Every Summer Show would end with the Laine's signature number 'Razzle-Dazzle' from the hit musical *Chicago*. The song became an unofficial school motto for Laine's, urging students to 'Give 'em the old razzle-dazzle'. The stage was a sensational extravaganza of tap. All the girls wore sequins and carried bowler hats, strongly influenced by Bob Fosse, the choreographer of the original Broadway show in 1975. Fosse also directed *Cabaret*, in which Liza Minnelli sported a very similar look. If you had blinked, you might have missed Victoria tapping her way across the stage at the back.

Despite her barely concealed dislike of Laine's, Victoria had learned the importance of image, begun to fashion her own and had three years of drama classes as well as dance. She chose the image that she felt suited her and then proceeded to play that part – a concept at the very heart of Victoria's ongoing success. Joy Spriggs noticed it: 'She was always very good at drama. She used to do very, very well in all of her exams. I mean, she's acting the whole time, isn't she really? She's acting her persona; yes, she's role playing.'

In her last days at Laine's, Victoria pored over the pages of the *Stage* newspaper for likely auditions. She saw an advertisement for a new show called *Bertie*, based on the life of the famous music hall performer Vesta Tilley. Victoria was not an expert on music hall but she had watched *The Good Old Days* with her grandparents and had seen acts imitating Tilley, who was the best-known male impersonator of that era. She was a huge star in both the UK and the US, presenting a dazzling array of male characters whom she brought to life in a daring and comic way. Her real name was Matilda Alice Powles but she chose the stage name Vesta Tilley. Away from the stage, she became a Lady when her husband, the impresario Walter de Frece, was knighted in 1919. Her huge reputation was augmented during the First World War when her famous monologues and songs were used as recruiting tools up and down the country – so much so that she was called 'Britain's Best Recruiting Sergeant'.

Vesta Tilley's amazing life was ripe for rediscovery in a musical. The writers Mike Margolis and Kenny Clayton called the show *Bertie* after one of her most famous songs, 'Burlington Bertie'. The star of the show was Anita Harris, who was married to Margolis. Victoria was auditioning to be part of the 'company', one of the all-singing, all-dancing members of the chorus who seem to be onstage rushing about all the time.

Victoria had continued to work on her image. Her persona in progress, as revealed in her photographic session with Geoff Marchant, had moved on. She had the look (moody), she had the costume (all black, which had the added bonus of making her appear slimmer) and she had the perfect song to match ('Mein Herr'). She was confident that she could 'put the song across'. She had done some singing at Jason, and subsequently at Laine's, but Victoria was primarily a dancer. She could sail through the dancing part of an audition but the make or break spot was the song. It went well but the competition was intense for every role, not least from the other students at Laine's.

You could have heard Victoria's screams in Broxbourne when the producer's assistant rang The Old School House to tell her the good news – she had secured a part. Mark was at home and thought her yells were real until he dashed downstairs and saw her sporting the widest grin in the world. In context, this was an astounding achievement. *Bertie* would have a regional run in Birmingham before moving to the West End – the West End!

Victoria had only just turned nineteen and was technically still at Laine's. She enjoyed telling her fellow students that she was the one going into a real show and not killing time dancing on a cruise ship.

The small cloud on the horizon was the Birmingham run, which would mean being away from home for three months. She and Mark chatted about it and decided to get engaged. Mark maintains, 'She said she wanted us to get engaged so our relationship would be permanent even though we were going to be apart for a while. I didn't say "Yes" right away because I knew my parents wouldn't be happy. But, at the same time, deep down, I knew Toria was the only one for me. She was the sweetest girl I had ever met and all I wanted was for her to be my wife.'

All Victoria wanted, it seems, was to be engaged – nothing more than that. You could almost imagine a finishing school in which the teacher – perhaps a Jean Brody figure – advised that all nice 'gels' should be engaged at least once before they reached the age of twenty-one. It was great fun. First of all, they took a trip to the jewellers of Hatton Garden in London to hunt for a suitable ring but she could not find one she liked, so they set about designing one at a cost of £1,500 ($3,000), an impressive amount for two young people starting out in life. In the meantime, Mark asked Tony Adams for permission to marry Victoria and he readily agreed.

Then they went for a romantic candlelit dinner at a restaurant near Tower Bridge with a view across the Thames. Jackie sent along some flowers and champagne to make sure the evening went well – if not a little too planned – and Mark slid off his chair, went down on one knee and slipped the ring on Victoria's outstretched finger. What was not to like about getting engaged, especially when Tony and Jackie threw a champagne pool party so that all their friends could celebrate the good news? Everyone seemed genuinely thrilled, except perhaps for her sister Louise, who had never warmed to Mark.

No date for the wedding was ever set nor was there any hint of how long they might stay engaged before moving to the next stage. The engagement seemed to be an acknowledgement that they were in a strong relationship. In *Learning to Fly*, Victoria says, 'I never for one moment thought that I would marry Mark.' Victoria was very young to be thinking of marriage and babies. She had powerful ambitions. Being engaged gave her added confidence and was one less thing to think about. She was never one for playing the field where men were concerned.

More important matters needed to be tackled – in particular, the rehearsals for *Bertie*, which were held at Sadler's Wells Theatre in Islington. Victoria had been to the ballet there and was excited that she was dancing on the famous stage, even if she was in a leotard and leggings. *Bertie* was a genuinely happy time in Victoria's career. She liked the other girls in the company and there was none of the bitchiness and jealousy that had plagued her life at college.

When it was time to move up to Birmingham for the final rehearsals, Victoria joined the others in 'theatrical digs', a wonderfully old-fashioned concept. These particular lodgings were in Edgbaston and were run by the magnificently named Marlene P. Mountain. Victoria was in her element, especially when she discovered she had a solo dance as a clockwork ballerina and wore a little white tutu with wings. Not everything was running smoothly, however, and the director left days before opening night amid rumours of backstage bickering. The choreographer was the marvellous Irving Davies, one of the best in the business and a treat to work with. He had been a star in theatrical circles for nearly fifty years and was in his mid-sixties when he put Victoria through her paces. He achieved international recognition when the great dancer Gene Kelly cast him as 'The Crooner' in his 1957 movie *Invitation to the Dance*. The film was an ambitious one in that it told the story without words, relying solely on a script of dance. Davies, who died in 2002, was a great admirer of Kelly and introduced the great star's athleticism into much of his own work. Victoria responded to that approach and worked hard to improve. She also appreciated the Davies calm, a reflection of his devotion to the teaching of the Maharishi Mahesh Yogi.

Bertie had quite a stellar cast for a musical. Big West End names like Ron Moody, famous for his portrayal of Fagin in *Oliver!*, Julia

McKenzie and Nicky Henson. The leading lady, Anita Harris, belonged to that peculiarly British tradition of middle of the road performers who retain their popularity over the years – Rolf Harris, Val Doonican and Jimmy Tarbuck are on a list topped by Bruce Forsyth and Cilla Black. Her heyday as a recording artist was in the sixties, when her biggest hit, 'Just Loving You', sold three-quarters of a million copies. She had kept in the public eye by appearing on television but, perhaps crucially, she did not immediately command attention as a West End star. Victoria's best friend in the cast was Anita's understudy, a trained ballet dancer called Camilla Simson, who really was posh and lived in Chelsea.

The world premiere of *Bertie* was at Birmingham's Alexandra Theatre. Mark travelled up with the family to support Victoria. She was not mentioned in dispatches after the show but the reviews were promising and, after a six-week run, everything looked set for the London opening later in the year. Victoria was paid £250 ($500) a week and enjoyed earning real money for the first time. What was the point in saving? She went straight down to London on her day off to buy a pair of must-have Patrick Cox shoes and a Prada handbag.

Victoria was taken by surprise when, after a few weeks of hanging around, the plans to take *Bertie* to the West End were abruptly shelved. This was not the script she had written for herself. Instead, she found herself in that classic show business state of 'resting' just when she was getting started. It was the start of months of mindless auditions and unsuitable 'promotional' work. Working on *Bertie* qualified Victoria for an Equity card, the actors' union membership that they have to hold in order to work. One unforeseen problem was that there was already a member using the name Victoria Adams, so she had to think of another. She cites this as the reason she adopted Mark's surname and started calling herself Victoria Adams-Wood. That is certainly a good explanation, although it does not quite clarify why she started using it on her chequebook – perhaps she was getting prepared to pay in all the money she was going to earn. She probably just liked the name and was in no mood to change it when she began a pop career, even though she did not need an Equity card for that. At least she decided against calling herself Victoria Wood.

Victoria had never had much luck finding modelling work. Both she and her younger sister were registered with a children's agency when they were younger but it was Louise, all grin and cheek, who was invariably chosen. Victoria found it hard even to get an agent. Eventually she signed up with an agency specializing in promotional work. Through it she did manage to pick up a few jobs, usually handing out leaflets at a shop opening or plugging a product in an arcade. Memorably, she even worked for the *Daily Mirror*, visiting newsagents wearing a tarty T-shirt two sizes too small for her. Most weeks she would sign on the dole and pore over the new issue of the *Stage*.

One week, in August 1993, she spotted a tiny advertisement asking for a girl singer for a new pop group and decided to send in her c.v. and a photograph. She chose one showing what would become a popular look for her over the years – all in black, wearing a pair of sunglasses in the manner of her fashion idol, Audrey Hepburn. The star of *Breakfast at Tiffany's* and *Roman Holiday* breathed cool, elegant glamour with a slender figure and cheekbones to die for. The ad had been placed by Steven Andrews, a professional model from South London, who harboured ambitions to be a pop star. He noticed Victoria straight away, 'It was just the image I was looking for.' Victoria's emphasis on image paid off again.

The process was a bit rough and ready. Victoria was called for an audition. She sang 'Mein Herr' and danced to 'Let Me Be Your Fantasy' by Baby D, which was a hugely popular club hit at the time and went to number one when it was finally released the following year. Once again, 'Mein Herr' did the trick and Steven invited Victoria for a second audition, this time at a club near Shepherd's Bush. She was one of a dozen girls who had to perform the classic party track 'Band of Gold' by Freda Payne. Steven observes, 'She wasn't a great singer but she had potential and I knew I had found the right girl.' The next day he offered Victoria the job. Nothing was signed and no deal was on the horizon. It was just a group of three girls and two boys hoping to make it. They called themselves Persuasion. Victoria was thrilled.

Twice a week they would meet to rehearse. Victoria was designated the lead singer. She was joined by Steven, Steve Monday,

Natasha McLauchlin, who, coincidentally, had been at Laine's, and a girl with a good voice called Nathalie Watkins. Steven concedes that Victoria was always prepared to work hard. 'She was never late or moody. She just got on with it. Everybody pulled together.'

Intriguingly, Steven remembers two things about those rehearsal evenings. First, Victoria, he thought, lacked confidence in front of the microphone and had a worrying tendency to freeze up. Secondly, the only times she seemed to get upset involved Mark, who would come along and sit in. Steven, who hated him turning up, put it down to Mark's possessiveness. A clue to Mark and Victoria's relationship is found in the birthday card that she gave him for his twenty-second birthday, which he later revealed to the world. It read, 'I'll still love you when you're old! Lots of love, your Little Pop Star! Victoria xxx.' One cannot imagine Mel B or Geri Halliwell allowing any man to call them a 'little pop star' and live.

'Some people feel embarrassed if they haven't slept with many people, but I don't think it matters.'

5

Getting In Touch

Chris Herbert was very clear about the plan for his group. He wanted one of the girls to appeal to the more mature man, the male consumer with a touch of discernment. As she walked down Oxford Street towards a dance studio next to Selfridges department store, on her way to yet another audition, Victoria Adams-Wood had no idea that her ability to sing and dance would prove to be a secondary consideration. You don't need to be posh to have a touch of class and that was the quality at the top of Chris's hit list.

Victoria had seen the advertisement in the *Stage*, which, like every other budding musical star, she read once a week from cover to cover.

WANTED

RU 18–23 with the ability to sing/dance?
RU streetwise, outgoing, ambitious, dedicated?

Heart Management Ltd are a widely successful
Music Industry Management Consortium currently
Forming a choreographed, Singing/Dancing
All Female Pop Act for a Record Recording Deal.
CVs/Photos & Demos (if applicable) are being collected,
with audition dates soon to be released.

Please send your CVs etc. to:- Heart Management Ltd

Heart Management were a father and son: Bob Herbert, fifty-two, a respected music business accountant, and his go-ahead son, Chris, a young man in his early twenties bristling with new schemes to rule the pop world. The all-girl group was exclusively his idea. Bob was keen to join forces with his son but he also wanted to bring his old music compadre, Chic Murphy, into the mix. Bob had done well in the entertainment world but, like all good accountants, he preferred to find someone else to absorb the financial risk, which is where Chic came in. The two had already been linked when they were part of the management team behind the Three Degrees, the most popular UK girl group of the seventies. Tall and silver-haired, Chic was a bit of a mystery man. He was worth millions though it was hard to know which of his many ventures had made his fortune. He had a tiny cross tattooed on his ear lobe and spoke in a 'Chas and Dave' cockney accent but he frequented the Surrey haunts more familiarly associated with stockbrokers and golfers. Chris Herbert describes Chic as 'old school', which in business terms means he played it tough and preferred an environment in which the music artists had very little control over their destiny.

Despite their British success, the Three Degrees, modelled more or less on the Supremes, were originally American and part of the Philadelphia stable. They had a big number one in 1974 with the disco classic 'When Will I See You Again', and were the first girl group to top the charts since the Supremes ten years earlier. The problem for the Three Degrees was that somewhere along the line the media decided they were the favourite group of the young Prince Charles, which gave them plenty of coverage in the diary pages but little credibility. He invited them to perform at his thirtieth birthday party at Buckingham Palace in 1978 and they were subsequently guests at his wedding to Lady Diana Spencer three years later, in 1981.

By the end of the seventies, the Three Degrees were moving inexorably towards the cabaret circuit. They produced *A Collection of Their 20 Greatest Hits*, which was a little tongue in cheek, considering they managed only eight top thirty hits. They were still very popular though – the sort of act that always gets work – and throughout the eighties Chic had been a familiar figure at their gigs.

Bob Herbert, who had a penchant for wearing white suits and was memorably described by Geri Halliwell as looking like an extra from *Miami Vice*, had, more pertinently, experience of nurturing young talent. In the mid-eighties, he spotted the potential of twin brothers Matt and Luke Goss, who were friends of Chris at the Collingwood School in Camberley, Surrey. At the time, they were only fifteen but Bob could see they had the looks to engage a female following. He was of the music school that was always seeking to copy a successful formula: in the case of Bros, he saw them as a late eighties version of the Bay City Rollers. When the brothers formed a band called Gloss with young bassist Craig Logan (Goss with an L for Logan), Bob gave them advice and, more importantly, space to rehearse in his summer house. The whole exercise would come back to haunt Bob Herbert with the Spice Girls. He plotted their futures, introduced them to songwriters and financed their demo tapes but, because of their age, could not sign them to a binding legal contract until they were eighteen. When they came of age, they were snapped up by Tom Watkins, the former Pet Shop Boys manager, who secured them a deal with CBS. Under the new name of Bros, they released their first single, ironically titled 'I Owe You Nothing', which, when reissued in 1988, would be their only UK number one. At this time a picture of Matt Goss was adorning Victoria's bedroom wall in The Old School House.

Undaunted, perhaps enthused by their success, Bob Herbert was looking to join forces with Chic Murphy to find a boy band when his son had a better idea: 'At the time the market was kind of saturated with boy bands – East 17, Take That, Bad Boys Inc. There was Worlds Apart. There were loads of them,' recalls Chris. It was a formula that was working and Bob and Chic originally thought that was the way they wanted to go too. 'But, to me, it only caters for fifty per cent of the audience and I just thought it would be better to put together a girl band, something that was sexy and sassy. Girls would aspire to be them and guys would sort of "admire" them.' To a large extent it is this simple formula that

Victoria has exploited ever since to cement and augment her popularity.

The first thing Bob and Chic wanted to discuss was the strength of the competition. It was anything but strong. An all-girl group called Milan had formed in 1992 and looked promising for a couple of years, opening for East 17 on tour and featuring a teenage Martine McCutcheon before she became a star in *EastEnders*. Eternal, which enjoyed a string of hits in the nineties, represented more serious opposition, but they were most definitely a vocal group even though they contained the lads' mag favourite, Louise Nurding. They were not an all-action equivalent of a boy band. If the Spice Girls were looked upon as forerunners of Girls Aloud, then Eternal were blazing a trail for All Saints or Sugababes. Chris Herbert did not set out to compete with an already established chart act: 'Vocally, you could not match them. Eternal were fantastic but that's not what we were setting out to do. We had our eyes on a different set of aspects – yes, an ability to sing and dance but also a good look. It was an overall package we wanted.'

Eternal had already had two top ten hits by the time Victoria made her way to Chris Herbert's auditions. She was not aware at the time that these auditions at the Dance Works studio were just one of a number of methods being explored to find the five girls. Chris Herbert was given a budget of a few thousand pounds to go out and make the initial search. He toured pubs and clubs, talent and karaoke nights, sat through stage shows and sent out flyers. He even trawled through the list of cruise ship entertainers. He recruited his girlfriend, Shelley Silva, a designer, to help him form the image of the group in his mind, mainly devouring magazines from which they would tear out what they liked and paste the pictures on a board on the office wall at Heart Management. It was their 'mood board' on which they would try to build up the looks and characters of the girls they were seeking. The one thing that was set in stone right from the start was that the group would consist of five girls.

On the day of the open audition, just before Easter, 1994, Chris Herbert was sure he wanted one of the girls to possess a touch of sophistication. 'There was a position in the band for a girl that appealed to an older man,' he explains. 'Victoria just came in and held herself differently. She had a more grown-up air about her than the rest of the girls there. They all came in and sang pop songs and they had styled themselves as if to audition for a pop band. Victoria was theatre school and sang "Mein Herr" from *Cabaret*.' Chris had no idea that 'Mein Herr' was Victoria's party piece and had already worked its magic in securing her a part in the musical *Bertie*. Certainly, it was an unusual choice. Melanie Brown, for instance, sang the much more predictable 'The Greatest Love of All' in her best Whitney Houston voice.

Victoria was strikingly dressed all in black with a crop-top showing off a very tanned midriff. She had no idea that she was making an impact, although she did notice that girls with what she perceived to be far better voices were picking up their bags and melting away into the Oxford Street afternoon. Her 'look' was keeping her in and the fact that she coped comfortably with the dance steps they were required to do. About four hundred girls turned up and they were whittled down to fifty before they were asked to do an individual song. The panel, consisting of Chris, Bob and Shelley, divided everyone into groups of ten and put them through their paces, ironically to the sound of Eternal's hit 'Stay'.

After she had finished her showstopper from *Cabaret*, Victoria picked up her bag and Chris told her they would be in touch. She had caught his eye and was already a strong contender. She was a curvy nineteen-year-old with a look suggesting a moody invitation to the bedroom. She was, however, only pencilled in at this stage. The girl who made the most impact was Melanie, soon to be Mel B, who sang everyone off the stage at the audition, standing out in a black top and a very short, brown mini skirt. Her hair even then was big, as if she had placed her fingers in an electrical socket. Chris Herbert observes, 'She looked the part. On first impression I thought, "Well, you're *definitely* in." She had a young, funky look, was an OK singer and a great dancer. She was absolutely right for the project. She always gave it one hundred per cent.' Melanie

Chisholm also made a good impression, boasting an impressive six pack underneath her mauve crop-top. She sang 'I'm So Excited', an eighties classic from the Pointer Sisters.

Another girl showing promise was Michelle Stephenson, who sang 'Don't Be a Stranger', a recent top ten hit for Dina Carroll. None of the other leading contenders had chosen a song from a musical. Neither Geri Halliwell nor Emma Bunton was at the audition. Geri had planned to go but had been skiing in the Pyrenees, where she became badly sunburnt and her face swelled up. Her absence would prove to be a wise career move. At this stage, none of the girls, including Victoria, had really had the time to notice any of the competition.

Chris was true to his word and did get back in touch with Victoria, a week after her twentieth birthday. Nearly a month had passed and she had put it to the back of her mind. She had no idea that they had held another audition and it was from both days that a final shortlist of twelve had been drawn up. He told her to present herself at Nomis Studios, around the corner from the BBC in Shepherd's Bush, west London, where they would hold the recall. Melanie C was invited but on the day had practically lost her voice, so her mother had to phone to say she would not be able to make it. Chris assured her mum that Melanie was still very much in their thoughts.

At the studios, it was the first chance for the girls to size each other up. In her autobiography, *Catch a Fire*, Mel B recalled meeting Victoria: 'She had big brown eyes and long legs and I thought her hair was really lovely, dark brown and glossy.' Coincidentally, Mel B also described Victoria as having a Hot Gossip quality, an enduring legacy from those leggings days at the Jason Theatre School.

Chris and Bob began the recall by chatting to the girls individually and then dividing them into three groups. Victoria was included in a group with Melanie Brown, Michelle Stephenson and a Welsh girl from Cowbridge, near Cardiff, called Lianne Morgan. They were given three-quarters of an hour to devise a dance routine to yet another Eternal hit; this time Chris had chosen 'Just a Step From Heaven', which was in the charts at the time. Not surprisingly, the ebullient Mel B took the lead and the others were happy to follow her ideas.

Just when they thought they were ready, Bob Herbert threw a spanner in the works by telling them to bring another girl up to speed – Geri Halliwell. The story of how Geri made it into the Spice Girls is a wonderful tale of blagging triumph. She phoned up Chris, despite missing all the auditions to date, and managed to charm him into agreeing that she should turn up as one of the final shortlisted girls sight unseen! While Victoria opted, as usual, to dress in her favourite black to make her appear slimmer, Geri was a riot of colour, favouring a tight pink jumper, purple hot pants and platform shoes, all topped off by her vibrant ginger hair, which she had styled into pigtails. Mel B put it succinctly, 'She looked like a mad eccentric nutter from another planet.' That may be so but Geri Halliwell is a force of nature and she certainly caught the attention of Bob and Chris – especially Bob. Chris asked her how old she was and Geri famously replied, 'I'm as old or as young as you want me to be. I can be a twelve-year-old with big boobs if you like.'

Geri was not much of a dancer, whereas both Michelle and Lianne were primarily singers. Their shortcomings allowed Mel B and Victoria to sail through the dancing part of the day. By the end of the afternoon, though, Chris and Bob had seen enough to think they had found their soon to be famous five. They sent each of them away with a tape of 'Signed, Sealed, Delivered, I'm Yours' by Stevie Wonder and asked them to return in a week's time to be put through their vocal paces to see how they blended together and whether they could harmonize. Chris explains, 'We wanted to create a band as a unit so it did not matter so much if, individually, they weren't so strong.'

Victoria is always at pains to point out that her voice was not up to much and that she only scraped in to the group by the skin of her teeth. It's a good story but it's just not true. Chris Herbert was always very impressed with Victoria's singing – once again it was Geri who was the weakest link. Victoria was well able to belt out a song and, luckily for her, she grew up listening to Stevie Wonder, one of her father's favourite performers.

When she returned to Nomis Studios the following week, Victoria was surprised that Lianne was no longer in the final five. The Herberts had decided to replace her with Melanie Chisholm, who had a powerful voice and was a terrific dancer. Lianne remains bitter about what she considers grossly unfair treatment. She received a note saying that she was being replaced because on reflection they considered her too old – she was twenty-three. She has nothing gracious to say about Victoria, telling the *Daily Mail*: 'She didn't smile, crossed her legs a lot, had long hair, trowelled-on make-up and bad skin.' She has also been unsympathetic about Victoria's singing abilities. Chris, however, reveals one of the great mysteries about Victoria's career. She used to be a far better singer than she is now. 'She was a better singer than the one I hear on the records. She had much more feel and was a bit more soulful than she is now.'

Lianne is still beavering away in the lower echelons of show business, planning a concert tour and hiring a PR person. The *Daily Mail* exclusive coincided with the Spice Girls' reunion in which she claimed she was a better singer than all the girls, which might have been true but is small comfort. Her new website makes no mention of age being an issue, instead it states that it was thought she was more of a solo performer. Lianne was unlucky but could hardly claim to be the 'fifth Beatle' of the Spice Girls – that dubious honour rightly belongs to another member of the 'final' five.

At the workshop day, Victoria met Melanie Chisholm, a good-natured Liverpool girl, who told her that she had been to Doreen Bird College, where Victoria would have gone if she had failed to win a place at Laine's. Melanie was lithe and athletic and created a good impression with the other girls. She also met Chic Murphy, who wanted to see for himself how his money was going to be spent. All the girls thought they sounded terrible together – definitely a cat's chorus. Victoria belted the songs out as she had been doing for Persuasion. To their surprise, Chris, Bob and Chic seemed a little hard of hearing that day and were impressed enough to move on to the next stage of the process – a week at a bed and breakfast in Knaphill village, Woking, which was down the road from the Heart offices in Lightwater, Surrey.

Ostensibly, the week was for them to rehearse, but that was only part of the reason. 'It was just for them to spend a little time together, see whether they actually got on, started to bond,' recalls Chris. 'Initially we wanted to observe and see if there was something there or if we had to make any changes.' He introduced them to working together in a studio, picking them up from the B & B and dropping them off at Trinity Studios in Knaphill, which was little more than a glorified village hall and in urgent need of a lick of paint and a decent central heating system. The building had once been a dance studio, so it did provide the space for the five girls to hone their dancing skills. Trinity was run by Ian Lee, who remembers that first week well: 'They were like five schoolgirls – a bit giggly and a bit insecure.'

The five 'schoolgirls' were given the name Touch by Chris Herbert, who began to assemble a team to help them improve. Yet again the Three Degrees provided the link when he asked their former musical director, Erwin Keiles, to come up with a song or two to get the girls started. The first they had to learn was called 'Take Me Away', a mid-tempo unchallenging number. He brought in the gloriously named Pepi Lemer, a voice coach of considerable experience and a backing singer since the sixties, when she missed out on stardom herself. Her professional view of Victoria: 'She had a pretty little voice.'

Pepi realized that collectively the girls had a lot of work to do: 'I remember them being quite attractive in their various ways, but terribly nervous. They were shaking and, when they sang, their voices were wobbling. It has to be said that they weren't very good.' At the end of the week, the girls gave Chris, Bob and Chic an exclusive performance of that first song. Intriguingly, they were dressed in a manner that they never wanted to repeat as the Spice Girls. They were colour coordinated in black and white.

Victoria, for the first time, gave Chris some cause for concern when he found out that she was already in a band. He spoke to her: 'I said, "Are you in or are you out? If you're going to move forward with us, then you need to make a decision." She told me she had made a decision. I think she kind of kept the other thing rolling but as time went on she realized where her future lay.'

Victoria had been keeping her options open, telling Steven Andrews that she was going away for a week and would have to miss rehearsals. Not for the first or last time, Victoria was being canny.

The precious commodity that the Herberts had managed to introduce to a bunch of seasoned auditioners was a sense of excitement. Even the cosy, old style guest house seemed thrilling. Victoria shared a room with Geri, who complained that she was taking up all the room with her two large suitcases full of designer clothes. They clicked immediately, in a way that became much more difficult once rampaging egos came to the fore. 'You must come with me to a car boot sale,' said Geri – as if that was ever going to happen.

Already a potential problem was building within the group. Four of the girls – Victoria, the two Melanies and Geri – were getting on famously, but the fifth, Michelle, seemed to be on the outside. This was not the gelling unit Chris Herbert wanted, 'Even when they stopped and broke for lunch or a coffee break, the four would be inside having a coffee and Michelle would be outside. She seemed a bit separated from the others. We spotted it and thought there was a problem developing even during that initial week.'

As is often the case with such an important decision, there are at least two sides to the story. The other girls questioned her work ethic and commitment, while Michelle was struggling to come to terms with a family crisis – her mother, Penny, had been diagnosed with breast cancer. Michelle, like Victoria, was brought up in the Home Counties and, it could be argued, was demonstrably posher, perhaps more intelligent and certainly more middle class. Her father, George, worked for Chubb security and her brother, Simon, was an art director. They lived in Abingdon, a lovely old market town on the Thames just south of Oxford. When she was chosen for the new group, Michelle was in her first year studying theatre and English at Goldsmith's College, part of the University of London. Like Victoria, she had progressed through the ranks of local productions but she had done much more acting, with work for the Young Vic and the National Youth Theatre on her c.v. She revealed, 'I actually wanted to be an actress. I just went along for the audition because I had not been to an open audition before. I just went along for the experience.'

The emphasis on drama reflects Michelle's true aspirations and why perhaps she failed to embrace the new group with the gusto of the other four. Michelle did not quit her university course nor did she give up her Saturday job at Harrods. The general observation was that she did not 'want it' as much as the others. Victoria thought that she did not have the dream. Mel B agreed, 'In our eyes, Michelle just didn't seem to be making the effort.' Their criticism of Michelle perhaps reveals more about them and their all-consuming drive than about Michelle.

At this early stage, Bob and Chris Herbert were more concerned with the lack of progress at Trinity Studios. They thought the girls needed more time to practise and improve. Chic came up with the solution. He happened to have a spare three-bedroomed house in Maidenhead. The girls could move in right away. It was basically a student house, a small, drab semi-detached in a grey estate in Boyne Hill Road. Geri bagged the tiny single room, while the two Melanies, the North Country girls, were in one double room and Victoria and Michelle, the two Home County girls, shared the third, twin-bedded room.

The girls were given £60 ($120) a week for expenses but they also claimed benefit. They were made to work hard for their money, squeezing every morning into Geri's old Fiat Uno to drive the thirty miles to the studios for a non-stop day of singing lessons, dancing movements and practising a repertoire that might become their showcase at a later date.

Relations between Michelle and the band continued to slide downhill. The four girls were exasperated when they thought she failed to put the work in to improve her dancing, preferring, they said, to top up her tan at lunchtimes rather than copy Geri's lead and practise to catch up the others. Geri was not a dancer but she was a maniacal trier. Mel B tried to motivate Michelle but in the end the gang of four told Bob and Chris of their misgivings, which largely was what the Herberts already felt. Bob commented, 'She would never have gelled so we had to let her go.'

Did she go of her own accord, was she pushed or was it a mutual decision? Chris Herbert diplomatically maintains it was a joint decision although Michelle was destined to always be famous as the 'Spice Girl who wasn't'. Michelle went travelling before going back to university to continue her degree. She explains, 'It wasn't my kind of music and I had different plans for the future.'

In her book, *Learning to Fly*, Victoria is quite rude and ungracious about Michelle, whom the gang of four called the 'sun-worshipper', describing her voice as 'cruise ship operatic' and her dancing as 'having less rhythm than a cement mixer' and stating that she 'couldn't be arsed' to improve.

Michelle, who until then had declared there to be no 'bad feelings', suddenly discovered some, observing that Victoria was 'the high and mighty one' and adding, 'I can't pretend that I wasn't very hurt by the things she said about my singing and dancing. But to say that I was turfed out of the group, when I left because I wanted to be with my sick mother . . . well, what kind of person does that? She knows my mother had breast cancer.'

Victoria's remarks, even if true, reflect badly on her. They are at best flippant. The Michelle saga does reveal something else about the girls, Victoria included, who would become the Spice Girls. They were all fiercely driven and very working class. Michelle, a nicely spoken university girl from Oxfordshire, would never have fitted into that world regardless of her abilities or family problems. Mel B described her as 'sweet, very upper class and very well turned out'.

Chris Herbert did not set out to create a working-class group: 'It wasn't premeditated in any way. It's just the way it turned out. In a way, though, that's what highlighted Victoria as being a little bit more sophisticated, a bit more upper-crust than that.' If Michelle had stayed in the group, Victoria would not have enjoyed that distinction. The irony is that Michelle was marginalized in the same sort of way as Victoria was by the rougher elements at St Mary's High School – this time Victoria had the opportunity to hunt with the pack and she grasped the chance.

Michelle once said, 'Of course I regret I'm not a multi-millionaire like them', which may be a massive understatement but she doesn't actually say that she regrets not becoming a famous Spice Girl. Eight years after she left, Chris and Shelley were in the Pitcher and Piano bar in Richmond when he recognized the waitress. It was Michelle. Chris recalls, 'We shared a fond welcome and had a good chat.'

Michelle can still be heard singing on YouTube and other websites. She was last reported to have married and settled in Los Angeles.

'We all knew what it was like to really long for it.'

6

Take Five

Victoria Adams-Wood, as she was still styling herself, had never belonged before. She was not exactly 'Vicky No-mates' but she had never been in a gang of friends or even in the netball team. Amateur psychologists could easily explain her apparent reserve as fear of rejection. She was always slightly on the outside looking in but here, for the first time, was the chance to be herself, laugh at others if she chose to and be part of something that really mattered to her. Yet Chris Herbert observes, 'I don't think it sat comfortably with her to start with, trying to morph into one of the girls. It wasn't that convincing but she was desperate to be one of the gang.' Later much would be made of 'Girl Power', an inspired marketing phrase, but Victoria actually *was* empowered by the group. In a small semi in Maidenhead, she found something that all the money and privileges afforded her in Goff's Oak could not give her. Chris Herbert notes simply, 'She grew in confidence.'

The original advert for the group highlighted a desire to find girls who were 'streetwise, outgoing, ambitious, dedicated'. Victoria might have been boutique-wise but she was nowhere near being streetwise, brought up as she was in her protected home environment. She was outgoing enough to want to perform but she was never going to be the Melanie Brown of Goff's Oak. Despite that, she had an ambition and dedication to match, if not surpass, the others. This would be the true bond of the girls who would become Spice.

Victoria would have run a mile to keep out of the way of Melanie if she had been a pupil at St Mary's High School. Fortunately, Melanie would have been in another class because, at nineteen, she was a year younger. Victoria hates being called Vicky, so it does not take a big jump of imagination to guess what Melanie called her, right from the start.

Mel B, as she became widely known, is a straight-talking down-to-earth Yorkshire girl who stands no nonsense from anybody and is ready to stand up for herself. She is mixed race, which even in modern Britain requires a degree of toughness in order to overcome outmoded prejudices.

It had been much more difficult for her parents. Her father, Martin Brown, was from Nevis, a beautiful island in the Caribbean. As a baby, he was left behind to live on a small farm with his grandmother while his parents came to Britain to build a new life, following a path trod by many West Indians in the fifties. As a boy, he played cricket on the beach while his parents tried to cope with the rampant racism of post-war Britain.

Martin had just turned thirteen when his parents brought him over to the depressed and depressing area of Chapeltown in Leeds, where the Yorkshire Ripper would prowl for victims in the late seventies. Melanie describes her father as a young man as a 'funky black dude', which must have come as more than a bit of a shock to the parents of Yorkshire lass Andrea Dixon, who had just turned seventeen when she met Martin on a Christmas Eve night out in Chapeltown. She lived in the district of Seacroft, an area on the east side of the city, where the black population was practically non-existent. For most of his life, Martin was a shift worker at a metal works while Andrea, who would soon be his wife, had left school at sixteen and took a variety of low-paid factory and office jobs. They had to deal with a lot of prejudice in their lives, which perhaps gave their eldest daughter such a strong sense of justice. Being mixed race brought its own special set of problems, with the locals unsure whether young Melanie was black or white and, as a result, she found it difficult to know where she belonged.

Melanie was a bundle of energy as a child but, fortunately, just as Victoria had done, she discovered the joy of dancing at an early age. Instead of the Jason Theatre School, her home from home was the Jean Pearce School of Dance. And, like Victoria, Melanie went every week until she left to go to dance college. Her mother took on more part-time work to pay for the classes. Some of her most memorable days out were dance school trips to see the big musicals like *Cats* and *Miss Saigon* on tour. She loved dancing so much that she enrolled in extra evening classes at a local school hall. They were 20 pence (40 cents) a time and Melanie enjoyed them because they allowed her to be creative and contemporary and to express her extrovert personality.

At fifteen, she skipped school to audition for a Blackpool show and ended up dancing in two productions for the summer. She wore a cheerleader mini skirt for a rock 'n' roll show on the beach and a see-through catsuit for a dance cabaret in the evening. That autumn she started at a dance college in Chapeltown and paid for her bus fare and lunches by teaching aerobics at the local Mandela Centre. She also won a beauty contest and became the proud owner of the title *Miss Leeds Weekly News*. College did not go smoothly, however, with the outspoken Melanie clashing frequently with all and sundry and, after the first year, she was not invited back for a second.

For Melanie, at age eighteen, it was time to earn a living. She worked as a podium dancer in a city centre club in Leeds, as an extra in *Coronation Street* and *A Touch of Frost* and, memorably, as a dancer on *Keith and Orville's Quack Chat Show* in Manchester. She also auditioned unsuccessfully for stage musicals. It was an eclectic mix of work, typical of a young wannabe trying to get a break. She returned to Blackpool for another summer season, this time in *The Billy Pearce Laughter Show*, which co-starred Joe Pasquale, before finding work as a dancer in a troupe entertaining the troops in the Falkland Islands and Northern Ireland. Her last show business job before spotting the advertisement in the *Stage* was in the pantomime *Jack and the Beanstalk* in Lewisham, starring Saracen from *Gladiators*.

Melanie Brown fitted perfectly into Chris Herbert's plans – she was vibrant, power-packed and black. Her dancing capabilities meant they did not need to employ a choreographer at this early stage. She was certainly something new for Victoria. Melanie said she knew she was among friends when they all laughed and joked when she puked up in a garden on their way back to the house in Boyne Hill Road. Victoria and Melanie were the last pair you would have thought would ever get on but they did, united in their ambition and their ability to laugh at others and at themselves – although Melanie's laugh was about ten times more powerful than Victoria's.

Geri Halliwell was drinking in the last chance saloon when the Herberts handed her the opportunity to be part of the new group. Uninformed media have jumped in to say that none of the Spice Girls could sing or dance. They have lumped them all together and Victoria, in particular, has come in for criticism. Pepi Lemer observes, 'I cannot bear that put-down, because I know differently. It's totally unjustified.' It might have been unjustified where Victoria was concerned but Geri really couldn't sing or dance. She lacked the training of the others and would have to work much harder to keep up. She was decidedly the weakest link but there was never any question of Chris Herbert saying 'goodbye' to her. He observes, 'She knew this was her last shot at fame. She had tried everything, and was incredibly hungry for fame.' Like Melanie Brown, Geraldine Halliwell ticked all four boxes of the original ad. She was streetwise, outgoing, very ambitious and very dedicated. While Melanie's effervescence stemmed from being a confident young woman, the impression was always there that Geri was strung tighter than chicken wire. Her continuous battle against eating disorders is perhaps a side effect of that nervous energy.

Geri Halliwell is one of the few girls whom Kylie Minogue could look in the eye. She is very petite – not much more than an inch or two over five feet tall in her stockinged feet. As a child, she showed no inclination to grow. Her Spanish-born mother was so concerned at her small offspring that when Geri was nine she was taken to see a specialist to see if she needed medical help. Her Spanish relatives helpfully nicknamed the little girl 'la enana', which translates as 'the dwarf'.

Her mother, Ana Maria, was a stunning Spanish girl from a

village in northern Spain. She came to London when she was twenty-one and fell for the dubious charms of Laurence Halliwell, whom Geri describes as an 'Arthur Daley-type' – a 'car dealer, entrepreneur, womanizer and chancer'. He was forty-four when they married after a seven-week courtship and fifty when Geri was born. He was not the successful businessman his new wife thought he was and throughout Geri's childhood her mother worked as a cleaner to keep the family above the breadline. It was a tough life in a poor area of Watford and Geri decided when she was six that she wanted to be famous as a means of escaping to a better life. Her parents split up when she was ten, and once a week she would go round to her father's flat to clean up the place. Despite his shortcomings, Geri loved her father and was very upset when he died, aged seventy-one, before she had become a star. She has a little Jaguar car tattooed at the base of her back in tribute to his memory.

Geri went to the Watford Grammar School for Girls but felt like an outsider there. Whereas Victoria felt removed because she was the rich girl in a working-class school, Geri struggled to belong because she was the token poor kid from the wrong side of town. Geri was a bright, if impulsive, girl and passed eight GCSEs and went on to sixth form college but left when she was seventeen. She was sucked into the rave culture that was so popular in 1989 and worked in a video store, lived in a squat in one of the roughest areas of Watford and danced on a podium at the Crazy Club in London's Astoria. For that job, she dyed her hair blonde and wore a conical bra. At twenty, she was dancing in Magaluf and had some topless shots taken. A subsequent attempt to be a Page Three Girl in the *Sun* did not work out but she worked as a glamour model and dancer until she was hired as the host of a game show in Istanbul. Her career path was distinctly tacky.

Victoria had met Geri a few months before at an audition for *Tank Girl* at the MGM Trocadero in Piccadilly. The producers were looking for a girl to play the comic book heroine in a new film. So many thought they could be Tank Girl that the queue stretched round the block and it took two hours to reach the front door. They could not have been more different: Victoria looked elegant in a suit, while Geri, anorexic and weighing little more than six stone, opted for denim hot pants and fishnet tights. They got on famously as they waited patiently, munching on some popcorn Geri had stolen from the foyer. The auditions were really to drum up publicity for the film, which had already cast the established actress Lori Petty in the title role. She had starred in the baseball hit *A League of Their Own* alongside Tom Hanks and Madonna. *Tank Girl* turned out to be a flop when it was released a year later. The audition did mean that Geri and Victoria remembered one another and could resume their friendship when they met again.

From the earliest days of the Spice Girls, Geri and Victoria were very close. Victoria observed touchingly in *Learning to Fly*: 'Geri was the first person I had ever felt I could say, this is my best friend.' They shared 'the dream' but Victoria also admired Geri's tenacity. Geri's 'bottle' would have a considerable effect on Victoria's life and career. In the short term, Geri's relationship with Melanie Brown would prove to be more significant. Geri oozed pure, naked ambition. She needed her drive to overcome her lack of singing and dancing experience. Her abilities did not reflect the amount of work she had already done as a performer. Victoria pointed out, somewhat bitchily, 'However you look at it, a few months as a podium dancer in Magaluf just isn't the same as ten years at the barre.' Admittedly, when she wrote that a few years later, she and Geri had fallen out. Geri also suffered from being top-heavy, which made graceful movement a touch more problematic for her.

The athletic, lithe Melanie Chisholm had no such problem. The second Mel had been properly trained as a dancer, just as both Victoria and Melanie Brown had been. Like them, she considered herself primarily a dancer and was studying for her diploma at the Doreen Bird College when, in the college cafeteria one morning, a fellow student handed her a flyer that he thought she might be interested in. It had been produced by Chris Herbert and was very similar to the advertisement in the *Stage*. At the time, she was feeling thoroughly fed up and disillusioned with her inability to pass an audition for any West End show. She was sure of one thing – she did not want to work on a cruise ship. In the best traditions of a

Hollywood script, she read the flyer and told her friend, 'This is it, make or break.'

Melanie C, as she became known, is the only member of the group whose family has any strong or consistent musical connections, albeit at a relatively low level. Her mother, Joan, has been singing in bands since she was fourteen, most recently in River Deep, a Tina Turner tribute group. She met Melanie's father, Alan Chisholm, a fitter at Otis Elevators in Liverpool, on a night out at the famous Cavern Club in the city. From an early age Melanie used to go to watch her mother perform: 'I'd sit at the front, miming every word she sang. I always wanted to be a pop star.' She was very proud of her mother and was inspired by her. 'I felt quite special,' she explained. 'You know, when you just want to go "that's my mum!".'

Melanie was only two when her mother and father split up, an event for which she later blamed herself. Both her parents happily remarried and had more children. Her extended family consisted of one half-sister, three half-brothers and two stepbrothers but in some ways she felt like an only child: 'I felt like a spare part but it made me determined and self-sufficient.' Despite those misgivings, Melanie has always been very close to her family. She lived with her mother and stepfather, Dennis O'Neill, a bass guitarist who joined Joan in River Deep, on a council estate in Rainhill, a suburb of Widnes, an industrial town about ten miles south of Liverpool. She was certainly near enough to develop a lifelong devotion to Liverpool Football Club. One could be forgiven for thinking that the wrong Spice Girl ended up with a famous footballer. Melanie Chisholm would have loved to have spent Saturday afternoons cheering on her partner, provided, of course, that his home ground was Anfield.

The first record Melanie ever bought was *The Kids From Fame* album that had proved such an inspiration for Victoria. She dreamed of being Madonna and would practise all the superstar's dance moves. The first song she ever performed in public, at Fairfield County High School in Widnes, was 'The Greatest Love of All', the Whitney Houston classic that Melanie Brown performed at the Dance Works auditions. Unlike Victoria, Melanie

Chisholm was genuinely good at sport, particularly gymnastics and athletics. Her declared ambition as a youngster was to be an Olympic gymnast, a prima ballerina or a pop star.

Even though she was more experienced as a dancer, Melanie found herself drawn to singing, much more so than the rest of the girls. It was while she was at Doreen Bird that she realized that, given a choice, she wanted to be a singer and that was the reason she found the advertisement for a girl group so attractive.

By general agreement, Melanie Chisholm was always the least tough of the soon to be Spice Girls. Muff Fitzgerald, who was their PR person when they first became famous, observes, 'Despite her initial boyish image, in many ways she is probably the softest and warmest of all five girls.' Melanie always wanted fame and the passport to a better life for her family but she wanted music to be the focal point of her celebrity.

The departure of Michelle Stephenson left a vacancy in the group. It was still very important to Chris and Bob Herbert that there were five. They did not want to go through the whole audition process again so they asked Pepi Lemer if she could think of anyone. She could – one of her former students, Abigail Kis, a pretty, olive-skinned girl with a stunning, soulful voice. Abigail impressed the Herberts and Chic but, at the time, lacked the commitment of the other girls. She had secured a place at university to study performing arts and decided to go ahead with that. She also had a steady boyfriend who, by all accounts, was not that keen on her moving into the house in Maidenhead. She became yet another 'fifth' Spice Girl. With hindsight she was probably a fraction too young for the rest of the girls, certainly in spirit. Boyfriends, it would soon become clear, were not very 'girl power'. She observed sadly, 'I would have loved to have been that famous. Every time I see them I think, "It could have been me."'

Victoria, meanwhile, had decided once and for all that her future lay with the all-girl band and not with Persuasion. She had talked it over with Jackie and realized that everything was much more professional with the Herberts and she could not keep both going while living in Maidenhead. Steven Andrews was angry and devastated, especially as he had set up a showcase for the group in late August 1993 at the Discotheque Royale in Uxbridge. She undoubtedly made the right decision but Steven says, 'I had to cancel the night. It was horrible. I lost all credibility.' It's stretching things a bit to lay the blame for Persuasion's demise at Victoria's door but she did let them down and the band folded. They could have kept going without her if the spirit had been willing. The likelihood is that they would not have made it with or without her.

It was back to the drawing board for Pepi Lemer, whose next thought was a bubbly blonde she had taught three years previously at a college in Barnet. She remembered that her name was Emma Bunton but, in those pre-Facebook days, had no idea what had happened to her. She had to go to the college to search through old records before eventually coming up with a phone number. Emma's mother, Pauline Bunton, answered and Pepi explained that she wanted to invite her daughter to an audition at Erwin Keiles's Surrey studio. She tried to play down the possibility of success but, later, when Pauline told Emma about it all, she was thrilled to bits. The audition proved to be a resounding success. She sang 'Right Here', a top three hit the previous summer for the American girl trio SWV. Emma had clearly thought of what might be best for an audition for a girl group – not 'Mein Herr', that's for sure. Chic, ungallantly, did express concern that Emma's legs were too big. Pepi recalls, 'I told him all young girls have weight problems and they didn't want some tall, skinny blonde untouchable.' Chic seemed generally concerned about the girls' weight, suggesting at one time or another, in his best cockney accent, that both Melanie C and Victoria could lose a few pounds. Chris Herbert thought Emma was perfect: 'She was very cute, very nice with a sweet voice, a very "pop" voice.' Emma was invited to Boyne Hill Road to see if she gelled with the other girls and could be part of a group both professionally and personally.

Emma was eighteen and the youngest of the group by a couple of years. When she moved to Maidenhead, it was the first time she had been away from home. She missed home and made sure she went back to North London every weekend. She grew up in East Finchley, where her father, Trevor, worked as a milkman and she would often go out on his rounds with him. She was, however, particularly close to her mother, who started her modelling when she was two. She signed Emma up with the Norrie Carr Agency and found that her daughter's blonde cherubic features were much in demand. Emma loved modelling but also started ballet and tap classes at a local dance school. Memorably, she played the Milky Bar Kid's girlfriend in a television advertisement for the sickly sweet white chocolate. More importantly, she was accepted at the prestigious Sylvia Young Theatre School in Marylebone, where her contemporaries included Dani Behr, the Appleton sisters and Melanie Blatt.

Her parents split up when she was eleven and, while Emma does not recall being too upset at the time, one effect of the upheaval was that her father and mother could no longer afford her school fees and Emma had to attend ordinary state school for a while, which she hated. 'I cried so much,' she later said. Fate was kind though and the Sylvia Young School contacted her mother a week later to offer Emma a scholarship. She loved the camaraderie at the school, wanted to be a professional dancer and, like all stage school students, proved particularly adept at auditions. Her dancing ambitions were ruined when, at fourteen, she fell and hurt her back. For the next few years she leaned towards acting, auditioning for the part of Bianca Jackson in *EastEnders*. She did make one episode in 1985, playing a young tearaway. She also had a small role in *The Bill*. She was yet another wannabe who found inspiration from Madonna, although, a little sheepishly, she admitted that her singing inspiration was Olivia Newton-John singing the saccharine classic 'Hopelessly Devoted to You', a top three hit in 1978.

Geri, the two Melanies and Victoria all made the trip to the station on a rainy July afternoon to welcome Emma off the train. She had travelled with her mother and the first sight the girls had of their new band-mate was her walking down the platform holding hands with her mum. Victoria echoed the view of everyone that Emma was very young – she certainly *looked* young, a petite, Geri-sized girl in a little white dress – but they soon realized that she was good fun. Melanie Brown recalled that she knew Emma was all right when she joined her the first night for a midnight snack of scrambled eggs. Emma was delighted to find someone in the house who liked to eat and who would join her for her favourite Indian takeaway, chicken korma. Chris Herbert recalls, 'After the first or second day they were all really getting on. They sort of embraced her and I said to the girls, "Look, are you interested in her becoming the fifth member?" And they said, "Absolutely."'

The five girls were set: Blagger Spice (Geri), Soft Spice (Melanie C), Korma Spice (Emma), Bashful Spice (Victoria) and, as it ever was, Scary Spice (Mel B).

'We were the bookends, me and Melanie C.'

7

Boyne Hill Road

Milkman, fitter, factory worker, car salesman, and electrician – these were the occupations of the gang of five's fathers. They are all traditionally jobs for working men supporting working-class families. Something, of course, had changed by the time the five girls came together: the list then would have replaced electrician with millionaire businessman. Surprisingly, considering that money was no problem for Victoria, she was able to fit in much better than might have been expected. She could be just as much fun as the other girls and her desire to be accepted by them was completely genuine.

She had better clothes than the others, and many more of them. She never minded the girls borrowing her stuff when she was back in Goff's Oak but she was exasperated that they never cared for them as carefully as she did. She always treated her things with the utmost respect and would blanch when she found a favourite top tossed back on her bed with make-up splodges all over it. It was, however, a small price to pay for acceptance. One side effect of Victoria's family money was that she did not have the rough edges of the other girls. She was able to exploit some quite obvious differences as her Spice Girl image gradually developed.

One person she unexpectedly found a natural sympathy with was Chris Herbert. They both came from working-class families who had made good and had plenty of money. Chris was surprised when Victoria's father, Tony, came to pick her up in the gold Rolls-

Royce; his father, Bob, had one exactly the same. Chic Murphy also drove one – Victoria could have been forgiven for thinking that every family had one. Tony was chuffed that Victoria was carrying on the family's pop career. When he and Jackie bumped into Joy Spriggs at a theatre do in Broxbourne, he proudly told her, 'Victoria and four girls are all living in this house and they're going to be a pop group.' Joy thought, 'Yeah, yeah.'

Victoria soon realized that she had to get over herself to fit in. Her customary reserve or shyness had no place in Boyne Hill Road. At first she used to shut the bathroom door when she was having a pee but none of the others bothered, so in the end she gave up. Pepi Lemer tells how she tried to coach the girls in how to act in social situations. One evening she made dinner for them, serving smoked salmon as a starter: 'One of them poked at the smoked salmon and asked me why it wasn't cooked. They were incredibly naive and sweet.' It seems hard to believe that millionaire's daughter Victoria Adams-Wood had never tasted smoked salmon.

Initially, she and Emma were the quietest of the bunch, although Emma was by no means as quiet as she first appeared. Victoria soon discovered she had a 'feisty' side to her. They found common ground by both missing their families. Victoria could not wait to get back to Goff's Oak at the weekend, especially as the weather was good and everyone would be lounging by the pool. She would always give Emma a lift to East Finchley on their way home. She had a Suzuki Jeep, a much nicer car than Geri's battered old Fiat Uno. She changed it soon afterwards for an automatic, black Renault Clio. It was not as flash but she found it easier to drive.

Unusually, from the outset the girls' quest for stardom was being filmed. Geri knew a young BBC researcher called Matthew Bowers and told him about their plans for stardom. He told a friend, Neil Davies, a former paratrooper turned independent film-maker, who was making a film about Muhammad Ali at the time. Neil liked the sound of a pop project; he met up with Geri and, as a result, the birth of the Spice Girls was fully documented in a film called *Raw Spice*. The girls gave it their full consent, although later, when it was broadcast on ITV in 2001, they were less keen on having their first faltering steps towards fame aired quite so starkly. None of them was the polished, finished article. Victoria had long brown hair and carried more weight than the rest of the girls. She was Chunky Spice. Depending on your view of this sort of thing, she either needed to go on a diet – Chic's view – or she looked fantastic, a budding Beyoncé. She looked nothing like the size zero woman of today.

Neil is most revealing about Victoria at the time: 'She was shy, quiet, retiring, bashful and slightly clumsy, bordering on the awkward.' His abiding memory of the girls collectively is that they lived to practise, to get better. This was a pop boot camp to strike fear into the pampered *X Factor* wannabes. During the week, the girls always piled in to Geri's car for the trip to Trinity Studios. Geri was the oldest and a natural leader, so it made sense for her to drive even though she was an awful driver and often had prangs.

The daily car trip intriguingly reflects the early hierarchy within the group. Geri drove and Mel B sat next to her in the front passenger seat. Victoria, Melanie C and Emma squeezed into the back. The seating arrangement is very revealing. At this stage, Geri was very much the driving force, an almost manic presence creating momentum for the group. In olden times, she would have been a spear carrier leading the troops into battle. Mel B urged her on, equally brave and fearless, a co-driver who always had one eye on the driver's seat herself. Together they plotted the best route to success, rally drivers negotiating a tricky passage through woods as fast as possible. The girls in the back fastened their seatbelts. Victoria, however, was never strictly a passive soul. She may initially have lacked confidence but she would always listen carefully, take advice and weigh up her options before acting.

The relationship between Geri and Mel B was very volatile. One minute they would be at each other's throats and the next they would be laughing and being loud just as if they were the best friends in the whole world. It drove Melanie C to distraction: 'I just stood in the middle with my fingers in my ears.' Ian Lee, who looked after Trinity Studios, recalls how they would have very 'heavy' disagreements there: 'It did get quite steamy at times but it never lasted.'

Chris Herbert identifies Geri as the one who undermined his hopes and aspirations for his girl group. The problem, which perhaps he did not realize at the time, was that these girls were never 'his'. The house in Maidenhead was far from luxurious but it cultivated a team spirit within the group, much as an army barracks might have done. The living room had an old grey carpet, a couch and a couple of chairs. The kitchen was always full of dirty plates. The bedroom shared by the two Melanies had pink walls and red carpet with matching bedding. Mel B put in a red light bulb, so the room had the air of an Amsterdam brothel about it. Geri's room was a cupboard with a mattress in it. Victoria and Emma shared the biggest bedroom, decorated in blue and yellow with a couple of white wardrobes. The single bathroom was a war zone with five young women fighting for time and space – Mel B usually won. Anyone visiting would have felt that this was a student house, especially with loud music blaring out and the remains of Emma's chicken korma in the sink. Despite her angelic appearance, Emma was the messiest of the girls. Melanie C did her best to keep everything clean and tidy but it was a losing battle. Geri tried drawing up a rota for domestic jobs – a typical student ploy – but none of the others took any notice.

Amusingly, Mel B maintained that she always had to clean the toilet. Victoria and Emma, she said, didn't know how to clean it 'because their mums always did it for them'. Victoria's mother, Jackie, and younger sister, Louise, were more than a little surprised by the furnishings when they went to visit but the girls all charmed them with a medley of the songs and dances they had been practising. They had the space to do it – one advantage of not having much in the way of furniture. Louise recalled being very impressed with their voices.

Food, in general, was one of the difficult aspects of life in the house and probably the most dysfunctional. Chris Herbert dismissed it as 'pretty much a student diet'. Pepi Lemer, who was quite protective of the girls, described their diet as a Pot Noodle one. She harboured ambitions to take them some healthy chicken soup. She observed, 'They were young kids and they used to be starving all the time.' She recalled that they were all obsessive about food and their weight. 'It was all terribly out of balance even then, but the pressure on them to lose their weight was huge.' As Emma observed at the time, 'My short-term ambition is to lose weight off my bum and my thighs and that goes for all of us.'

Victoria had always felt under pressure to be thinner, especially since her days at Laine's. She was a naturally curvaceous young woman but was chronically insecure about her shape. Early film of her as a Spice Girl is quite revealing about the day-to-day importance of food. She says, 'I'm feeling in a better mood now 'cos I've had something to eat, so I'm not going to be as moody. I'm just really fat now. I'm even fatter than before.'

Mark Wood, whom she would still see every weekend, put it succinctly, 'She didn't really eat.' He recalled her diet was one that included crisps, carrots and apples. Her fad at Boyne Hill Road was dips. Geri was no help, barely eating at all and, when she did, opting for a tasty helping of beansprouts. Melanie C preferred mashed potato and tomato ketchup. Only Mel B, never beset by personal insecurity, ate properly and often, confident that she would be working off the calories dancing at Trinity Studios.

The girls may not have eaten much together but they played together and, more importantly, they worked exceptionally hard, day in, day out. When they returned after a day at Trinity Studios, they were too tired to go out and collapsed in the lounge. Mel B said, 'We eat, sleep and drink it really. Wake up in the morning, go to the studio, rehearse all day, come back from the studio and just go to sleep.'

They did work hard but they were not nuns. Sometimes they would go clubbing. Maidenhead was not exactly at the coalface of popular culture. The girls thought it totally dead and most nights the television seemed more exciting. Occasionally, Mel B would suggest going to the town's only disco, The Avenue, when it was cheap booze night but Victoria seldom bothered. Chris Herbert sometimes promoted a night at a club called Tuskers in Sandhurst and the girls would pop in. Sometimes they would try a club called Pantiles in Bagshot. Chris recalls, 'We used to go to some clubs together or they would come out with me and my friends because they didn't really have many friends in the area.' Victoria and Emma both liked going clubbing but during the week work tended to take priority so they never sampled too many of the night-time delights of the local area. At weekends Mel B and Geri would go out, preferably into London to something like Ministry of Sound, while the others went home, or in Melanie C's case went to Sidcup to see her college friends. During their weekends together, Geri and Mel B would spend ages talking about the future and how best to achieve their aims.

The original name of the group, 'Touch', sounded a little cabaret and it was time to think of a better one. Various stories have circulated over the years about how the girls finally became Spice. The favourite is that Geri had an eureka moment while she was taking one of her regular aerobics classes. She literally turned to Melanie C and said, 'I've got it.' Geri has always said it was her brainwave and Victoria has confirmed it. Like all brilliant ideas, the inspiration probably came to her from something close at hand. One theory is that she unconsciously thought of her elderly neighbour's dog, a Lakeland terrier called Spice. According to the neighbour, Mabel Brobyn, she and her husband were often in the back garden shouting for their dog. It's rather like speculating where J. K. Rowling thought of the name Harry Potter. It probably popped into her head from more than one source. Chris Herbert is in no doubt that the name came from a song the girls had co-written: 'I was also managing a songwriter called Tim Hawes. I put a little song-writing session in with Tim and the girls and Tim came up with a song called "Sugar and Spice" for the girls. And I came in at the end of the day and they played me this song and I said, "That's the name; that's what you should be called." And they all agreed. There was kind of a little rap in this song that went on about the whole Spice thing and about the whole Spice stuff. And it just sort of became their little anthem.' The girls recorded a demo of the song but it was never released.

The name Spice had five letters just like Touch but was slightly edgier. Chic's idea of Take Five was too similar to Take That, so Spice was an instant hit. It may have been Geri or it may have been Chris who thought of it. They did not know it at the time but there was already an American rapper called Spice. The name would need a readjustment at some stage.

The downfall for the Herberts was their apparent reluctance to draw up a firm management contract with the girls. Chris Herbert recalls that while he was keen to formalize things, Chic was less enthusiastic: 'Bob and I were having conversations and I was saying, "I'm happy with this and we need to engage them formally." Chic's position, I think, was that he didn't want us to let the girls feel secure in their position so that they would be reliant on us – their position would always be in the balance so that we could chop and change them if we pleased, if they played up. Chic had managed a lot of American acts and that was his way of management, ruling with an iron fist really and that's how he wanted to do it. So we just continued to roll on a sort of verbal agreement. It didn't sit comfortably with me and definitely not with my father.'

As the summer of 1994 wore on, the girls were desperate to persuade the Herberts to sign them properly. They were collectively suffering from a massive dose of insecurity. The problem for the Herberts was that putting the girls together, improving their abilities and strengthening their confidence would all ultimately undermine their position. The girls began to display an 'all for one, one for all' mentality. A unified group is always stronger than one in which the individuals look after themselves. Perhaps the best example of this was the six-strong main cast of *Friends* who always negotiated together. Nobody was ever marginalized. As a direct result of this bargaining strategy, Jennifer Aniston et al. were being paid $1 million (£500,000) each per episode by the end of the hit series' ten-season run.

Behind the scenes, Chris Herbert was trying to get a buzz going about the girls. The idea was that after six months of hard graft they would be ready to do a showcase. He explains, 'We wanted to get it to a point where they could put on a twenty-minute show, fully choreographed, live vocals, four-part harmonies and put on a showcase for our contacts within the industry, both writers and producers.' Chris wanted most of the first album recorded before he courted labels. In the meantime, it was like the film *Groundhog Day* for Victoria and the gang – repeatedly rehearsing the same four songs written by Erwin Keiles and his writing partner John Thirkell. Pepi Lemer recalls the growing tension: 'They started to get frustrated because they were getting good.' Even Geri was showing progress, helped by the extra classes she was given in singing and dancing.

Geri, most of all, was beginning to grow impatient. She was incredibly hungry for fame. She used to badger Chris to find them a single and try to release that while he attempted to explain his strategy was longer term. 'I told her we had bigger aspirations but I think that was where the tension started. She wanted to get there quicker than we were prepared to go with it. I think Geri, with all her Geri frustrations, managed to get Mel B on board with it. I think that's where the whole thing kind of started.' What Chris did not know was that Victoria was the first to suggest tentatively that they might split from Chris and Bob.

The showcase, when it happened, was a great success. Once again Chris had chosen Nomis Studios in Shepherd's Bush. Among the hundred or so 'guests', he specifically invited certain writers who were to prove to be hugely significant when the Spice Girls were up and running. The girls performed their four-song set throughout the day to the assembled mix of producers, A & R men and writers. Everybody was impressed. The girls wore Adidas tops and jeans. Pepi Lemer observes proudly, 'The buzz was here from the moment they came out on stage. They looked brilliant and they started with that energy.' One of the most significant things about the showcase was that Geri and Mel B together realized that they could talk directly to people of influence. Afterwards, Boyne Hill Road seemed very small beer and their own plans for world domination seemed to stretch far beyond the horizons offered by Bob and Chris Herbert. The problem for father and son was that everyone at the showcase knew the girls were not tied to contracts. Geri, in particular, lapped up the attention. Film-maker Neil Davies says, 'In Geri's eyes, she immediately thought, "Bye-bye, Chris. I have seen the promised land" – guys in Armani suits and chauffeured cars – and she thought, "Go with the money."'

Soon after the success of the showcase the girls were presented with the long-awaited management contract tying them to Heart. It was full of the usual legal jargon mandatory for such documents but the girls drew in their collective breath when they saw the management percentage, later revealed by Geri to be twenty-five per cent of everything. There were five of them, so they would only be getting fifteen per cent each. The maths did not appeal. Victoria persuaded the other girls to do nothing until she had shown the contract to her father. Tony was a very shrewd businessman and, advantageously, had been given a management contract himself many years before when he, too, harboured dreams of becoming a pop star. He had signed it and bitterly regretted doing so. In her book, *Learning to Fly*, Victoria describes his reaction when she took the contract home to Goff's Oak and showed it to him: '"It's like throwing hundred pound notes on the fire. Forget it," he said, succinctly.'

There are many key moments in a career. For Victoria Adams-Wood, this was one of them. Geri and Mel B did not need more than a second to agree with Tony Adams. The girls wanted to shape their own destiny. They had come a long way in little more than six months – from a ragtag bunch of wannabes to a well-drilled professional group. No longer the pursuers, they were now the pursued.

'Something got us out of bed and working. I don't know what it was.'

8

A Kick in the Nuts

Spice never wanted to sing about the moon rhyming with June. It did not reflect their collective attitude to life or the image they wanted to project. They were not a girl group that wanted to be soppy about men. There was never any likelihood of them covering hits by the Three Degrees, like 'When Will I See You Again' or the slushy ballad 'Woman in Love', in which the girl tells her man to give her love when he can. They wanted something far funkier.

Their first tentative steps towards writing a song were taken, like a million students' before them, when it was a really boring night on telly and they were sprawled out in the lounge in Boyne Hill Road wondering what to do before bed. Someone suggested writing a song – it was probably Geri – so pen and paper were produced and the girls started to scribble down a few ideas for lyrics. None of them could play an instrument so they could not gather round the piano and try out a melody or two. Instead they had a giggle working out raps.

The first proper song they concocted was called 'Just One of Those Days', which adopted the tried and trusted principle of writing about what you know – in this case, the boring routine of their lives in Maidenhead. After the showcase they had the opportunity to work with some of the songwriters who had come along to Nomis Studios. Respected songwriter Alan Glass invited them to his London studio and, during a month with him, they started to develop the sort of sound that would become recognisably the

The Return of Posh Spice at the O2 Arena, London, in December 2007.

Victoria discovered a love of performing at the Jason Theatre School in Broxbourne.

She was a pink cat in the school's big production, 'Let Us Entertain You'.

When she was eight . . .

All in gold, Victoria danced to
'If My Friends Could See Me Now'
at the Jason School choreography
competition. Sadly, she only won
the bronze medal.

Victoria had her
chance to be a
bridesmaid at the
wedding of a family
friend in 1982.

Everyone looks smart for their
school photo and Victoria was no
exception for the annual photograph
at her junior school in Goff's Oak.

Twelve-year-old Victoria performs a Czech Easter Egg dance.

Victoria takes centre stage during a jazz class at one of the Jason's special workshop days where professional dancers would put the girls through their paces.

At fourteen, Victoria used this photograph to send to children's modelling agencies before she decided a moody image suited her better.

The hair was bigger and the figure was fuller. Victoria pictured with principal, Joy Spriggs, on her graduation day from the Jason Theatre School when she was sixteen.

Posing for the National Dance Magazine's coverage of the day.

When she was at Laine's Theatre School, eighteen-year-old Victoria went to photographer Geoff Marchant for some publicity shots. She wanted to be moody but he persuaded her to smile. She liked the results so much she took boyfriend Mark Wood along on a second shoot – it was back to moody, however.

Becoming a Spice Girl was a gradual process: Victoria and Geri dancing in 1994, two years before the release of 'Wannabe'.

Both Emma and Victoria missed home so made sure they took their cuddly bears with them to the group's house in Boyne Hill Road, Maidenhead.

Spice Girls. More significant, however, was their meeting with two writers, Matt Rowe (Matthew Rowebottom) and Richard 'Biff' Stannard. With Matt and Biff, Spice found their songwriting soul-mates.

Biff Stannard recalls that it was by pure accident that he heard the girls at the Nomis showcase. He knew Chris Herbert and had worked with one of Heart Management's acts but he was at Nomis that day to meet Jason Donovan and literally bumped into Mel B in the corridor. He told *Gay Times*, 'She ran into me – loud and every-thing – and asked me straight up who I was, what I did, what hits I'd written, was I gay or straight, the complete thing!' The girls instantly loved Biff and were impressed to learn that he and his songwriting partner, Matt, who was not there that day, had co-written the East 17 hits 'Around the World' and 'Steam'. They all became good mates and within a week were working together, transferring the personal chemistry they had to the songwriting process.

Matt Rowe was a former chorister and classically trained musi-cian from Chester. Biff Stannard was an East Ender and had worked as a dancer and fashion stylist. Perhaps his early career gave him the common ground to hit it off with the all-dancing, fashion-conscious girls. The other factor was the way that Geri and Matt clicked. Mel B let slip in her autobiography that she knew what was going on when they started making eyes at one another. Geri fails to mention it in hers, describing Matt as 'tall, slim and a bit preppy' and Biff as 'round and cuddly'. All Biff would say on the subject was that Matt and Geri were close. And all Matt would say is that they indulged in a bit of flirting, noth-ing more.

During the very first week at Matt and Biff's Strongroom Studios in Shoreditch they came up with a hatful of songs, including some X-rated, never-to-be-released material. Two other tracks, however, would become very well known – one entitled '2 Become 1' and, best of all, a catchy little tune called 'Wannabe'. It was the second song they wrote, squashed together in a small room and it took only about twenty minutes to put together. The inspiration for the song, explains Biff, was the 'madness in the room'. They were all sitting around talking about the film *Grease* and, in particular, the way John Travolta moved and the general fun, high school energy he created. If one song is a starting point for the Spice Girls' sound, then it is probably 'You're the One that I Want', the number one for Travolta and Olivia Newton-John.

Much space has been devoted over the years to speculating on the origin of the words 'Zigazig Ha!', which became a catchphrase for a generation of young girl fans. Mel B thought it up, but not specifically as a lyric for this song. It was just something stupid she started saying one morning that the rest of the girls latched on to until they were all shouting it at one another. In the context of the whole song, the sexual connotation is unmistakable. Generally, Matt provided the basic music for a track while Biff had a great feel for lyrics. Biff heard them saying 'Zigazig Ha!' to each other like a 'gang of girls'. He adds, 'I just picked up on it. It was nonsensical, we were messing around. It really was all very innocent.'

The only person not over the moon about 'Wannabe' was Victoria. She had to miss going to the studio that weekend to go to a wedding with Mark and made do with hearing the tune down the phone. When she next joined up with the girls, she discovered that she did not have a solo line to sing – the others had carved it up among themselves. All Victoria ever did on the Spice Girls' most famous hit was sing a few backing vocals.

Victoria is quite correct in her judgement that this very first song coloured how the public viewed her singing. It was assumed that she did not have a solo line because she could not sing, which was quite untrue but did not do wonders for her confidence. Celebrity writer Kate Randall explains, 'It might have changed the perception of her if she had been there and got a line in the song. As it was, everyone thought she was pointless.' By her own admission, she made the least contribution to those early brainstorming studio sessions. Like most things in her life, she became better at them through practice.

Here are some names of those who never found the limelight: Reg Jones, Danielle Ditto and David Price. There are many more like them. They are the first loves of famous teenage pop stars – Britney

Spears, Justin Timberlake and Billie Piper – who did not survive their partner's first taste of fame. In Victoria's case, one can add the name of Mark Wood. It was time for her to become Victoria Adams once again.

With twenty–twenty hindsight, Mark did not stand a chance. He sat on Tony and Jackie's comfy sofa or stretched out by the pool while Victoria worked ferociously to grab what was clearly becoming a golden opportunity. Perhaps he never grasped how much progress was being made nor the confidence that was beginning to flow through Victoria's veins. How could he, cocooned as he was in Goff's Oak, understand the collective strength of the gang of five or the individual power and drive of Geri Halliwell and Melanie Brown? These young women would never let a man stand in the way of their ambitions and Geri, in particular, was none too happy when Victoria went to the wedding instead of choosing to stay behind and help with 'Wannabe'. They would also never keep their opinion to themselves – and Mark did not impress.

Mel B admits that she did not like him and could not 'connect' with him. She would tease Victoria mercilessly about him, especially over his dress sense. They all did. He would come to Boyne Hill Road to visit her occasionally. Victoria relished being one of the girls and needed their approval. Despite that, Mark's days did not appear numbered on Valentine's Day, 1995. Victoria's card to him read: 'Mark, I know this is meant to be a secret, but I guess you know already who this is from! Anyway, it's no secret how I feel about you even though we have our ups and downs. I'll love you forever, Victoria xxxxx'

The 'downs' had taken over for good a couple of days before Victoria's twenty-first birthday in April. Mark's present was a pair of shoes that Victoria had already chosen. She was going out that night without Mark and wanted to wear them for a special birthday celebration with the girls. He objected because he said they were a present and she should wait until her actual birthday to wear them. Mark, perhaps, should have realized that one should never come between a girl and her chosen outfit for the night. Even so, it was a silly row. He later told the *Sun* newspaper, 'She flew into a rage because she wasn't getting her own way and said I was selfish. She told me not to pick her up later on because I would ruin her night out.'

Mark claimed he moved his belongings out of The Old School House that night. He had been there for three years but had bought a small flat in Hertford. Would he and Victoria have lasted as long as they did if they had not been living under the same roof? They were together for her family birthday celebrations a couple of days later but, according to Victoria, barely spoke and had a wretched evening. It was a very upsetting time for both of them and they have given different versions of who dumped whom. Victoria may have wanted them to stay together at first but that changed within a very few days. By chance, she met her first Hollywood star.

Corey Haim was a colourful character. He was born in Toronto and was the same age as Mark but had been a teenage star in the eighties. He gained an international reputation when he starred in the cult vampire movie *The Lost Boys* alongside another child star, Corey Feldman, and a very young Kiefer Sutherland. To date he has made a total of eight movies with the other Corey but they never recaptured the success of the first one. Haim's subsequent life reads like a script of a child star's descent into nightmare. The *Sun* revealed that he became so hooked on drugs that he nearly died. Corey revealed that he smoked his first joint on *The Lost Boys*. He later explained, 'I lived in Los Angeles in the eighties, which was not the best place to be.' He reportedly went into rehab. When he met Victoria he was not yet at rock bottom. That would happen a few years later, in 2001, when he suffered a stroke that was allegedly drug induced. He's clean now and making a successful comeback on television with his old friend Feldman.

Victoria came across him at the Strongroom Studios, where Matt was helping Corey with his music career. He fancied himself as a rock singer and was making a demo tape. He instantly took a shine to Victoria and the two became inseparable for a week. He was a hurricane of fresh air as far as she was concerned. He thought she was a 'rocking babe'. The *News of the World* would later allege that

Victoria and Corey had a week of sushi and sex at the Ritz. Corey never confirmed that anything intimate had happened between them but did concede that he 'had a great time with Victoria'. The lady herself could not have been clearer in stating that they did not have sex. They only kissed, apparently.

Corey was in London for only a week but during that time Victoria took him home to Goff's Oak to meet Jackie and Tony. She genuinely had a good time with Corey. He was so different from what she was used to – he was funny and unpredictable. It was just a week and then she dropped him off at Heathrow for his flight back to Los Angeles. He served a purpose in showing Victoria that there could be life after Mark, although about a week of Corey was about all she could manage. For one thing, he never seemed to sleep – perhaps the effect of too many pills.

On the night of the shoes row, Victoria was going out on the town with the girls. Chic had decided that they should do something to mark her twenty-first birthday and had organized something special. The evening began in a style to which Victoria was already accustomed with a trip in a Rolls-Royce. Chic drove them to a suitably posh Chinese restaurant in Knightsbridge, where the meal ended in a birthday cake fight. Victoria was traumatized when a splodge of cream landed on her smart Karen Millen suit. Beneath the restaurant was a casino and Chic gave each of the girls £100 ($200) in chips to play the roulette tables. This was by far the most glamorous evening yet for the Boyne Hill Road girls. Revealingly, Victoria was the most careful player of the five girls, making sure she came away with a tidy profit – an early example of her business acumen that would have made her father proud.

For that evening, at least, the prospect of the girls splitting from the Herberts was put to one side. Barely a month after that jolly evening, the girls did a runner. Chris Herbert had been getting more and more uneasy. He was well aware that the girls were employing stalling tactics by picking on little things in practically every line of the written contract. He recalls, 'I began pushing for them to sign. It wasn't a big, long form of agreement, but quite a simple management contract.' The sequence of events was quite bizarre – more like a piece of bad television fiction than the reality of five girls taking a momentous step.

Chris Herbert had arranged for the girls to travel to Sheffield in the middle of May for a recording session with acclaimed song-writer/producer Eliot Kennedy. The Chris version of events is that Geri was pestering him to give her all the details, which made him smell a rat: 'I was reluctant to give her this information. They didn't need to know until they were ready to go up there. A day or two before they were due to leave, there was a big argument down at Trinity Studios and a couple of the girls, including Victoria, stormed off. That left Geri and Mel B in Maidenhead together. We couldn't work out what had gone on and the other girls now seemed pretty uncontactable. They'd gone back home, basically. I wasn't prepared to let the girls go to Eliot Kennedy's until we'd sorted out these problems internally.

'So, on the morning the girls were supposed to be up at Eliot's, I rang him and said, "I'm sorry but the girls are not going to be able to make the session; they've all come down with the flu." To which Eliot said, "OK, fine." I said, "Look, I'll let you know when they're all feeling a bit better and we can reschedule the session." And he hung up and that was that. The next thing I know, about twenty minutes later, he rang me back and he said, "Look, I've got to let you know that Geri and Mel are already up here."

'Unbeknown to us, we were covering for the girls because of this argument, which turns out to have been a big staged argument between them. In the meantime, Geri and Mel had gone up there. They couldn't get the information out of us as to where the session was, so they had literally gone on a wild goose chase, got in the car, driven to Sheffield and went knocking on doors until they turned up on Eliot's doorstep and said, "You don't know us but we need your help." Geri asked him if he would still work with them if they cut from their current management and Eliot said yeah because he had already bought into the project. They stayed over that night and continued the session. We had no idea they were up there. With the session secured, the other girls went up there.'

That version of events paints a far from attractive picture of duplicity from the five girls. In Geri's book, *If Only*, she maintains that she and Mel B were in the house in Boyne Hill Road on the second weekend in May when Bob Herbert rang and insisted they sign the contract the following day. They were due to go to Sheffield on the Tuesday but feared that the session would be cancelled if they did not sign, so they took responsibility for their own destiny. They quickly packed up their clothes in bin bags, loaded up the old Fiat Uno and shut the door behind them. Geri says she left a note which read: 'Thank you for all you have done. We can't agree to the terms of the contract.' And that was that. Geri makes no mention of any staged row but also, intriguingly, she makes no reference to how the others – Victoria, Emma and Melanie C – collected their belongings – unless, of course, they had already done so. In Mel B's version, they all left the same night with her and Geri the last to go. In Victoria's account, they left after Geri had managed to get their demo tape from Bob and Chris's office in Lightwater. Her description is all a bit cloak and dagger.

Everyone agreed that Geri and Mel B headed off to Sheffield to find Eliot not knowing whether it was all going to fall down like a pack of cards. The other undeniable fact is that they ran out on Bob, Chris and Chic. Chris tried talking to Eliot's management and stated his position that he thought the right thing to do was to hold off until the problem was sorted, but basically it was too late. A few days later he heard they were coming back to Maidenhead and got through to them for the first time since the Sheffield flit: 'I said, "What the bloody hell is going on?" And they said they were clearing out, leaving the house and "we're gone" sort of thing. And that was pretty much it.'

In the murky waters of the music industry, five young women ruthlessly ditching the man who put them together is nothing to get too excited about. If, however, the question is: 'Was it a decent way to behave?', then the answer is almost certainly 'No.' The Spice Girls' biographer, David Sinclair, described their behaviour as 'incredibly self-serving and underhand'. As Neil Davies observes, 'Chris Herbert scored the bull five times.' The most precious thing the Herberts and Chic Murphy gave the girls was time. They had a full year to improve and develop with no real time limit set upon their goals. It was an intensive year of further education – they were given somewhere to live, pocket money, teachers, songwriters and somewhere to practise and rehearse. At the end of the year, they were very nearly the Spice Girls. Could Chris Herbert have taken them that extra step? Probably not. He himself admits, 'I was a young, inexperienced manager.'

During that year Victoria had grown in confidence, and, just as pertinently, had begun to evolve her later Spice Girl persona as Chris had imagined it at the very beginning – a slightly classier, more composed young woman. She may not have been posh but she certainly had no rough, in-your-face edges.

Without Chris Herbert's initial vision, the Spice Girls would almost certainly have never found each other. The well-known singing coach Carrie Grant, who later worked with the Spice Girls, observes, 'Would they have made it individually? No.' Mel B and Geri would have been on cruise ships, Emma in *The Bill*, Mel C in a tribute band and Victoria in provincial stage musicals – perhaps.

The Sheffield phone calls spelled the end for Chris Herbert and the girls. He recalls, 'I felt gutted about it; more so because I had spent time with the girls and I felt more of a connection with them. We were all friends as well. I felt that it was a real kick in the nuts for me.' Chris Herbert was an ambitious young man and did not dwell too long on what might have been. Fortunately, the experience at the hands of Spice was not the end of his career, although plans for world domination via a girl band were quickly put on ice in favour of a return to the more tranquil waters of boy bands. While the Spice Girls bathed in the glory of being one of the biggest acts in the world, he and Bob went back to the route that had worked so well before. In 1997, they placed an ad in the *Stage* for a boy band and immediately caught the imagination of the media. The headlines read: 'Spice Boys Wanted, Boy Power!' – publicity that resulted in thousand of young hopefuls turning up. Once again the Herberts were seeking five boys to try to cover all the bases with a young public. They succeeded almost as well as before and this time chose a better name than Touch. The group, 5ive, had three number one singles and a number one album before disbanding at the end of 2001. The original idea had come full circle: the Spice Girls came about from the belief that a girl band could emulate the success of Take That. Five was born from a desire to emulate the success of a girl band, the Spice Girls. In their first year, they were on twenty-three magazine covers and followed in the girls' footsteps by securing a deal with Pepsi.

Chris and his fiancée, Shelley, were due to marry in August, 1999. Sadly, the Monday before the wedding, Bob Herbert was killed in a car crash. He was fifty-seven. The wedding went ahead as planned on the Saturday and Bob's funeral was the following Wednesday. Chris cancelled the honeymoon. In her autobiography, Victoria said of Bob, 'I always liked him. He was killed in a car accident at the end of 1999.' Collectively, the Spice Girls paid tribute to him during a press call.

Chris continued with 5ive and subsequently managed Hear'Say, Kim Marsh, Stephen Gately, Alex Parks and the kids from *Fame Academy* and, recently, a new band called Ben's Brother. He bears no grudge whatsoever against the Spice Girls: 'I knew the girls were going to be successful and we could have had success with them, but I couldn't be confident that I would have been able to guide their careers in the way that Fuller did.' The Fuller in question, Simon Fuller, would have a powerful and lasting effect on Victoria's life and career.

Mark Wood, meanwhile, was history. The pace of Victoria's life suddenly moved into the fast lane and he was stuck in the slow one. She had enjoyed the glamour of her night at the casino and the mad whirl that was Corey Haim. She found that she could move on much more quickly than she might have anticipated. Mark came round to The Old School House and spotted a photograph on the kitchen counter of a smiling Victoria and Corey with their arms entwined. Tony had taken it in the garden when Victoria brought him home. The picture may or may not have been left out on view on purpose but it had a volcanic effect on Mark. Victoria left him in no doubt that he needed to get on with his life. She was getting on with hers.

'Every time we performed it, I just felt like a gooseberry standing at the back not doing anything.'

9

'Wannabe'

A couple of demos, even if they were for 'Wannabe' and '2 Become 1', were not enough to build a career for five girls with no contract, no manager and nowhere to live. They were camping out in a Sheffield flat that belonged to Eliot Kennedy, who had been their knight in shining armour when they needed to escape from Boyne Hill Road. Eliot was a Sheffield lad but had been brought up in Australia before returning to Yorkshire as a teenager. He worked as a singer and guitarist before gaining experience as a studio engineer and producer. His first chart success as a producer was on a track called 'Independence', a comeback hit for Lulu at the beginning of 1993. Take That's manager, Nigel Martin-Smith, liked the track and brought in Gary Barlow to start working with Eliot. The result was the classic 'Everything Changes', which was number one in April 1994, just when the girls were getting started.

Eliot lived in the same semi-detached house that his parents had owned and was very relaxed about having five girls descend on him. He enjoyed working with them and having them around, dressed in pyjamas, watching *Star Wars* movies with him late into the night. The songwriting process with him was remarkably similar to that with Biff and Matt. He would sing them a chorus or melody with no lyrics and then they would all produce pen and paper, bounce ideas around and come up with the song in about ten minutes. 'It was a really quick process,' he recalls.

The girls were very fortunate that Eliot took an instant liking to them because it could have made life very difficult indeed if he had decided to defer to the Herberts, whom he had worked with before. He chose not to and the result of their week with him in Sheffield was two tracks, 'Say You'll Be There' and 'Love Thing', both destined to become Spice Girls' classics. Victoria shared a room with Geri, leaving Eliot, whom she described as a 'total sweetheart', to sleep on the sofa with his large woolly dog.

After a busman's holiday of a week in Sheffield, it was time to return south and take stock of their situation. They were making things happen but the advice they were getting from Eliot and from everyone they came across was that they needed a brilliant manager to realize fully the ambitions they were all working so hard to achieve. Once again, it was the showcase at Nomis that provided the introduction. One of the invited audience that day was Mark Fox, creative director at BMG Music Publishing and one of the best-known A & R men in the music business. He had been a founder member of teenybop favourites Haircut 100 while working as a teacher. He was the group's drummer and took over as lead singer when Nick Heyward left. When the group folded in the early eighties, he moved behind the scenes. The first thing he did for Spice, as they were still called at this stage, was introduce them to a songwriting team called Absolute, who would become the third key component of their sound after Matt and Biff and Eliot.

'Absolute' were Andy Watkins and Paul Wilson, who met when they were students in Bristol. Paul had been a classically trained musician, studying at the Royal College of Music, while Andy had played guitar in a band covering classics by the Clash. Together they went into partnership, getting a government grant to start their own studios in Bath and building a reputation as go-ahead producers, re-mixers and writers. They had moved to London by the time they first met the girls, to their new studios on Tagg's Island, which is in the Thames not far from Hampton Court. They had recently signed to BMG Music Publishing, so it was potentially good business for Mark to put them with a promising act like Spice. Amusingly, Andy and Paul were not that enthusiastic when they first heard 'Wannabe' and thought it would be difficult for them to fit in with that kind of sound. It took them longer to click with the girls so that they could move forward creatively. They found the girls fantastic fun, but the sound favoured by Absolute in their work with artists like Lisa Stansfield was much more soulful than the pop orientation of Biff and Matt. Absolute loved modern black music and wanted to work with a girl group producing R & B – that was not Spice.

To their credit, Absolute quickly realized that the problem was trying to impose their music too much on the girls. Instead, they tried starting off with absolutely nothing, a blank canvas, and seeing where the session took them. It was a blinding success and, in no time at all, they had the basis for the future number one 'Who Do You Think You Are'. Andy and Paul also realized that the girls were imagining how the dance routine might go and the video might look while thinking of a catchy lyric for the chorus – this was total concept product. From there, the partnership with the girls grew in strength so that Absolute would end up co-writing more tracks on their first album than anybody else.

The much maligned phrase 'co-writing' is an interesting one where the Spice Girls are concerned. In the sceptical world of pop, it would be too easy to assume that their names were stuck on to the song in order to take a percentage of the publishing royalty, where vast sums of money can be earned. Sometimes that's true – perhaps more often than not – but it was not the case with the girls. They were a team and, while contributions varied, they always wanted to be involved in every part of the process that would take them to the top. They also made sure that each of the five members always received an equal share for songwriting. There were never any squabbles over who thought of a particular line. The principal writers, like Matt and Biff, never had a complaint with this – they became rich and successful riding in the slipstream of the Spice Girls.

Spice continued to hunt for the right manager with Geri, in particular, maniacally arranging meetings all across London. Victoria and Melanie C would slightly hang back while the other three went into action. They were a heady mixture of full on sexuality and schoolgirl allure, rampaging through the offices of hapless managers like a bunch of St Trinian sexpots. Geri and Mel B were

Olympic standard bottom pinchers, while Emma would put her hair in bunches and wear the shortest skirt. Despite creating a stir wherever they went, they could not find the right person until a conversation with Andy and Paul on the dock near their studio one afternoon changed their lives. Absolute explained that their manager had recently joined forces with a company called 19 Management, run by a rising star called Simon Fuller. He had negotiated the deal with BMG Music Publishing on Absolute's behalf. They had already sent him a tape of one of the songs they were working on with the girls and he had responded enthusiastically. It was a promising start.

Ten years later, Fuller recalls, 'My first impression of them when they bounded into my office was of an abundant energy and optimism that couldn't be ignored.' He noted in his foreword to the Spice Girls' biography that they 'feared nothing and challenged everything'. Ever since that first meeting, he has been inextricably linked with Victoria's destiny. He has been the man guiding Brand Beckham through the years. Strangely, for a man who has had so much influence on popular culture during the past two decades, he remains something of a ghost figure, shunning all limelight. The whole world it seems knows the name of Simon Cowell but it is Fuller who is the third richest man in music, with an estimated fortune of £450 million ($900 million).

When Victoria and the girls marched into the offices of 19 Management in Battersea, he was thirty-five and had been building a reputation in the music business for ten years. He was born in Cyprus, where his father was stationed with the RAF, and enjoyed a nomadic childhood in Germany and Ghana before his family came back to England and settled on the south coast in Hastings. His father became a primary school headmaster and Simon was very much a product of a middle-class, provincial environment. From an early age he seemed to appreciate that he could make money from music, managing his school band and leaving school to run local discos. He followed a tried and trusted method of gaining a foothold in pop by being hired as an A & R man with Chrysalis Records. He was noticed straight away when he recommended that the company buy up Madonna and her first hit,

'Holiday'. In the end, they chose to pick up the song but not the artist.

After a couple of years, Fuller decided to go it alone and manage a young keyboard player and producer called Paul Hardcastle. It proved a very wise move. They struck gold almost immediately when Hardcastle's anti-Vietnam War song, '19', went to number one. Nineteen was the average age of US soldiers serving in that pointless war. The record was number one in fourteen countries and sold more than four million copies. At the age of twenty-five, Simon Fuller had made his first million. Not surprisingly, he called his newly formed company 19 Management and kept the prefix as his company expanded into the 19 Entertainment Group. Hard-castle could never repeat that first success, although he continued to be successful as a writer and producer. Ironically, the record proved more of a stepping stone for the manager than the artist.

The next two artists Fuller took on were Cathy Dennis and Annie Lennox. The former demonstrated his acumen in getting the best out of a client; the latter his ability to work with an estab-lished star. Cathy was the dance music darling from Norwich with a much copied bob haircut who had five top ten hits in the early nineties. Her biggest hits were 'Touch Me (All Night Long)' and a version of the Kinks' classic 'Waterloo Sunset'. Fuller, however, saw her more as an international artist and she became a bigger star in the US, with three consecutive number ones in the *Billboard* dance chart. 'Touch Me' reached number two in the main chart. He would use the blueprint of her success to move the Spice Girls into the American marketplace at the earliest opportunity.

Cathy Dennis had a self-deprecating style, rather like Kylie Minogue and also strikingly similar to the one Victoria would adopt for herself. Cathy once said, 'It never crossed my mind that I could be a pop star because I came from Norwich. Pop stars don't come from Norwich.' By the end of the nineties Cathy had tired of per-forming and reinvented herself as one of the most talented and in-demand songwriters. One of the reasons she was in demand was the way in which Simon Fuller wove her career into the paths of his other clients. For instance, she wrote the majority of the hits for S Club 7, who just happened to be his brainchild. It is a superb example of management that turned Cathy into a multi-million-airess. She would also co-write one of the first Spice Girls songs, 'Bumper to Bumper', which would coincidentally be on the flip side of 'Wannabe' and contained the Girl Power sentiment that they wanted to 'drive your body all night'. To date she has written six number ones. Looking at an image of Cathy Dennis from her early chart days is quite an eye-opener: the dark black bob, the sultry look upwards at the camera – it is Victoria Beckham, 2007.

Annie Lennox was an excellent credential for 19. Arguably the most successful female singer in Britain and one of the richest, her connection with Fuller improved his prestige in the eyes of Spice. When he took her on she had had a number one album, *Diva*, and was about to have another, *Medusa*, which included the beautiful 'No More "I Love Yous"'. Coincidentally, the album was number one in the charts as the girls were leaving the Herberts and looking to rule the world. Simon Fuller was an impressive figure even before they met him.

They bounced in to his office ready to do their 'number' on Simon only to find that he was the first manager they had met to keep them waiting. They had to wait until he chose to appear, a dapper, perma-tanned figure with shiny black hair and a quietly imposing manner. Author David Sinclair described him nicely as cutting a 'neat, slightly camp figure'. The girls did their well-rehearsed impromptu office version of 'Wannabe' and waited for the reaction. There was no 'I'm gonna make you stars.' That would have been stating the obvious. Instead, Fuller explained what he thought he could do for them to maximize their impact both at home and internationally, using Cathy Dennis as an example.

He also asked them what they wanted to achieve and that's when Victoria came out with one of her most famous sayings, 'We want to be household names. We want to be bigger than Persil washing powder.' At the end of the meeting, Fuller did concede a rare compliment to the girls. 'I think you're fabulous,' he said, which really meant something coming from him. Here was a man who smoothly oozed success and the girls were of one mind that they wanted him to be their manager. Victoria had always appreciated the need for the right image and had worked hard to present herself in the most effective way. From Fuller she would learn the importance of strategy, marketing, publicity, media and the ability to make good business deals. Geri Halliwell praised Victoria's ability to keep her feet on the ground, a characteristic well in tune with the Fuller approach and one reason why he has remained a key element in her life.

Simon Fuller has become something of a legendary Svengali figure over the years – so much so that many think he in some way manufactured the Spice Girls. That was not the case. The concept for the girl group came from Chris Herbert. He and his late father, Bob, also chose the members. Nobody, however, 'made' them. Victoria, Geri, Emma and the two Melanies worked furiously in an undistinguished studio in Knaphill to turn themselves into a formidable gang of five. They were an extremely accomplished, driven and wildly entertaining slice of show business when Fuller took them on – or rather they took him on. Not only that, they had already linked up with premier songwriters to produce most of the tracks for their first album. He was not a Svengali for Spice. Geri described the girls as the captains of a ship and him as the navigator. His job was to harness and guide their energy and talent into a marketing strategy that would appeal to as many people as possible, beginning with record company executives.

One advantage of no longer being at Boyne Hill Road was that Victoria could once again live in her favourite place, The Old School House. She was officially single and for the first time in her life had the chance to play the field. Victoria, however, has never been that sort of girl. She was with Mark for five years and was used to being in a settled relationship. Nobody has ever come out of the woodwork and revealed a one-night stand with the Spice Girl. Revelations of bed-hopping in Boyne Hill Road would have jarred with the image she had carefully constructed. She might enjoy a glass of wine and a cigarette but, Corey Haim aside, that seems to be the sum total of her rock 'n' roll behaviour. She is someone who seems to function better within a relationship, preferring that stability. She is the only one of the Spice Girls whose parents are not divorced and Jackie and Tony are the role models for her life and values.

She was single for just a couple of weeks before her brother Christian introduced her to Stuart Bilton in a local wine bar. He was a year older than Victoria, fair-haired, fashion-conscious and handsome in a Jude Law sort of way. Victoria had heard his name mentioned around the school corridors when she was a teenager and knew he enjoyed a local reputation as a ladies' man. He had already had two high profile girlfriends in Patsy Palmer and Daniella Westbrook, both familiar faces from the golden years of *EastEnders*. He was the nearest you could get to a local celebrity in this corner of Hertfordshire or, at least, in the Prince of Wales pub at the end of Victoria's road.

Stuart was a part-time model, but mostly worked in his father's florist's shop in Wormley, near Broxbourne, and lived in a flat next door to the shop. Victoria did not seem bothered by his low-flying career. Stuart remembers it as Victoria making the running, 'driving him mad to go out'. She was smitten and her parents liked him. Even Louise did not seem to raise any objections. Victoria described their relationship as 'hearts and flowers' and, after the unsatisfactory end to her time with Mark, he was perfect. At least he didn't call her 'his little pop star'. Stuart was very easy company and always ready with a smile. He also seemed happy to stay quietly in the background while Victoria took her first ride on the Spice Girls' merry-go-round. He did offer some constructive help, however, by driving her over to Bethnal Green to visit his old girlfriend Patsy Palmer because Victoria wanted to ask her about how to deal with the press and the paparazzi. She told the *EastEnders* star, 'I'm in this girl band and we are going to be really famous.' Patsy leaned across in a concerned manner and said, 'Don't be too disappointed. It's always the rejections that we learn from.'

Simon Fuller, meanwhile, did the rounds of his major contacts, sent the girls in to do their 'Wannabe' act and sat back to wait for offers. Major interest came from Sony, London and Virgin. London was an attractive option because, among others, it was the label for East 17 and therefore had a link with the songwriters Matt and Biff. Virgin, however, were especially keen because they did not have a major pop act on their books at that time. If the girls signed with Virgin, they would be joining a roster that included the

Verve, Lenny Kravitz, Massive Attack and Neneh Cherry. From the point of view of Spice and Simon Fuller, Virgin had a reputation as a cool and hip label and one that could give them the care and attention they wanted. For their part, Virgin declared their intentions by flying the girls over to the US before they had signed a contract. It was all a bit different from chicken korma in the lounge of Boyne Hill Road. The girls were treated royally by the Virgin executives in a good old-fashioned piece of schmoozing. Virgin were determined not to lose the group.

The girls decided to go with Virgin, persuaded in part by a deal for five albums and an advance, if all went to plan, of £1 million ($2 million). Simon Fuller was delighted to obtain such a figure for an unsigned band. The girls literally went from the dole to riches overnight. Behind the scenes Fuller had set about reaching an amicable agreement with Bob and Chris Herbert and Chic Murphy. They settled for a one-off payment of £50,000 ($100,000) to cover their time and expenses. The figure may not seem much for missing out on millions but nothing is ever guaranteed in the music business. In this case, everybody was happy and Spice were able to sign to Virgin bringing no excess baggage with them. Chris looks back wryly, 'We worked out the financial settlement with them. It didn't take account of sixty million albums!'

London Records did not give up and invited the girls to a party on a boat on the Thames. By coincidence, the date, 13 July 1995, was the same day they were set to sign the Virgin contract. Both companies knew what was going on. The girls arrived at the boat and happily knocked back the wine and the food and revelled in all the attention from a real rock 'n' roll party. One can only imagine what the sober-suited executives of Virgin were thinking as they waited nervously back at their offices in Notting Hill for the girls to arrive. As the old adage almost goes: 'It's not over 'til the fat lady signs.' Their nerves were not helped by a practical joke the girls played on Virgin. Their limo arrived outside the HQ but inside waiting for the welcoming committee were not Spice but five blow-up dolls from the Ann Summers sex shop in Charing Cross Road. The girls had dispatched their new personal assistant to buy them and send them on as an advance party

When the girls finally arrived, they were each presented with a bouquet of flowers and a goodwill payment of £10,000 ($20,000), which made their collective eyes light up. Victoria was in a bit of a daze from enjoying a glass of wine too many. One of the side effects of not eating very much was that alcohol tended to go straight to her head. After signing the £1 million ($2 million) contract, the girls, all in high spirits, were bundled into a taxi bound for the fashionable restaurant Kensington Place, where Simon had booked a table for them all to celebrate. Victoria by now was very tipsy and shrieked, 'Hang on to your knickers!' whereupon the other four pulled hers off and Geri threw them out the window. The taxi was in such a state of beer and fags, Simon had to give the cabbie an extra £50 ($100) to send him away happy.

It was one of the most memorable days of Victoria's life so far and it was a shame she could not remember anything about it.

'Hang on to your knickers. It's going to be a bumpy ride.'

PART TWO

VICTORIA BECKHAM

10

Becoming Posh

The Spice Girls signed their contracts with Virgin sixteen months after Victoria had walked down Oxford Street towards the auditions. They had worked in a thoroughly dedicated manner towards their goal and were now absolutely ready to take the world by storm – or so they thought. They had a brilliant manager and back-up team, songs already written and an album set to go and they looked sensational both individually and collectively. The record company, however, had made a large financial commitment and did not want anything to go wrong. Behind the scenes, many powerful people were agonizing about the girls' image and where to position them in the pop market. Executives were worried that they might sell a few singles with a quick blast of publicity but they would not have enough substance to shift the number of albums needed to justify such a big outlay.

One of the first big issues to address was the choice of their debut single. Nobody could afford to make a mistake. Even though they signed in July, it was considered too close to Christmas to be able to cash in properly on that lucrative market, so nobody seemed in any great hurry. In the meantime, Geri and Mel B wanted 'Wannabe' to be the first single. They were convinced that it best represented the nature of the group – upfront and sassy. Ashley Newton, head of A & R at Virgin, did not agree and strongly lobbied for 'Say You'll Be There', which had a mellower feel and a stronger melody. Geri, the appointed representative for Spice, stood her ground. Victoria may not have been that bothered about 'Wannabe' but she never let on in public. She was smart enough to understand the importance of creating interest in the band. They had to sell the sizzle.

They started off by flying to Los Angeles. The trip was typical of their forward thinking: they would start off in the world's biggest marketplace before the UK even knew they existed. They were also already thinking of a movie before they had a record out. Then it was a holiday in Hawaii. The girls posed for a rare picture of them all wearing bikinis; Victoria never normally wears a two-piece swimsuit. At this stage they were still called Spice, but not for long. To everyone's annoyance, they discovered that there was an American rapper called Spice 1. They did not want to be confused with the man who brought the world the notorious albums *AmeriKKKa's Nightmare* and *1990-Sick.*

Simon Fuller had noticed that when the girls were in the US they would charge into a room and inevitably someone would say, 'Here come the Spice girls.' He suggested in passing to Geri that Spice Girls might be an even better name for the group. From that moment on they were known as the Spice Girls. At last they had found the right name.

They kept on being given dates for the release of the first single only to have it postponed – again. After a while they could have been forgiven for wondering if there was ever going to be a single. The stumbling block was still 'Wannabe'. The problems with it were not resolved until Simon Fuller sent the song to engineer Mark 'Spike' Stent. It proved to be an inspired move. Spike, so called because he had spiky hair as a young man, had established a solid reputation for his work with Depeche Mode, Erasure and Massive Attack. At the time, he was in Ireland working with U2 on their album *Pop* but would come home for odd weekends to see his family and catch up on business at his London studio. During one of those weekends, he turned his attention to 'Wannabe'. The song had been mixed about half a dozen times but still nobody was completely happy. The track did not gel together in a radio-friendly manner. There was a world of difference between sticking the demo on while the girls danced around the desks and sounding good on Radio One. Spike recalls, 'The problem was that the vocal balance hadn't been quite sussed. It's a very quirky pop record, and there's not a lot going on with it, and my work was all about getting the vocals to sound right. It was quite tough to do, even though it only took six hours.' He did the job so well that Virgin pronounced themselves happy to release 'Wannabe' as the first single.

The 'buzz' for the Spice Girls began in the unlikely surroundings of Kempton Park Racecourse, when the record company arranged for them to spend the day being photographed and generally larking about at the Sunbury racetrack south of London. A few journalists turned up to take advantage of a free day at the races and one of them had the treat of a live performance of 'Wannabe' in the ladies' loo. Victoria wore a short black mini dress that revealed how she had been spending her time since they signed with Virgin: she was clearly losing weight. They all frolicked around a statue of the famous racehorse Desert Orchid and generally made a nuisance of themselves – job done.

The girls were paraded by Virgin at the Brit Awards in February 1996. They mingled with Lenny Kravitz and Vanessa Paradis. Lenny made everyone laugh by declining the food on offer in favour of a Jamaican takeaway he had brought with him and proceeded to share with them. The girls were not the talk of the night. That accolade belonged firmly to Jarvis Cocker, who took umbrage at the sight of Michael Jackson appearing Christ-like on stage among a throng of adoring children and promptly ran up and waggled his bottom at the man who was then the biggest star in the world. The highlight for the girls was being introduced to Take That. They had always idolized the boys; they had posters of them on the walls in Boyne Hill Road and would sing their hits and copy their dance routines. Chris Herbert had even treated them all to a night at a Take That concert. The Spice Girls were noticed at the Brit Awards but not as much as Jarvis and Jacko.

Something far more significant to the careers of the Spice Girls than the Brit Awards happened in February 1996: Take That split up. They were the most popular band in the country and their demise made *News at Ten*. The split left a huge hole in the teenage market and record companies were falling over themselves to fill it. The perceived wisdom was that an all-girl band would not appeal to the teenage girls who adored Take That. That 'wisdom' would emphatically prove to be wrong.

Virgin were still trying to think up publicity angles for the girls, who were not getting enough media coverage. The then head of press, Heather Finlay, asked music journalist Sonia Poulton to interview the girls at the studio in West London where they were finishing off the recordings for their first album. Sonia recalls that Virgin were tearing their hair out. 'People don't get them,' said her friend. 'They think pop bands need to be all synchronized and dressed in matching outfits. Nobody in the press is interested.'

When she went to the interview, Sonia was greeted at the door by Geri, who was always, it seems, at the front. Upstairs she met the others, who all talked at once, except Victoria, the 'pouty brunette', who remained slightly aloof, watching everybody. Sonia observes, 'She looked more like a corporate executive than the "next big thing" in her pencil skirt and smartly tailored jacket.' Geri, by contrast, was wearing a teal green piece of BacoFoil. Despite her general impression that the girls were a bit of a ragtag bunch, Sonia was impressed by their 'formidable energy' and set about more readily identifying them as individuals.

Her conversation with the girls just before they were launched into the public eye is fascinating. Mel B she thought was 'feisty and strong with lots of attitude'. She told Geri, 'You're a vamp – seaside saucy meets exotic dancer.' She said blonde Emma was cute and needed protection: 'I see you as the Baby Doll of the group.' Melanie C was easy: 'Obviously, you're the sporty one,' observed Sonia.

Finally, she turned to Victoria, still the least talkative of the bunch. Victoria was in the habit of watching and listening in those early days, working out the best way to present herself. 'You are the sophisticated one,' said Sonia. 'You have a snobbish quality about you.' Geri, who had been listening intently, piped up in her best East End landlady voice, 'She's a Lay-dee.' Sonia also noticed that Victoria, while very pretty, had 'angry, red acne' marks on her face and kept pulling her hair to try to hide them, unsuccessfully. Over lunch that day Sonia discussed her impressions with Heather and the Spice Girls' personas began to take shape. Feisty, Saucy, Baby Doll, Sporty and Snobbish were not exactly the right sort of nicknames for the girls but this was definitely the right idea, a starting point for creating their separate identities.

The girls had treated Sonia to an impromptu version of 'Wannabe'. They had literally performed this routine a hundred times and more before the song was released. Sonia hated it but did think the girls were going to be a huge hit. She could see that as a group they were a force of nature but individually they were different enough to be easily identifiable. That difference would prove to be the ace for the Spice Girls. Sonia told the girls to 'stick together', which, of course, they had every intention of doing.

Victoria was constantly working on her image. Sonia noted that her dancing lacked the rhythm of the other four. She recalls, 'Victoria shimmied her hips and smoothed her skirt down. She lacked the dance rhythm of the others but she made up for it with lots of pouting and pointing her fingers in strange positions.' Perhaps Sonia did not realize that Victoria was already in character. How do you remain sophisticated leaping around like a 'ferret in a bag'? As Victoria herself said about her persona, 'Onstage I have to pretend to be the cool Spice Girl, and I find it really hard to look so miserable! I look really bored, but the fans seem to love it. All the other girls are working really hard, running about and kicking their legs, and there I am – just standing there and not doing any work!'

The girls were due to be interviewed by *Top of the Pops* magazine to coincide with the release of 'Wannabe', which had eventually been set for July 1996. The editor, Peter Lorraine, wrote a fun, quirky piece illustrated by a row of Spice jars underneath the girls' heads. The nicknames were set: Scary, Ginger, Baby, Sporty and Posh. Exactly how much input Virgin had into the creation of these names and this article is a bit of a grey area. The simple fact is that it totally suited publicity purposes for it to be a journalistic idea rather than one planted by the PR machine.

Victoria was now 'Posh Spice' and that was that. Geri, incidentally, wanted to be known as Sexy Spice but that was felt to be a little too overt for the young female fans. Ginger Spice, which she never particularly cared for, was second choice. Posh was altogether a better deal for Victoria. A dictionary definition revealed it meant 'Smart, rich or fashionable, exclusive; refined or upper class' – all complimentary qualities with which to be associated and far better than the arrogance and affectedness of a snob. All the nicknames were ideal for headlines and they literally launched a thousand of them. It made everything so easy for the tabloid press. Victoria was delighted, not least because her mother loved her nickname and hoped she would be called 'Posh Mum'.

The other vitally important ingredient for the launch of a new 'pop sensation' was the video. The idea was to film the girls running riot through a building, terrorizing the people there in much the same way as they had when performing 'Wannabe' at record company offices all over London. The initial plan was to film in Barcelona but that fell through. Instead, the shoot took place on a freezing morning at the St Pancras Hotel. The director, Jhoan Camitz, was best known for filming commercials for Diesel jeans and Nike. He was very keen to film in one take, which did result in one or two blemishes. Geri stumbled into a chair and Mel B's nipples were noticeably erect – a sight too much for some puritanical parts of Asia where the video would subsequently be banned. Victoria wore her uniform of a little black cocktail dress. The overall effect was brooding, high energy anarchy, which was perfect for their image. The last thing they wanted was to look pretty-pretty.

The video, which had cost more than £100,000 ($200,000), quickly became the most requested on the Box channel, staying at number one on their viewers' chart for thirteen weeks. Six weeks before the designated release of the single, the video was being shown more than ten times a day. It would be voted number forty-one in Channel 4's *100 Greatest Pop Videos* (Michael Jackson's *Thriller* was number one). When 'Wannabe' was finally released on 8 July 1996, everything was in place for a massive hit. Not everybody bought in to the Spice Girls, however. Chris Evans, then presenter of the breakfast show on Radio One, famously told them to 'f*** off back to *Alive and Kicking*'. He proceeded to be rude about them on air practically every day, although he did later change his mind about them and decide he liked them after all.

The first week, 'Wannabe' went to number three in the charts. Simon Fuller promptly flew the girls to Japan in a canny move to make them appear an international group. The very first time they featured on *Top of the Pops* – a huge ambition for Victoria – they mimed the song by satellite. Victoria would much rather have been in the garden of The Old School House, where her parents were throwing a big Sunday 'chart party'. Instead, she had to make do with sending postcards to practically everybody she knew when the song went to number one the following week. Symbolically, they knocked Gary Barlow off the top spot with his first solo record, the saccharine 'Forever Love'.

'Wannabe' sold more than one and a quarter million copies in the UK alone while, worldwide, it sold more than six million. It remains the biggest selling single in the UK by an all-girl group. Even careworn pop writers had to admit its appeal. Rick Sky observes, 'It really is a beautiful pop song – one of the very best of the decade.' The *Independent*'s critic, Andy Gill, however, was disappointed that, 'the initial tough gal rap style dissolves into a harmless cutie pie chorus.'

One of the most surprising things about its success for Virgin was the realization that pre-teen girls were the ones singing the song at school. Robert Sandall, director of press at Virgin, explained it to author David Sinclair: 'Whether it was Bangkok, Tokyo, Paris or Buenos Aires, you got the same gaggle of girls, roughly the same age, all absolutely obsessed with that song.' Celebrity journalist Kate Randall, who was a twelve-year-old schoolgirl at the time, recalls, 'It was a catchy, easy song and all of us wanted to be one of the girls. You could identify with them so easily. I wanted to be Geri because she was the most fun. Nobody wanted to be Victoria at first. She didn't seem to quite fit in and she didn't smile. It was just her role and she got to wear all the nice clothes!'

Back in the UK, the girls went to Elstree to realize their ambition and perform in the *Top of the Pops* studio. Victoria had admitted the ambition when she was filmed by Neil Davies at Boyne Hill Road. Emma recalls, 'It freaked me out. Marilyn Manson was watching us and I forgot the words. I've been on countless times but I never got over that feeling of excitement.'

The song was at number one for six weeks and the girls made the trek to the studios three times. They made a great impression and always flirted with the crew and remembered everyone's name. They were novices and complete professionals at the same time. One of the floor crew observed, 'All the guys thought they were up for a shag with one of the Spice Girls.' A fan base of impressionable little girls and lusty geezers would prove to be a formidable commercial alliance.

Victoria had become a genuine pop star just two weeks after the release of her first record, though in reality it had taken two years and four months. She swiftly became a local celebrity in Hertfordshire and was not yet jaded by exposure to the media. A photographer, Nick Stern, followed her one afternoon when she went to get her nails done: 'I thought it would be worth getting the first picture of the girl in this new wonder girl band. She saw me and said, "Hi, are you paparazzi, where's the picture going and can I get a copy of it?"' This was the low-key start to the total madness that would engulf her life. Few could have predicted the Spice Girls' rapid rise to global fame.

The week that 'Wannabe' was released, another record crept into the lower echelons of the charts at number twenty-five. The track was by a female duo from Plumstead called Shampoo and was entitled 'Girl Power'. Shampoo vanished but Girl Power lived on when it was adopted as a slogan, primarily by Geri. So much of the impetus for the Spice Girls came from the mercurial Miss Halliwell. 'Girl Power' is really a slogan for little girls and those who have had a lager too many on a hen night. It may have been simplistic but it was also good fun and contributed to building the Spice Girls brand. Victoria enthusiastically embraced the concept, realizing that it would do wonders for their image. It remained at the heart of the group's popular appeal.

The Golden Rules of Girl Power, as defined by the Spice Girls in an MTV video, were:

Be positive.
Be strong!
Don't let anyone put you down.
Be in control of your own life and your destiny.
Support your girlfriends,
and let them support you, too.
Say what's on your mind.
Approach life with attitude.
Don't let anyone tell you that you can never do
something because you're a girl.
Have fun!

Slogans and catchphrases clearly work in promotion and marketing. Individually, the Spice Girls had their nicknames, now Girl Power gave the whole group a strong persona. For one thing, it took them out of the pages of the *Sun* and the *Daily Star* and gave more serious media an excuse to write about them. In 2001, the *Oxford English Dictionary* defined 'girl power' as: 'Power exercised by girls; specifically, a self-reliant attitude among girls and young women manifested in ambition, assertiveness, and individualism.'

At the beginning of the Spice Girls, Victoria was feeling her way as the classy and cool member of the group. She was walking a difficult image line between remaining aloof and entering into the bum-pinching shenanigans that would be the group's energetic interpretation of Girl Power. Sonia Poulton found Victoria pleasant but dull, monosyllabic in her responses and not funny. She observes, 'I would think that her images and poses were gleaned from pop videos and fashion magazines.' As Victoria's fame grew, so did her confidence. After a relatively short time, Victoria started to emerge as a stronger personality. She had always embraced at least the first two golden rules of Girl Power but now she was a disciple of all ten.

The first time the public realized that Victoria had as much of a voice within the Spice Girls as the rest of them was in the notorious interview in the *Spectator*, conducted in an inspired and original fashion by writer Simon Sebag Montefiore in December 1996. Victoria famously said, 'John Major is a boring pillock.' The article was a gentle satire on politics but the irony was that the views the girls expressed were followed up in all the national newspapers and became the subject of much discussion. Sebag Montefiore, tongue firmly in cheek, concentrated much of the interview on Victoria, because it gradually emerged that she was the only true Tory in the group, and Geri, because she was outspoken and always gave good quotes.

'We Spice Girls are true Thatcherites. Thatcher was the first Spice Girl, the pioneer of our ideology – Girl Power,' said Geri, voicing the opinion that would launch a thousand articles about their political views. At least one headline was a matchless piece of deadpan nonsense: 'Spice Girls Back Sceptics on Europe'.

Geri had so many opinions that she was practically a walking one-woman manifesto but Victoria was not slow in voicing her own views. They included: 'The single currency is an outrage'; 'My favourite [royal] is Princess Di'; 'These new passports are revolting, an insult to our kingdom, our independence. We must keep our national individuality'; and 'Earls and Dukes are good for tourism'. Victoria was, in some ways, revealing the good old-fashioned values of new Hertfordshire money. Of course, her famous opinion about John Major was only half a quote. What she actually said was: 'He's a boring pillock. But compared to the rest, he's far better. We'd never vote Labour.' Victoria might never vote Labour but she was not speaking for the rest of the girls. Melanie C, a staunch socialist, was very unhappy about the tone of the interview.

With hindsight, the most penetrating quote arguably came from Geri about Tony Blair, who was not yet prime minister: 'The real problem with Blair is that he's never had a real job. In the olden days a politician could be a coalminer who came to power with ideals. Not Blair. He's just a good marketing man. No ideals!'

The *Spectator* article, which avoided ridiculing the girls, broadened the Spice Girls' arena and kept them on the front pages for a week – although, throughout the years, barely a day would pass when they failed to feature somewhere. They were on *Newsnight* with Jeremy Paxman and Major himself discussed them on the *Today* programme and said he wanted a Spice Girls album for

The girls were determined never to wear the same clothes as the uniform-obsessed boy bands did. The best laid plans . . .

She joined Prince Charles to meet Nelson Mandela. The great South African leader described meeting the Spice Girls as 'the greatest day of my life'.

By Royal Appointment. Victoria is chief hand-holder to thirteen-year-old Prince Harry on his first public engagement in Johannesburg in November 1997.

The Spice Girls after collecting a special Brit Award as Best Selling Album Act in February, 1998. Victoria looks dazed as if she had just caught sight of her giddy dress in the mirror. Geri left the group three months later.

Quintessential Spice Girls – a riot of colour and flesh at the MTV Europe Music Awards in Rotterdam, 1997.

For once there was no pouting: Victoria cannot conceal her happiness when she and David Beckham announce their engagement outside a Cheshire hotel in January, 1998.

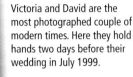

Victoria and David are the most photographed couple of modern times. Here they hold hands two days before their wedding in July 1999.

And four years later Victoria was at his side when David went to Buckingham Palace to receive an OBE from the Queen in November 2003.

Victoria threw herself into promoting her first solo venture alongside Dane Bowers. Here, backstage at G.A.Y. in London in August 2000, three weeks before 'Out Of My Mind' reached number two in the charts.

Victoria, Damon Dash and fans at a charity event in California in 2003 when she was hoping to break into the world of hip hop.

Her family is one of the closest in show business. Victoria's father Tony carries his tired grandson, Brooklyn, home from a Manchester United game in May 2001.

The Adams girls – mother Jackie and sister Louise join Victoria for the *Elle* Style Awards in 2000.

The world thought Victoria was overcome with emotion when the Spice Girls were honoured for their Outstanding Contribution to Music at the Brits in March 2000. In reality she had been targeted with a death threat and was shedding tears of relief that she had not been shot.

Christmas. Victoria said she never read the article although she made an incisive comment about politics: 'I just think it's a bit ridiculous that at the time of the election the main question to all the MPs was, "Who's your favourite Spice Girl?"' When election day came in May, Blair won a landslide victory, although his success was probably not due to Victoria calling John Major a pillock.

During their first year of soaring success Virgin assigned a young press office called Muff Fitzgerald to try to make sense of the chaos surrounding them. He saw them literally all day, every day as they set out to conquer the world under the expert guidance of Simon Fuller. His view of Victoria was: 'She is a little darling and was always a pleasure to be around.'

He added, 'Victoria is definitely not posh; however, she has a markedly refined aesthetic sensibility. Her taste in clothes and design is very sophisticated. She adores the finer things in life. She says in a lot of aspects her life is very much the same as it was before she joined the Spice Girls, only now she has twenty-five pairs of Gucci shoes instead of one.'

Victoria's new buying power was a direct result of the Spice Girls earning so much money so quickly. At the 19 Management Christmas party in 1996, Simon Fuller ushered them into an office and handed them each an envelope. Inside was a cheque for £200,000 ($400,000). Mel B did not even have a credit card. They would soon be getting cheques with an extra nought on them but for the moment it was more money than any of them had ever seen. Tony Adams never had cheques for that sort of figure. Victoria celebrated by buying a bright purple MGF sports car. Unfortunately, she was away from home so much that most of the time she lent it to her boyfriend, Stuart, to drive.

The Spice Girls had yet to go on tour or release a record in the US. Their third UK single, '2 Become 1', was the Christmas number one and their third chart topper, after 'Wannabe' and 'Say You'll Be There', in five short months. Even more importantly, their debut album, *Spice*, had been released in November and went straight to number one. They had a songwriting credit and therefore a royalty on every single track. *Spice* sold 1.8 million copies in seven weeks, making the Spice Girls the fastest-selling UK pop act since the Beatles.

It was a licence to print money. Simon Fuller was not content to stop there and negotiated lucrative deals with Pepsi and Mercedes-Benz. The branding of the Spice Girls would act as a prototype for the branding of the Beckhams.

'I don't mind being called Posh Spice. It's just a nickname.'

11

Parallel Lines

While the teenage Victoria Adams was putting her dance bag over her shoulder and heading for the Jason Theatre School, a pale, floppy-haired boy was leaving his East London home to play for the Brimsdown Rovers youth team. The distance from The Old School House to the Goldsdown Road stadium was just seven miles but it might as well as been from the earth to the moon. Victoria was never going to urge her father to get the Rolls out to go to watch a game. She was not the slightest bit interested in football nor was her father. If she had been, she might have met David Beckham when he was the under-15 'Player of the Year' in 1990.

Just as Tony was hugely proud of his daughter, so David's father, Ted, was always there to cheer on his boy. Tony had harboured an ambition to be a pop star when he was a young man but Ted was a footballing man through and through and a lifelong supporter of Manchester United. Those were the days when you would earn more in a regular nine-to-five office job than you would bashing a ball around once a week. Both dads were from similar working-class backgrounds. Ted's father was an East End gas fitter and Ted followed in his footsteps. Ted's wife, Sandra, David's mother, was a hairdresser, a profession shared at one time by Jackie Adams. Throughout his early childhood, the family lived in a modest terraced house in Leytonstone. David would escape from his sisters by joining his father to watch the local Sunday league side he coached.

Later, when they moved the few miles to Chingford, David went to the local comprehensive, Chingford High, but did not suffer the same sense of isolation and unpopularity that Victoria did at St Mary's. Sport breaks down barriers at school in a way that ballet does not. He and Victoria did share two personality traits, however: they were both shy and they were also both single-minded in their ambition. David would spend hours by himself, or being coached by his father, practising kicking a ball and taking imaginary free kicks and corners. Just like Victoria, he dreamed of the glory to come. All he ever wanted to do in life was to play for Manchester United. He was a devoted fan, like his father, even though the glamorous Tottenham Hotspur played just down the road. Every Christmas Ted Beckham would buy his son a replica United kit.

Victoria may have had no luck in her pursuit of a spot on *Jim'll Fix It* but David did far better when, aged eleven, he watched *Blue Peter* and saw an item about a competition run by the Bobby Charlton Soccer Schools. Young players from all over the country would test their skills in regional heats with the chance to win through to the final at Old Trafford. David went straight to his mother to ask if he could enter. The entry fee was £125 ($250), which was quite a lot for the Beckham family, but his grandfather, Joe, stepped in and gave him the money. David said, 'How can I ever thank him enough? It was a defining moment in my life.' He went on to win the competition easily.

Neither David nor Victoria was that impressed by academic work, but Victoria was diligent in making the best of it and left school with five GCSE qualifications, whereas David had none. He was the living proof that spending every available moment kicking a ball around the park was not a gateway to exam success – not that it mattered to David. On his fourteenth birthday, he signed a schoolboy contract with Manchester United. He had been spotted by talent scout Malcolm Fidgeon, who recalls, 'He was very frail and tiny, but could do things the other boys couldn't.'

The parallels between David and Victoria continued. He, too, left school at sixteen. While she was enduring serious dance coaching at Laine Theatre Arts, he travelled north to Manchester to join United's training scheme. He cleaned the famous players' boots, swept the changing room and coveted the gleaming sports cars in the club car park during what amounted to an old-fashioned apprenticeship. He also came under the watchful eye of the manager, the legendary Scottish firebrand Alex Ferguson. He gelled with the other trainees, especially Gary Neville, who would become his closest friend and, eventually, his best man.

In 1994, when Victoria was training to be a Spice Girl in Boyne Hill Road, Maidenhead, David had become a notoriously conscientious and disciplined young player. He still lived in digs and preferred to watch TV and grab an early night to going out on the town. He, too, kept his eye firmly on the main prize. Throughout his apprentice years, his mother and father were unswerving in their support. They knew every inch of the motorway to Manchester as they travelled up and down from Chingford to watch their son play in various youth and reserve teams. He observed, 'With that kind of support behind me from the outset, I have learnt to stand on my own two feet and not be afraid to make the right choices.' Eventually, he made his debut in the first team in a home match against Leeds United in September 1994. He never looked back.

David's first sighting of Victoria Adams is the stuff of legend. In November 1996, he was in a hotel room in Tbilisi, Georgia, for an away game against Dinamo Tbilisi. He and Gary were lounging around watching television when the new Spice Girls video 'Say You'll Be There' came on. This is the famous one filmed in the Mojave Desert in which the girls parade as comic strip warrior queens, capture a hapless male and tie him up. The girls adopted screen identities for the film. Victoria was the highly dominant Midnight Miss Suki, sporting a black PVC catsuit and a black wig. Goodness knows what it had to do with the song but it was fun and sexy. The girls did not enjoy having to film in 112°F (44°C) heat but David certainly liked what he saw. He turned to Gary and, pointing at Victoria on screen, said, 'That's the girl for me and I'm going to get her.' Many young men were pointing at the screen and expressing similar sentiments but David was going to get the opportunity sooner than he might have expected.

Fortuitously, not long afterwards, the Spice Girls were dressed in football strips for a photo feature for the football magazine *90 Minutes.* Victoria knew little about football but had chosen to wear Manchester United's jersey because Simon Fuller supported the team. She soon regretted it because she hated the colour and did not fancy having 'Sharp' emblazoned across her chest. At the end of the interview, she was shown photographs of various footballers and asked to name them. 'Ooh, he's nice. Who's that?' she asked enthusiastically. 'David Beckham' was the reply.

The week before the Brit Awards in February 1997, Simon Fuller asked Victoria if she would like to accompany him to watch Manchester United play Chelsea at Stamford Bridge. United were Premier League Champions and were heading towards another title. Simon was almost as big a United fan as Ted Beckham. The finer points of the game were lost on Victoria but afterwards she joined Simon in the VIP lounge and was thoroughly bored while everybody talked about the match. The other drawback was that she had forgotten to put in her contact lenses, which she had started wearing as a teenager, and was peering foggily about the room trying to put names to faces when Simon suddenly introduced her to David. 'It was the moment I'd waited for and I blew it,' Beckham would later recall, claiming that he had lost his bottle. Did Simon Fuller have some sort of Machiavellian plan to pair off Victoria and the most promising footballer in the country? David was already capped for England and there was every likelihood that he would star on the biggest stage of all, the World Cup tournament, which would be held the following year in France. Spice Girls' biographer David Sinclair says Fuller 'engineered' the introduction, although surely not even he could have foreseen what would evolve from that first meeting. Rick Sky observes, 'Fuller is a very Machiavellian person. I don't think he would see that as a negative thing particularly.'

Victoria basically thought David was a good-looking bloke, from what she could vaguely see, but he was not on her mind when the Spice Girls took to the Earls Court stage at the Brit Awards. Was it just a year since they had been star-struck newcomers worrying their minders that they were going to be sick over Lenny Kravitz? Three number one singles and a number one album had changed all that. This time it was a triumph. The Brits might become a slightly jaded affair from time to time but the awards jamboree is still the biggest night in UK music. All the girls were more than a little nervous, especially as their families would be there beaming encouragement.

The whole idea of these award ceremonies is to win the main prize, which is not presented on stage. It goes to the act that gains the most coverage in the next day's newspapers. In the US, Madonna and Britney Spears are the queens of this art form. Who could forget the kiss they shared on stage one year or Britney bouncing out with a huge python around her neck? At the Brits, there was only one winner the moment Geri Halliwell came out wearing a super-tight Union Jack mini dress with stitched-in knickers, arguably the most famous pop costume of all time. It looked as if she had forgotten to put on the bottom half of the outfit. The headlines were assured. Nobody was that bothered that the Spice Girls won two Brits – for best single, 'Wannabe', and best video, 'Say You'll Be There'; they had been nominated for five so it was not all good news. Victoria met Lennox Lewis and Diana Ross for the first time and, unusually in public, she spent much of the night smiling.

Two weeks later, on 15 March, Simon invited Victoria and football-mad Melanie C to Old Trafford to watch United play Sheffield Wednesday. This time after the match David was more forward when he saw her in the Players' Lounge. He chatted to her before blurting out an invitation to dinner. It was too difficult to settle on a date at the time, so Victoria asked for his number, saying she'd call him. David, fearing the brush-off, insisted she give him her number. She did. As she left, she uttered the famous remark that would have been unthinkable coming from the mouth of Victoria Adams before she became a world-famous Spice Girl: 'If you don't ring me, I'm going to kick you in the bollocks the next time I see you.'

Victoria, of course, still had a boyfriend, Stuart Bilton, who was spending his time cruising around the old haunts in Victoria's sports car. He was on a skiing holiday in France with, among others, her father, when she was giving out her number to a famous footballer. She did not know it at the time but Stuart had broken his leg in an accident on the slopes. David wasted no time and gave her a call the next day. They arranged to meet up the following day, on the Monday, in an Essex pub car park. It was not a romantic first date. They were both concerned that nobody see them in public and as a result spent the evening chatting to Melanie C at her flat. The important thing was that the ice had been broken, although nothing more happened than a little goodnight peck on the cheek. Victoria had to fly to New York the next day, so they had to make do with talking on the telephone for the foreseeable future.

David Beckham and Victoria Adams clicked immediately. They understood each other. One reason why so many stars date each other is that they recognize what it's like to be a celebrity and what they have gone through to achieve that status. It may be a cliché but the fact is that David and Victoria did have a huge amount in common. They came from working-class family backgrounds, they were single-minded if not obsessive in their ambitions, they had overcome a natural shyness, they were not rocket scientists but they were smart about their own identities and their place in the world, and they laughed at the same things. All those reasons allowed them to forge a relationship quickly – and they fancied each other.

David was not dating anyone but there was still the problem of Stuart. Everyone liked Stuart but he worked in a flower shop whereas Victoria was already a very wealthy woman, one of the biggest names in the UK media and recognizable throughout the world. He would never have the same type of shared experience that Victoria had with David. Victoria was fond of him and did him the courtesy of not stringing him along while she waited to see how things developed with David. She finished with him when she returned from the US and before she and David had had their first proper kiss. Technically, she had gone behind her boyfriend's back but she had rectified the situation with due speed. She was now free to pursue a new romance with enthusiasm.

Victoria soon realized she was falling in love, which meant she had other things on her mind when she was told there was an interesting article in the *Sun* newspaper. Victoria's first taste of someone selling a story to a newspaper was when a childhood friend passed on a picture of the Spice Girl dressed up as a pierrot when she was ten. Victoria thought she 'looked like an idiot' and that it was 'so un-rock 'n' roll'. At least hers was a nice story, although she was still upset. 'It makes me think everyone's got a price,' she said.

At the time, Victoria could count herself very fortunate because Geri and Mel B were being hit from all angles with former boyfriends' lurid tales of sex. Even poor Emma discovered that every ex-boyfriend seemed willing to sell a story about her. She spent a week in tears when her first teenage sweetheart told all to the *News of the World*. 'What really hurts is the fact that I really loved him,' she said. Mel B adopted the 'I'm not bothered' attitude towards stories about her. The other Melanie may have escaped any old boyfriend stories but she did have to deal with the *Sun* finding out that she had a sister she had never known about. Within a year of the release of 'Wannabe' there had been, give or take, *thirteen* kiss-and-tell stories about the Spice Girls.

Victoria had two possible kiss-and-tell suppliers – Mark Wood and Stuart Bilton. Muff Fitzgerald tells a poignant story of how, in January 1997, Victoria was worried that Mark was being harassed by a journalist and photographer from the *People* newspaper. He spoke to Mark about it on the phone. 'Listen, I love Victoria,' said Mark, 'and I would never do anything to hurt her.' Muff advised Mark to shut the front door in their faces.

Victoria could have done with a little of Mel B's coolness when the *Sun* newspaper was published on 1 April 1997. The headline on the exclusive read: 'Posh Spice was just 17 when we had sex on a speeding train.' Mark Wood had sold his story after all. He was extremely hurt by a throwaway remark Victoria had made during a television show. She said she had finished with him but kept the ring.

His account read that they had enjoyed some lusty moments on an express train to Scotland. Victoria had apparently been wearing her Bros-type jeans. It was, he claimed, the most exciting sex they had enjoyed in their five-year relationship. In fact, their sex life as described in the article seemed rather dull. 'Toria would never initiate anything or do anything to me,' he said, plaintively.

The other highly personal story he told was of a pregnancy scare while on holiday at her parents' villa in Spain. They could not obtain any morning-after pills, so Victoria took a huge dose of the pill, which meant she spent the day being sick. This was day one of a tabloid three-day Posh spectacular and it was the most lurid of the stories. Day two was all about their engagement and how he had cried himself to sleep when they split. Day three was a picture feature containing previously unpublished pictures Mark had taken of Victoria in her pre-Posh days. They included one of them posing before a charity dinner and dance in 1990 when Victoria, aged sixteen, wore a long black evening dress and sported a big, frizzy perm.

Victoria has scarcely missed an opportunity to lay into Mark since then. She did not forgive and forget. In an official Spice Girls book published the same year as the charity picture appeared, Mark was not by her side. He 'is cut out of the picture because he's so disgusting – not just in looks but as a person too!' In her autobiography she lets him have it with both barrels, claiming he sold her down the river for £60,000 ($120,000). She calls him a 'tight-arse who treated me like shit'. Four years had certainly not calmed her down. On the subject of the couple having sex in a train toilet, she could not have been plainer. She wrote: 'In your dreams, mate.'

She repeated the denial in a TV documentary, *Being Victoria Beckham*, in 2002, which, of course, gave the *News of the World* the chance to run Mark's story again under the headline 'Posh did go like a train on the Glasgow Express'. This time he didn't mince words: 'She was rampant.' The piece was unintentionally funny when it said that Mark had maintained a 'dignified silence' since his original interview when he had first claimed they had had sex in a train toilet. All good knockabout fun except that Victoria was by now married with a small child.

Mark stayed in the Hertford area. In November 2000, he went on *Blind Date* and engaged in some banter about 'Posh' with the host, Cilla Black. He eventually chose a girl called Julie Gibbs for the date in Tenerife. She later complained that he spent the entire time talking about Victoria. These days he finally seems to have put Victoria behind him and is now a married man. He did, however, appear on *Deal or No Deal* in 2008 and smiled when the host, Noel Edmonds, told the audience that one of the contestants used to be engaged to Victoria Beckham. Mark Wood will never live down his time with one of the world's most famous women.

Stuart Bilton, by contrast, has never spoken at all. His story, which might have read 'How Becks Stole My Girl' or some such nonsense, would probably have been more valuable than Mark's. He did not spend any time crying into his beer in 1997, but promptly started dating his third *EastEnder*, Martine McCutcheon. He clearly had the knack where the girls of Albert Square were concerned, but that relationship lasted only a few weeks. He also dated Mandy Smith, the former wife of ex-Rolling Stone Bill Wyman, bringing the celebrity count for this particular Hertfordshire flower seller to a highly respectable five. Victoria seems genuinely fond of Stuart, who has never spoken about any of his famous girlfriends. She described him as a 'sweetie' and remained on good terms with him. Her parents always liked him and his family. They could not have foreseen that within a year she would be engaged to a footballer.

'I fell in love with David very quickly.'

12

A Schedule, Not a Life

Victoria may have been a woman in love but, in 1997, she was also in the middle of what would prove to be the *annus mirabilis* of her professional career. The Spice Girls were absolutely everywhere. Victoria would have to find a place for David among the madness. As biographer David Sinclair wryly observed, 'When it came to endorsements, it seemed the Spice Girls didn't know the meaning of the word "No".' They were taking commercial exploitation to a new level. Within an astonishing space of time, they had become completely woven into the fabric of British life. *Forbes* magazine, which produces a world-famous rich list, estimated the girls' first year fortune at $47 million (at the time, approximately £29 million), a quite astonishing figure, particularly considering they had been claiming dole three years before. They were ranked at number thirty-two in a list of the highest paid entertainers.

Victoria somehow managed to keep David a secret from the world for a couple of months. Like millions of couples before them, their first proper night out was a trip to the pictures. They slipped into a cinema in the King's Road, Chelsea to watch *Jerry Maguire*, starring Tom Cruise and Renée Zellweger. The film, a comedy drama about a sports agent and his clients, was quite an apt choice, but it would be nice to think the couple spent the movie kissing in the back row. That same evening she took the young footballer home to meet her parents in Goff's Oak. Her father, Tony, famously asked a nervous David, 'Which team do you play for then?' Tony had particularly liked Stuart Bilton but he was a man fiercely loyal to his daughter and both he and Jackie would do everything they could to make David welcome, especially if they thought he was going to be around for a long time.

In the early days, much of Victoria and David's romance was conducted on the telephone. It did not take long for David's teammates at Manchester United to find out what was going on and to act accordingly. Ryan Giggs, for instance, was in the habit of ringing David and pretending to be Victoria murmuring sweet nothings down the phone. 'I love you, I love you,' he would purr before collapsing into a fit of giggles. David was falling in love. His best friend, Gary Neville, observed, 'He was coming to training every day and he was like a little schoolboy.'

One of the most endearing qualities David Beckham has is that he comes across as a great romantic. He's a soppy bloke. He did not announce to his teammates that he had met a Spice Girl and she was really 'fit'. He told everyone he had met a 'lovely girl', which is, of course, why everyone felt they had the licence to have fun at his expense.

The Spice Girls were concentrating on America at this point and were preparing to sing live for the first time. They performed 'Wannabe' and 'Say You'll Be There' on the top-rated 'cult' show *Saturday Night Live*, a stalwart of the American entertainment scene and filmed in New York. The Spice Girls always had to fight against the perception that they were a completely manufactured band and, therefore, unable to sing or perform to any standard. These girls were exceptionally well trained and used to performing. They had sung the songs a thousand times and more already, so once more live before an audience of twenty million viewers was no problem. They were, in fact, very nervous. The headlines had already been written: 'Can they really, really sing?' The girls rehearsed for five full days at a Manhattan studio with the show's house band, which reflected just how seriously everyone was taking this 'live gig'. They were all acutely aware that, up until then, they had spent six months miming their two most famous hits. Before they went on, they had a group hug. Rob Lowe was the host that night, Will Ferrell was one of the resident performers and actor

Joe Pesci was the main guest. One of the cast accidentally said the F-word, which became more of a talking point than the first live performance by the Spice Girls.

Geri thought she was a 'bit squeaky' on one line but everybody else declared themselves satisfied and thought they sounded pretty good. Not everyone was impressed. One critic called it a 'fleshy train wreck'. Others were kinder. At least Noel Gallagher of Oasis would have to shut up about them not singing live now. They looked fantastic too. Geri wore a figure-hugging white dress with 'Girl Power' across her chest, while Victoria wore a little black dress that barely covered her bottom and a pair of killer heels.

By now, Victoria was displaying progressively more assurance in her role within the group. She was watching less and saying and doing more, particularly on their numerous publicity trips to the US. A prime example was the first time the girls appeared on the prestigious *Late Show with David Letterman*. This programme, like its rival, *The Tonight Show*, is a peculiarly American entity, scripted within an inch of its life and subject to gales of laughter and general hollering from the audience at every opportunity. Their appearance in May was to mark the sensational news that *Spice* had reached number one in the US album charts.

Letterman introduced Posh as the group's 'fashion and style guru', which she liked. It was a good deal better than poor Geri's description as a 'former nude model and lap dancer'. At the end of the interview, the girls subjected the host to a lipstick attack, while one of them ruffled up his hair. Surprisingly, it was not Geri or Mel B but Victoria who was messing up the expensively coiffeured Letterman locks. He hated it. The girls were not the main guests – Bill Clinton was followed by Olivia Newton-John – but they were the memorable ones, which was always the point.

Spice was the top-selling album of 1997 in the US with sales of 5.3 million copies, a phenomenal success and achieved despite a lukewarm reaction from the critics. Christina Kelly in *Rolling Stone* magazine described the album as a 'watered down mix of hip hop and cheesy pop balladry'. She compared the girls to the Village People, the disco act of the seventies in which each member had a very distinct and unsubtle identity, from American Indian to policeman. They were simply guys dressing up, whereas the Spice Girls were expressing individual personalities, albeit in a rather simplistic and cartoon-like manner. Kelly also dismissed Girl Power: 'Despite their pro-women posing, the Girls don't get bogged down by anything deeper than mugging for promo shots and giving out tips on getting boys into bed.'

Critics, understandably, were not really tuning in to the right frequency. The Spice Girls' audience was a great deal younger than had at first been realized. Virgin's A & R chief, Ashley Newton, explained to the group's biographer, David Sinclair: 'The girls completely understood that really the people they were talking to were young kids. And it was something they did with incredibly good grace.' The day after the Letterman show, Victoria joined the others at a studio overlooking the Hudson River for the photo shoot for their first *Rolling Stone* cover. The magazine's publisher, Jann Wenner, made a rare appearance at such an event because his children pestered him that they wanted to go to get autographs. The same sort of thing was happening throughout the world. Children, sometimes as young as three or four, were nagging their parents to buy something connected with the Spice Girls, whether it was a record or a packet of Walkers crisps – one of the mountain of products they endorsed. When children get their hooks into something, it can become a formidable franchise very quickly. The Harry Potter phenomenon is one example of this, the Simpsons another. A further characteristic the Spice Girls share with these two success stories is that adults could like them as well. The range of ages enjoying the group was impressive.

Rolling Stone ran the Spice Girls cover in July for their summer double issue. Victoria was particularly pleased that, for a change, they all wore black, not just her. She was even more chuffed that she was firmly displayed in the centre of the Mark Seliger photograph, looking very thin in a two-piece outfit and displaying a hint of cleavage and a lot of leg. She looked like a brunette Barbie doll. The headline on the cover was: 'Spice Girls Conquer the World', which was just about right. Amusingly, there was a small heading above it entitled 'Pop Tarts', an article unrelated to anything Spice. It may or may not have been done deliberately.

Victoria's blossoming romance with one of the best-known footballers in the UK put her centre stage in the Spice Girls. The rest
of the world found out about it when back in the UK she was photographed coming out of his house. They were both relieved it had
become public and they could dispense with subterfuge.

Victoria did not see David again until the day of the Prince's
Trust Concert in Manchester, the second occasion on which they
would sing live. Geri was in genius form when the girls met Prince
Charles at the Manchester Opera House. She gave him a full lipstick smacker on the cheek before patting the heir to the throne's
bum and telling him in her best Watford accent, 'You know, I think
you are very sexy. We could spice up your life.' Once again, Geri
had the Midas touch when it came to maximizing publicity for the
Spice Girls.

David had been at the concert but had to dash off afterwards.
Later that night, however, Victoria was asleep in her room at the
Midland Hotel when she roused by a knock at the door. It was
David and he had caught her without her make-up on. She let him
in anyway. At least the media did not have tickets to this event.
When they eventually read about it in her autobiography, the *News
of the World* exclaimed, 'Posh's Bedroom Bliss'. A 'pal' recalled,
'Victoria wasn't at all nervous about meeting Prince Charles
because all she could think about was David. She didn't actually go
into details of his performance but her smile was enough to tell us
that she was totally, blissfully satisfied with her man.' Amusingly,
the pal and the newspaper had the wrong first night because
Victoria had already stayed with David the night before the
concert.

David was an intoxicating interlude amid the hectic reality of
her life as a Spice Girl. Victoria had to leave at the crack of dawn
the morning after the concert to catch a flight to Cannes to start
the hype for *Spice: The Movie*, as it was then called, which had yet to
be made but was the next stage in their plan for global supremacy.
The Spice Girls stayed on a yacht in the harbour and lapped up
the glamour of the biggest film festival in the world. It was
madness. The van taking them to a party at Planet Hollywood was
practically hijacked by crowds hammering on the doors and

rocking it from side to side. A cameraman was punched in the face and the girls arrived quite shaken by this aspect of the fame they had so desired.

The group had always wanted to make a movie and had talked about it during those very early days in Boyne Hill Road. Subsequently, it was one of the first ambitions they had spoken of to Simon Fuller. He had just the man to help – his elder brother, Kim Fuller, who was an experienced television comedy writer. Kim had started writing sketches as long ago as 1979, when he contributed to *Not the Nine o'Clock News*, which launched the careers of Rowan Atkinson and Griff Rhys Jones. He had subsequently written for Tracey Ullman and Rory Bremner but was principally known for his work with Lenny Henry. A movie would be a major development in his career, while his family connection with Simon kept the project very much 'in house'.

The blueprint for the film was obviously *A Hard Day's Night*, the hugely influential 1964 movie fictionalizing a day in the life of the Beatles. The Spice Girls' success was so often being compared to the sixties' icons that reworking the formula seemed a sensible option. Instead of a day, the idea was to portray a fictional week in their lives and its inherent, manic chaos in the build-up to a concert at the Royal Albert Hall in London.

Once again, it was Geri who was the primary mover. She really threw herself into the project and during much of the previous year had been available by phone or fax to discuss ideas. Kim found her the most ambitious for the film and the most helpful with the script: 'She would say to me, "Well, actually, Victoria wouldn't say that." So then I would change it round to make sure the lines were ringing true.' On the rare occasions when the girls were in London, they would go round to Kim's house in Notting Hill and tell him tales from their travels, including one in which they had all leapt off a double-decker bus and made a run for it. A London bus, driven by Victoria, would feature prominently in the film.

Filming was set to begin in London in June 1997. The locations were kept top secret to try to limit the opportunities for paparazzi bagging pictures of the girls on set. Somehow they always found out, as was the case when two photographers were discovered dressed as a cow grazing in a meadow next to where they were film-ing. The girls waved as the men were escorted off carrying their cameras and a cow's head. It was a game and everyone knew they would be back to have another go in the morning.

The two main characters in the movie – other than the girls themselves – were their manager Clifford, played by a sardonic Richard E. Grant, and his inscrutable boss. A former James Bond, Roger Moore signed on for that role in his seventieth year. These two were joined by a who's who of popular British actors and enter-tainers, including Stephen Fry, Hugh Laurie, Alan Cummings and Jonathan Ross. Michael Barrymore, then one of the biggest names in light entertainment, took the role of Mr Step, the dance teacher, when John Cleese turned it down.

The director they chose was Bob Spiers, one of the most respected names in British comedy. He had directed *Fawlty Towers*, *The Comic Strip Presents* and *Bottom*. In the nineties he was best known for directing *Absolutely Fabulous*. The Spice Girls' movie, however, would for him be a very rare foray into feature films.

In the early sixties, films and music seem to have been more closely linked. Cliff Richard and the Shadows followed the Elvis Presley path of flimsy stories showcasing new songs. The mock *cinéma-vérité* approach of *A Hard Day's Night* somehow set the bar too high. The problem for future bands is that they would always be judged against that classic film. Kim Fuller was trying to blend Dick Lester's film with the equally popular satire *This is Spinal Tap*. The result was far better than many expected. Janet Maslin in the *New York Times* said, tongue in cheek, 'Nothing about it should disturb its target audience of media-wise, fun loving eight year old girls.'

The plot is more about energy than complexity but does feature some of the distractions in the world of the Spice Girls – the paparazzi, being stalked by a documentary film-maker and, most intriguingly, becoming increasingly dissatisfied with a manager who refuses to give them any time off. By the end of the year this fictional storyline would become the reality of their situation with Simon Fuller. Victoria and Emma, who had taken the most drama classes growing up, probably do best of the five in the acting stakes.

Maslin commented, 'Emma and slinky Victoria come closest to showing signs of life after Spicedom but the whole group radiates energy, colour and good cheer.'

Kim Fuller later told David Sinclair about a conversation with Victoria about her role that highlights her professionalism and good humour about sending herself up. She asked, 'You know my character in the movie? I'm just a laughing stock really, aren't I?' 'Yes, you are', said Kim. Victoria replied, 'OK, that's fine. As long as I know.'

Critics, in general, found it hard to be too nasty about the film, perhaps because the movie had a finely tuned self-deprecating style. When Geri casually says, 'Is the Pope Catholic?' in response to a reporter's question, 'Pope Shock' headlines appear. Victoria sends herself up in a way she has generally employed ever since. Her funniest piece of dialogue involved a Gucci dress. She complains that she never knows what to wear. Sporty chips in, 'It must be so hard for you, Victoria. I mean, having to decide whether to wear the little Gucci dress, the little Gucci dress . . . or the little Gucci dress.' 'Exactly,' says Posh. 'I know,' says Baby Spice, 'why don't you wear the little Gucci dress?' Posh replies, 'Good idea. Thanks, Em.'

While not exactly of Academy Award-winning standard, it was a film full of vitality. *A Hard Day's Night* did, in fact, win two Oscars, whereas the Spice Girls had to make do with being nominated for Razzie Awards. The Razzies, otherwise known as the Golden Raspberry Awards, are part of the annual fun in Hollywood but still not something a serious actor wants to win. They 'salute' the worst offerings of the year. *Spice World*, as it was finally titled, was up for six awards but 'won' only one – all five girls collectively won in the Worst Actress category. The citation read: 'A five member girl group with the talent of one bad actress between them!' They were in good bad company. Both Madonna and Mariah Carey have received this dubious accolade. The public were not at all bothered by what the critics thought. When it was released at Christmas time, the film was a huge success and ended up the second most successful British film in the UK for 1997, with receipts of £8.5 million ($17 million), beaten at the box office only by *Bean* with £18 million ($36 million). *Spice World* would eventually take more than £11 million ($22 million) in the UK alone and $30 million (£15 million) in the US. Worldwide figures suggest that it made at least ten times its original budget of £4 million ($8 million).

The most quoted line in the movie is when Richard E. Grant as their manager tells them, 'You don't have lives, you have a schedule.' That was proving to be the case and the girls did not like it one bit. They were filming during the day. When the cameras stopped rolling at 5 p.m., they were whisked off to the recording studio to work on their second album. Hardly any material had been written, so everyone was scribbling lyrics on bits of paper and taking them to the Winnebago where a mobile recording studio had been set up. Broadly speaking, it was the same cast of characters as before, with Matt and Biff, the Absolute boys and Spike Stent all involved. Only Eliot Kennedy had moved on to other projects. Victoria's working day began at 6.30 in the morning and ended at 11 at night. She was seeing far less of David than she would have liked – a situation that was about to become even trickier.

Simon, who was fast becoming the target for all the girls' malcontent, persuaded them that a year in tax exile was the only sensible thing to do. His argument made good sense and was not one they were about to ignore. They had earned so much money so quickly. By the end of filming, their portfolio of commercial alliances was astounding, and included Pepsi, Polaroid cameras, Cadbury's, Impulse deodorant, Benetton, Sony and Chupa Chups lollipops, which were the biggest thing in Spain. And that was not including merchandise with Spice labels all over it – dolls, skates, satchels, pencil cases, bicycles, sportswear and *Spice* magazine. Geri Halliwell called the commercial phenomenon, the 'Spice Juggernaut'. It was certainly a corporation. They were paid a reported £500,000 ($1 million) to launch Channel Five and then signed a deal to be the Christmas face of the Asda supermarket chain. It was spectacularly good business, not just for the vast sums involved but also for the exposure it gave the group all over the world. As Geri memorably put it, 'I couldn't walk down the street without seeing my face on a T-shirt or a coffee cup.'

On the last day of shooting *Spice World*, their new deal with Mercedes saw the arrival of five different coloured coupés. Victoria's SLC was in racing green. She no longer needed her MGF, as David was already building an impressive fleet of high performance cars, so she sold it to Cathy Dennis. Victoria enjoyed driving the Mercedes but not as much as Jackie did, so she bought it for her mother when the year's free lease was up.

What more could the girls possibly want? Simon Fuller did not realize it but they simply wanted a day off. None of them was happy about spending a year away from her family even if they were going to be on their first world tour for most of that time. Victoria had first left The Old School House to go to Laine Theatre Arts in Epsom. Then she became engaged for the first time. This time she was going much further afield but the outcome would be the same. Two days before she was due to leave, David got down on one knee and proposed. This time Victoria became engaged with no help from Jackie. David chose an idyllic setting at the rural Rookery Hall Hotel near his home in Cheshire. The proposal was very romantic except perhaps for the white towelling guest dressing gowns they were both wearing. Gucci, for once, was nowhere to be seen. It was fitting, however, that they wore matching outfits for the occasion. Victoria observed, 'We've got matching dogs, matching watches and similar wardrobes and I like that. I know it's really tacky but it makes us laugh.' David was only twenty-two, a year younger than Victoria, but he craved a happy family life – this would endear him to the British public.

Typically, rumours of the engagement somehow leaked to the press before David had the chance to ask Tony for Victoria's hand. Her father was totally unphased by the speed of their decision and readily agreed. They had known each other for just six months, but David said, 'As soon as I met Victoria, I knew I always wanted to marry her, to have children, to be together always.'

Victoria, too, had known from the beginning that she and David were compatible. She explains, 'Everyone used to ask if my initial attraction to David was the fact that he was famous. I always said it wasn't but actually that was a lie. If someone is really talented, as a footballer or an artist or an academic, the point isn't that they are famous, but they are talented and dedicated. The fact that we are in the same position makes us equal and it is quite ironic the way our careers run parallel . . . We are equally famous and we attract equal attention.'

David and Victoria were together for just a few days before saying goodbye. Simon Fuller had rented a villa near Cannes in which the girls could rehearse for a month before their first full-length live gig, which would be in Istanbul at the end of October 1997. The house, complete with swimming pool and high security, cost £10,000 ($20,000) a week to rent and was a considerable improvement on the semi in Boyne Hill Road, but the girls were not at all happy. Geri called it Spice Kampf.

The strange irony of their success was that it took away Girl Power. Richard E. Grant's words rang true. They felt they were no longer in control of their own destiny. They had lost the collective spirit. In her autobiography, Victoria explained, 'None of us were happy. But instead of talking about it like we would have done in the old days, we just kept to our rooms.'

Victoria's engagement to David was the first of three events that would shape the rest of her life. The second was the death of the Princess of Wales in a Paris car crash. Diana was the most famous woman in the world and the celebrity above all others whom editors wanted on the front pages of newspapers and magazines. She boosted sales. Without her, there was an enormous void that needed to be filled. Individually, neither David nor Victoria had a chance of filling that gap but together they would be welcomed with open arms by a desperate media. The third event was of a more personal nature. Victoria had always loved fashion and loved shopping. When she became rich in her own right, she enjoyed the opportunity to wear the famous labels. The joke about Gucci in *Spice World* was funny and self-mocking but true. In October she was invited to the Versace Show in Milan. This is one of the biggest fashion events in the world, made especially poignant that year because it was held just a few months after Gianni Versace was murdered in Miami. For the first time Victoria rubbed shoulders with the most famous – and tallest – people in fashion, including Kate Moss and Naomi Campbell. The superficiality of it all did not impress her but it was an introduction and she did stay at the Versace villa, which made her feel part of everything.

The deaths of Versace and Diana had some practical effect on the Spice Girls. First of all, references to the pair had to be edited out of the final cut of *Spice World*. Making movies is an inexact science and fate can never be factored in. A further four minutes, for instance, ended up on the cutting-room floor when Gary Glitter was arrested on child pornography charges.

Victoria had almost been to a fashion show before. *Tatler* magazine flew her to Paris for a front row seat at the Karl Lagerfeld show but, annoyingly, there was no time in her 'schedule'. It took eight hours to be fitted for the various outfits she wore for the fashion shoot at the Ritz Hotel in Paris. She was disappointed to miss the show but had the consolation of being the magazine's cover girl for the first time. She wore black but for once not a little cocktail dress. Instead, she was pictured in a 'nightie' dress topped off with a black flying saucer hat, which would have looked very stylish at Ascot. The cover line read: 'Posh Spice Goes to Paris – Victoria Adams wears haute couture'. She may not have shown the panache of Audrey Hepburn, but she looked perfect for a high society wedding.

The *Tatler* piece itself was pretty inoffensive, although the writer, Vicki Woods, did point out that Victoria wore very heavy make-up for a girl in her twenties. She also acknowledged, 'Victoria's learned to pout for her publicity pictures like a moody supermodel, smouldering away with mouth closed.' Woods did seem to have an aversion to Victoria's voice 'spraying around her Hertfordshire vowels and her north London syntax with feeling' and using speech rhythms that are 'not what you'd call Sloaney'. She gives examples of Victoria's conversation: 'When we get in the studio we all vibe off each other', as well as, 'When we met Prince Charles we was all really, like, cheeky with him.' They come across as very cheap shots.

Four years on, Ms Woods, writing in the *Spectator*, revealed what she really thought of 'little Victoria Beckham' at the time: 'It was a tiresome nonsense of an interview. She posed and pirouetted about and tossed off smart-ass one-liners and wouldn't sit still or answer questions.' She continued, 'She struck me as diamond-bright in a streetwise sort of way, pretty damn thick in every sort of way and overloud, shrewish and quite prickly in a wearisome sort of way.' She once again found fault with Victoria's 'tiresome Hertfordshire-cockney'. The writer clearly loathed Victoria and had strained every writing muscle not to reveal her true feelings in the original *Tatler* piece, which is quite amusing in retrospect, especially when Victoria tells Vicki that her mum didn't want her to shorten her name. Perhaps Vicki could not distinguish between Posh Spice and Victoria Adams. Unintentionally, Ms Woods throws some light on why so many commentators in the media do not understand Victoria's popularity – it's a class thing. Millions of ordinary young girls and women, who would never buy a copy of *Tatler*, adore her.

The girls had expected to have the number one record at this point but 'Spice Up Your Life', the first single from the yet to be released album and film, was delayed following Diana's death. The Elton John tribute single, 'Candle in the Wind 97', completely took over the charts throughout the world, becoming the most successful single ever. Waiting a month resulted in the Spice Girls having their fifth successive number one. It also coincided with one of the proudest moments of Victoria's professional career when the Spice Girls flew to South Africa for a charity concert and met Nelson Mandela. They were introduced to the great man at his home in Pretoria. Their now firm friend Prince Charles was there, undertaking just about his first serious public engagement since the death of his former wife. He brought along an excited Prince Harry, then aged thirteen. The meeting between Charles and the President was light-hearted, with both men entering into the spirit of a Spice Girls occasion. Mandela produced his grandchildren so they could all be introduced and obtain autographs. 'This is one of the greatest moments of my life,' said Mandela. The Prince said it was the second greatest of his life. 'The first time I met them was the greatest,' he added.

On their return to the UK, the Spice Girls sacked Simon Fuller. He had been in hospital in New York for an operation for a troublesome back condition. In his case, absence did not make the heart grow fonder. Instead, left to their own devices in France, the girls made the decision to dispense with his services – after consulting their lawyer to make sure they could do it. Once again, Victoria took part in the decision-making process and then left Geri and Mel B to get on with it. Fuller was informed on the day of the MTV Europe Awards after flying to Italy to recuperate. He was therefore not part of the celebrations when the Spice Girls won best group. It seems scarcely believable now but they beat a list of nominees that included U2, Radiohead and Oasis.

Victoria was as relieved as the rest of them that Fuller had gone. She might actually get a day off now. Some reports suggested that part of the reason for the fallout was Fuller's closeness to Emma Bunton but this was never confirmed. He had an almost paternal relationship with Victoria – always making sure she was eating properly, a concern that irritated her. Nobody likes to feel they are being checked up on like a naughty schoolgirl. On one occasion in Hong Kong when Victoria pushed away her food uneaten, Fuller reportedly told her, 'You are not going a whole day on just a bowl of rice. Don't be stupid. You've got to eat properly.' Victoria sullenly ate her meal. One theory, however, is that someone worked out that Fuller might actually have been earning more from the Spice Girls than they were. If he was on twenty per cent commission, they were sharing the other eighty per cent – a total of sixteen per cent each. They were soon to embark on a 106-date world tour. For every million they earned, he was getting £40,000 ($80,000) more than they were. Victoria was always quite good at maths. She revealed that she felt 'much more in control' since the sacking and that everyone was much happier.

Reading between the lines, she also might have been fretting about Fuller interfering in her romance with David. She wanted to keep her love separate from her role as Posh Spice. 'I've never felt like I do now,' she said. 'I feel like I know what's important in life now. I know some people think I've got no depth but that's all part of the Posh Spice thing – it's not me. I don't mind people thinking that way and I understand that's my image. But there is a lot more going on in my head.'

The girls had to deal with the release of the *Spiceworld* album without Simon. It went straight to number one. David Wild in *Rolling Stone* was almost complimentary: 'The Spice Girls take us deep into pop's heart of lightness, a happy place filled not with music of good taste but with music that tastes good – at least to a substantial portion of the planet.' He concluded, 'Their message is this: Have a good time, believe in yourself, and while you're at it, don't forget to buy a lot of Spice Girls merchandise.' Overall, the album was generally acknowledged to be an improvement on their debut. David Browne in *Entertainment Weekly* thought it had better songs and stronger vocals than their debut. He summed it up: 'Anyone with a brain can see that *Spiceworld* is superficiality incarnate. But anyone with a heart can see that its very goofiness, its very crassness, makes it not only a better album than *Spice*, but the true essence d'Spice experience.' One track, 'Saturday Night Divas', did have a more serious subplot. The lyrics were a dig at those ex-lovers who kiss and tell on the famous, something the girls knew all about from their former boyfriends. When she recorded it, Victoria had no idea that she would suffer even more in the future from this modern malaise.

Second albums are notoriously difficult to pull off, especially when the first one sells so many copies. *Spice* sold 22 million copies, while *Spiceworld* shifted a very respectable 14 million. If the first album had not been such a sensation, then *Spiceworld* would have been regarded as a huge success, finishing the year in the top ten bestselling albums in both the US and the UK. Having sacked Simon Fuller, Victoria and the girls were about to suffer the inevitable backlash, the popular media sport of building someone up, giving them big love and then turning on them, rather like the spider who eats its mate after sex. 'Too Much', their classiest ballad and Victoria's favourite track, was the Christmas number one – the first time a group had achieved that in successive years – so the outlook was not all gloomy.

Victoria spent Christmas at the K Club, a beautiful leisure complex near Dublin and close enough for David to pop over to exchange Christmas presents. They gave each other Rottweiler puppies called Snoopy and Puffy. It was time to let the public know officially that she was engaged to the most handsome young footballer in England. They went back to the Rookery Hall Hotel in Cheshire but this time they were sporting their engagement rings and happily posed for invited photographers. Nobody realized at the time that it was a rerun.

Her engagement ring was a £40,000 ($80,000) solitaire diamond designed by Boodle and Dunthorne. Victoria seemed delighted by her ring. 'It's my dream ring,' she confided to the press. 'It's just what I wanted and it was a big surprise' – which, of course, it wasn't. His ring was a £50,000 ($100,000) diamond encrusted gold band that she had bought in Rodeo Drive, Beverly Hills, when she was in Los Angeles promoting *Spice World*. On arriving home, she inadvertently walked through the nothing to declare channel at Manchester Airport and was sent a £3,000 ($6,000) bill by HM Customs and Excise after the couple showed off their rings at the photo call.

While the media looked to have it in for the Spice Girls, they seemed genuinely to like Posh and Becks, as they were soon known. Victoria could look back on her year with immense satisfaction – she had fallen in love, become engaged, made millions, met Nelson Mandela and Donatella Versace, made a movie, and had a number one hit record in the US and the UK.

'We're not promoting drink, drugs and alcohol. We're doing nice things here and we're nice people.'

13

Brooklyn

Victoria has never given the impression that she enjoys a surprise. She likes to know exactly what's going on. She hates being shocked. In her younger days, people were always remarking on her lack of confidence. As she grew older, they tended to notice her growing desire to be in control of her life. Perhaps the two are connected: the greater her control, the more confidence she had. She had no influence over the abrupt departure of Geri Halliwell from the Spice Girls in 1998 and she reacted very badly.

From day one, when they were five girls together in Touch, Geri provided the impetus that meant failure was not an option. She was a brassy ball of fire whose whole being seemed engaged in driving them on. She never flinched from working all hours to improve so that she would not be left behind. She brought the group her flair for promotion and publicity: she wore a Union Jack dress that became a symbol for Cool Britannia in the nineties; she patted the behind of the heir to the throne; she embraced Girl Power and wrote many of the catchiest lyrics in the songs. When they met Nelson Mandela, the great statesman told his guests, 'I think I'm too old for them.' 'No, you're not,' exclaimed Geri. 'You're as young as the girl you feel, and I'm only twenty-five.' It was another moment of genius from the Spanish cleaner's daughter from Watford, the oldest of the group and, by some margin, its most articulate and intelligent member. She was also, at least initially, the most popular. In a poll conducted by *Sky International*

Magazine, she was voted the most popular Spice Girl with more than thirty per cent of the vote (Victoria came second). Admittedly, this was a probably a lads' vote for Geri's boobs but for many she clearly represented the Spice Girls.

Away from the gaze of the world, Geri suffered from chronic insecurity and eating disorders. At Boyne Hill Road, she was beset by loneliness, bingeing and self-disgust. In her disarmingly honest account of her life, *If Only,* she describes it, 'I'm paralysed by a black, relentless cloud.' Secretly, she spent a week in a psychiatric unit after New Year, 1995, as she struggled to come to terms with her father's death. In her mind, Geri left the group while they were on tour in early 1998. After a performance in Milan, she claimed she told them she would be leaving in September after their Wembley concert, the final night of their world tour. In the event, she left much earlier, in May, the day the girls appeared on the National Lottery show on television and told the world that Geri had a stomach upset. Nobody could have guessed the truth, which revealed how accomplished the girls now were at acting. Geri said the catalyst for her abrupt departure was an interview she wanted to give to ITN to promote breast cancer awareness. The girls, she claimed, vetoed it. Instead of the gang of five, it had become four against one.

Mel B had a different version and said she did not have a clue that Geri was planning to go her own way until they had a call from the group's lawyer, Andrew Thompson, on the morning of the lottery show. Victoria said the same, revealing they all talked to Geri that day to try to persuade her to change her mind. The last time she saw Geri was when they embraced at the airport before having a day off prior to the lottery appearance. She had no idea that it would be the last time she would see her for years. Her verdict on the whole distressing business is: 'Geri Halliwell left us totally in the lurch.' Now she was gone, Victoria was in no mood to forgive and forget in a hurry.

The whole world knew what was up when 'ill' Geri was seen catching a flight to France. Geri issued a statement saying she had left because of 'differences' between her and the rest of the group. The other four responded by saying they were 'upset' and 'saddened' and ended their statement with the slogan 'Friendship never ends.'

Victoria echoed the general well-wishing: 'There are no hard feelings. We wish her all the luck in the world. We are totally behind her. We've always said that if anybody was unhappy, they should leave. The most important thing is our friendship.'

The friendship *had* ended. There *were* hard feelings. Three years later, in her autobiography, Victoria revealed what she truly thought: 'I'd known Geri for four years, we'd shared a room in Windsor, we'd been through the most extraordinary experiences of our lives together. She was one of my best friends. And now she had walked out without a word. What I felt was first anger at the selfishness of it all, then betrayal. Total betrayal.'

The remaining four girls did not have time to dwell on the matter or feel sorry for themselves. Perversely, it worked out well and Victoria, despite the gruelling schedule, thrived on it. They had to rearrange all the choreography and the harmonies but that was not too hard for four well-trained dancers. Best of all, Victoria at last had the chance to sing a solo line in 'Wannabe'. One of the strange coincidences at the time was that Geri's boyfriend, Christian Storm, a dancer in the show, turned out to be none other than Christian Horsfell, who had been at Laine's with Victoria and whom she had quite fancied. He and Geri did not last long and he married Shaznay Lewis of All Saints in 2004.

The abrupt departure of both Simon Fuller and Geri Halliwell from Spice World re-emphasized two important aspects of Victoria's character. In the case of Simon, she was ruthless or, at least, shared in taking a difficult decision. She reveals a surprising toughness whenever she needs to, whether it's dismissing Persuasion from her life or dispensing with the services of Bob and Chris Herbert. She is not a ditherer. Her feelings towards Geri, meanwhile, reflected the resentment she felt towards those she perceived to have her treated badly at school and again at Laine's. Victoria followed the fourth Golden Rule of Girl Power: 'Be in control of your own life and your destiny.'

David Beckham was in floods of tears and it had nothing to do with football. Victoria had just told him she was expecting their first child. The tour had reached New York and he was in Saint-Étienne preparing for the crucial World Cup quarter-final against Argentina. 'He must have cried for about an hour and I had tears running down my face too. It was a very emotional moment for both of us. The baby wasn't planned so it was surprise mixed with real delight.' His euphoric mood did not last long.

In 1998, as a result of a second's petulance, David Beckham was briefly the most hated man in the country. It was all very silly. Becks had clashed with Argentine midfielder Diego Simeone, which resulted in him lying pole-axed on the pitch. As Simeone walked by, Becks flicked his leg at him and Simeone went down as if hit by a speeding car. It was the sort of playground incident that football authorities take very seriously and the England midfielder was sent off. England lost the game on penalties and Beckham took the blame. The manager, Glenn Hoddle, said he should not be made a scapegoat but, privately, was reported not to have spoken to his player in the dressing room.

The media put the boot in. The respected sportswriter James Lawton echoed the views of many when he said it was 'an act of crass stupidity'. His manager at Manchester United, Alex Ferguson, was the voice of reason and noted that he could not have been more vilified if he had committed murder or high treason. Sir Bobby Charlton, the legendary United player, also rallied round: 'You cannot throw him to the wolves. I saw him straight after the match and he was terribly affected by it. He realized what he had done. Someone has to take the blame and David Beckham will take the blame this time.'

The first person Becks called in the dressing room was Victoria and she told him to catch a plane to New York. She had been watching the game on television and even she realized that it was serious. Two Concorde flights later, David was in New York in time for the Spice Girls' concert at Madison Square Garden, probably the most famous venue in the world.

The US tour, which had begun in West Palm Beach, Florida, was quite a triumph and exceeded everyone's expectations. The girls thrived on the busy schedule and liked being able to take a day off when the workload became ridiculous. This was the first time any of them had spent an extended period of time in America and they loved it. They revelled in the enthusiasm of the audience and the fact that famous people came to see them – Stevie Wonder, Prince, Cameron Diaz, Demi Moore and Drew Barrymore were some of those they met. Most memorably, Madonna came backstage in New York, bringing her two-year-old daughter, Lourdes, to meet the girls. David and Victoria's family, who had also flown in, were very impressed.

America took to them and it was mutual. The tickets for Madison Square Garden alone sold out in twelve minutes. In the *New York Times*, critic Jon Pareles wrote, 'For a sold-out house filled with little girls, like an elementary assembly with parents invited, the Spice Girls worked the stage like a fashion-show runway. Through nearly a dozen costume changes they touted "girl power", a mandate to enjoy female bonding, push men around, wear snazzy clothes and sell things along the way.' He thought Victoria held herself with a 'hint of reserve'.

David was able to stay for ten days, which was just about the longest time they had spent together. The press did not have the pregnancy news yet but it did not take them long to find out. The best story was that, amazingly, Mel B took a positive pregnancy test the same day as Victoria. The two of them would be expectant Spice Girls at the same time.

Victoria spent much of the latter part of the tour throwing up. She also had to answer questions about whether the two pregnancies, following the departures of Simon and Geri, signalled the demise of the Spice Girls. She said, 'I don't want people to read all this negativity.' On her return to the UK, she could have done without reading the revelations in the *Sun* of a Page Three Girl from Manchester called Emma Ryan, claiming all sorts of shenanigans with David, stopping short of claiming an affair. He had allegedly gone out on dates and got her tickets for a couple of games. The *News of the World* continued the 'fun' by suggesting that David wanted Emma to play strip Scrabble, putting a whole new slant on a triple word score.

In public, Victoria brazened it out, smiling broadly for the photographers as she patted her fiancé's behind. She later wrote: 'It's Posh Spice giving the performance of her life. Don't anyone say I can't act.' In private, she was devastated and would reveal in her autobiography that she punched David in the face. He has always vigorously denied anything untoward. In the end, they took legal action when the *News of the World* printed another story in which a lap dancer said she performed a dance for David at Stringfellows club in London. The girl said she slipped an ice cube down her naked body and popped it in Beckham's mouth. David had never been to Stringfellows and reached an out-of-court settlement with the newspaper. That didn't make Victoria feel any better. Up to that point, it was the worst thing that had ever happened to her and she felt nothing but contempt for the girls who sold their stories. The Spice Girls had been plagued by former boyfriends telling tales but this was the first time a current relationship was threatened.

Victoria fought back. 'We're very strong and this hasn't damaged us at all,' she said. 'Right from the beginning we've talked about this happening – and I'm surprised it hasn't come up before because, wherever we go, there are always guys who try to talk to me and girls who try to speak to David. But we trust each other.' Emma, sadly, was not the last time that trust would be tested. Victoria would have been a saint if she was unaffected by it but she never wavered in the belief that David was telling the truth and was completely innocent of the allegations.

One of the most famous images of the Beckhams is of David tenderly kissing his pregnant fiancée's stomach while they are sunbathing on a beach in Marbella, Spain. By Christmas, at least, all was back to normal. She surprised David with her most extravagant gift to date – a red Ferrari costing well in excess of £100,000 ($200,000). Victoria was eating for two at the couple's new flat in Alderley Edge, Cheshire, fifteen miles from Old Trafford. She would never really settle in the north but at least it was their first home.

One of the many urban myths about the Beckhams is that they named their first child after the place where he was conceived. It's a good story but Brooklyn Joseph Beckham would probably have been called Copenhagen if David and Victoria had used that method of choosing a name. Instead, they went with Brooklyn for two reasons: first, Victoria had always liked the name Brooke and her train of thought went from there to Brooklyn; and secondly, she was in New York when she discovered she was pregnant. Joseph was in honour of David's grandfather, who all those years ago gave him the money to enter the Bobby Charlton soccer skills competition that set him on the road to football glory.

Brooklyn was reluctant to be born. On the day he was due to be induced David and Victoria travelled down from Goff's Oak to the Portland Hospital in London only to return home disappointed. Her obstetrician, Dr Malcolm Gillard, had explained that the baby's head needed to be engaged – the widest part of the head had to enter the pelvis prior to labour – before he could be induced. They had decided to try to have the baby a week early because David was desperate to be there and he had lots of important games coming up. In the event, they had to be patient as the days went by and Mel B was able to slip in to the Portland, have a baby girl, Phoenix, and be on her way home while Victoria was still at the starting gate. Someone suggested that curry and raspberry leaf tea might help. Victoria laughed, 'As soon as David heard that he was dragging me out to a curry house every night and force feeding me raspberry tea. It was ridiculous.'

The situation became a little less amusing during one routine check at the hospital when Mr Gillard suggested that a Caesarean might be the answer. He was concerned that Victoria might go into labour without the baby's head being engaged and then she would need an emergency Caesarean, which was always more risky. David was in Manchester and was due to drive down that afternoon. Victoria decided on the safer option and just had time to be driven back to The Old School House to collect her overnight bag and her mother before returning for the operation in the early evening. She arrived at the hospital wearing blue tracksuit bottoms and a blue hat – quite a good disguise for Posh Spice. David, meanwhile, was hurtling down the motorway to make sure he made it in time. She explained, 'The baby wasn't in a good position. We had to decide really quickly if we were going to do it normally or perform a Caesarean. I chose the second option. I didn't want to be stressed and have the baby suffer as a result – all I was interested in was having a healthy baby.'

Both David and her mother, Jackie, were with her when she gave birth at 7.46 p.m. on 4 March 1999. David wanted to cut the umbilical cord but a doctor was too quick for him and he did not get the chance. Jackie was armed with a video camera. 'She videoed me being stitched up,' said Victoria. 'I remember looking up and her saying, "Smile!".'

Right from the very beginning, Victoria worried about the health and security of her newborn. She told David while they were in the theatre exactly what to do if nurses took the baby away for any reason: 'Just leave me here, half dead or whatever, and just go with the baby – make sure you don't let him out of your sight.' She was horrified to turn on the television and see the crowds outside the hospital and realize that they were broadcasting live: 'That completely freaked me out. David was supposed to stay the night in the room next door but I made him make up a camp bed in my room, so that if anyone tried to get to Brooklyn, they'd have to trample over David's head first!'

'Anyone would think I'd given birth to a royal.'

14

It's My Wedding, OK!

David Beckham came of age as a modern-day icon when he became a father. Until Brooklyn came along, David was a good-looking, talented footballer who dated a pop star. He was living the life many young men could only dream of but it took something universal to give him fulfilment. He was completely besotted by his child from the moment he first held Brooklyn in his arms. While Victoria seemed beset by insecurities as a young mother, Becks, just twenty-three, approached being a dad with a masculine confidence and an almost feminine affection. It was entirely genuine. He did not play with his son just for the clicking camera. His family instantly became the most important thing in his life. As he himself put it, Brooklyn made him grow up. Victoria echoed the views of millions of women up and down the country when she said that there was 'nothing nicer than seeing a man who was good with a baby.' And David was good – bathing his son, changing his nappy, holding him in his arms and just watching him start his life.

A couple of nights before Brooklyn was born, David had been with his own father, who told him, 'When the baby's born and you first set eyes on him, you'll understand how your mother and I feel about you.' David soon understood what he meant. He enthused, 'It's a wonderful feeling, being a father. Both sets of parents would love to have Brooklyn every day, but they've stood back and let us get on with it. That's what we wanted because it's our first child. We've got to learn and it's nice that we can learn together.'

Among the things they had to learn quickly was that a baby with colic is not much fun. Poor Brooklyn was one of those unfortunate babies who seem to spend more than half the night screaming. Whereas David seemed to take it all in his stride, Victoria fretted about everything. The baby was also Olympic standard when it came to being sick and would demonstrate his prowess at every opportunity until it was established that he had a milk intolerance. When he was six weeks old, Victoria detected a small lump and Brooklyn was whisked into hospital for a hernia operation.

The essential difference between Victoria and David after Brooklyn's birth was the classic one that affects a man and a woman in this situation. David barely broke stride in his life. He was still the glamorous footballer, kissing his partner and baby goodbye before jumping into his Ferrari and going to the training ground. The great English public had gradually forgiven him for the World Cup debacle. He could indulge his love for his son by having his name tattooed in large letters at the base of his back, a particularly painful procedure. David was still Becks but Victoria was living a life that was not remotely Posh Spice.

The couple returned with their son to the luxury apartment in Alderley Edge and, when David left for training or a game, she felt completely isolated. Jackie would drive up whenever they needed her but there were many days spent staring out the window and sobbing for no reason. She explained, 'It's hard going from Spice Girl/Pop Star to a flat on your own with a baby, no friends, no family, no nothing.' She hated being up north, away from the things that gave her confidence and security. The chief among those would always be her family back at The Old School House. The £300,000 ($600,000) penthouse flat in Alderley Edge was modern and minimalist with wooden floors and an open-plan design. Much of the wall space was filled with photographs of great moments in David's career, mainly goals he had scored. The biggest painting was of his Manchester United teammate Eric Cantona dressed as an emperor. David, notoriously clean and tidy, did most of the washing, ironing and vacuuming. He also did the cooking, specializing in spaghetti bolognaise or lasagne. By contrast, Victoria was notoriously untidy, admitting that 'messiness must be my most annoying habit.' It was certainly the one that most irritated her fiancé. Victoria never settled at Alderley Edge. She much preferred, whenever she could, to drive down to Goff's Oak and sleep in her old bedroom. David would have to get used to a long commute to work. The bonus of being at 'home' was that she, Louise and Jackie could plan the wedding of the year. It raised her spirits.

Victoria Adams officially became Victoria Beckham on 4 July 1999. Many little girls want a fairy-tale wedding and, like many before her, Victoria had cut out pictures from magazines of something she might like for her own big day – perhaps a dress or a cake or a fabulous setting. Most fairy tales are left to gather dust in a bottom drawer but Victoria could afford any wedding she wanted. A perfect fantasy for a little girl might be marrying a prince, travelling to the church in a glass coach while thousands of adoring subjects cheered her progress. For Victoria, aged twenty-five, the day would be the ultimate glossy magazine spectacular. Instead of thousands waving, millions could pick up a copy of *OK!* magazine and marvel at the fashions, the jewellery and the lavishness of it all. The most talked about wedding of the eighties was the magical one between Lady Diana Spencer and Prince Charles. Victoria and David would have the most famous one of the nineties.

OK! magazine paid £1 million ($2 million) for exclusive rights to the pictures and text from the wedding. It was an obscene amount of money and dismayed those who thought it demeaned the ceremony. Victoria sought to justify it by claiming that it gave them complete control over this aspect of the event. She had a point – anarchic chaos would have been the result of a photographic free-for-all. She was not the first and she will not be the last celebrity to change their view of the paparazzi from friendly tolerance to contempt and irritation. Britney Spears, for one, had a reputation for being one of the easiest going of stars before developing a hatred for the posse that followed her every minute of the day. The catalyst for the about-turn for both women was becoming a mother. There is a world of difference between a throwaway shot coming out of a department store and a deeply personal one of you playing with your young son.

Control is something that Victoria values very highly. Her natural desire to keep her hands on the reins was developed in those early days of the Spice Girls when she absorbed the skills of Simon Fuller. Early on he employed a lawyer to police the media where the girls were concerned. He also made sure that they retained copyright over posed photographs to maximize income and control over their image.

One million pounds ($2 million) would have been a great deal of money to turn down. In the world of Goff's Oak, where she grew up, success is still judged by money and the material world. A wedding worth a million was the ultimate in showing off, Hertfordshire-style. It was also good business to balance the books because no expense was spared and the wedding was reported to have cost £500,000 ($1 million). Victoria enlisted the help of a party organiser, Peregrine Armstrong-Jones, the half-brother of Princess Margaret's ex-husband, Lord Snowdon. Peregrine was very well connected in both royal and pop circles, having organized both Elton John's and Princess Anne's fortieth birthday parties.

Peregrine thought Luttrellstown Castle, near Dublin, might be an enchanting venue, so a then pregnant Victoria flew out to take a look on a cold and miserable January day. She instantly fell in love with the place. With its turrets and eerie Gothic façade, one could imagine Rumpelstiltskin scaling the walls, yet Victoria also noticed how much light the rooms let in. It had a fairy-tale feel, although it was built in 1794, and, best of all, the building was very private and would be receptive to tight security. Victoria explained, 'Privacy was really important. I wanted somewhere that had a big wall around it so I wouldn't feel paranoid every time I walked past a window.' In the grounds, a short walk from the main house, was a broken-down old folly that, when done up, would make a perfect venue for the actual ceremony, like a tiny Welsh chapel. Peregrine thought it might take about thirty guests. Victoria loved the idea of restricting the exchanging of vows to a few family and closest friends, then throwing open the doors for an unbeatable party.

For some reason that has never been properly explained, David and Victoria chose a Robin Hood theme for their wedding. The hero of Sherwood Forest apparently had no connection with the couple. They had never named it as a favourite story or film of their childhood. He was, however, a fun choice. A football, musical or Hollywood motif would have been a dreadful cliché. In reality, the Robin Hood theme amounted to little more than lots of greenery around the place and there was no sign of men in tights or bows and arrows.

Only two dramas needed to be faced before the big day. The first involved the wedding dress, which was travelling over to Dublin with Victoria, David and her family in a private plane chartered by *OK!* At the last minute, the dress in its travelling case proved too bulky to fit in the small hold, so it had to be unpacked and hung in the toilet for the trip. Nobody was allowed to use the loo during the flight, especially David, who was ordered to keep his eyes shut when the dress was being disembarked so that he could avoid the traditional bad luck of seeing the bride's gown before the big event.

The day of the wedding, the star guest, Elton John, fell ill. His partner, David Furnish, rang to say he had been rushed to hospital. Victoria is fond of Elton and was very worried about her friend, notwithstanding that he had promised to sing at the event. Fears that it was a heart scare were misplaced and he turned out to have an ear infection.

Victoria's £50,000 ($100,000) champagne-coloured dress took fifteen months to make and had been in preparation almost from the day David and Victoria announced their engagement. Victoria and Jackie had toured the best bridal shops and stores in London and New York before commissioning the leading American designer Vera Wang to make the dress. A Vera Wang dress was very exclusive. She made only about six a year and was much sought after in the celebrity community. She had made wedding dresses for, among others, Mariah Carey, Sharon Stone and Uma Thurman. Amusingly, Victoria, tongue in cheek, said she did not want to sell the wedding to *Hello!* magazine because she thought everyone who had their wedding in *Hello!* ended up saying goodbye and getting divorced. She obviously had failed to notice that Vera Wang's three most famous previous clients also became ex-wives.

The strapless satin gown was one that appeared to stay up by magic. The front of the dress had a fold that is known in the business as a crumb catcher, although Victoria was scarcely likely to eat anything that might result in crumbs. *OK!* proved to be breathlessly enthusiastic in its detail. She wore 'something borrowed' – a brooch pinned inside the dress that both Jackie and her grandmother, Doll, had worn at their weddings; 'something blue' was a series of taffeta bows sewn inside the dress, while 'something old' was a gorgeous diamond-studded crucifix that David had given her as a Christmas present – so seven months 'old'. Victoria had never worn it, choosing to save it for the wedding.

Victoria had been over to New York for fittings some half a dozen times. She enjoyed meeting Vera, whom she described as a very 'family-orientated person'. She said, 'It's an exciting time when you are planning a wedding and it's nice to have people around who are excited about it as well. I've had certain designers before now who thought they were too cool, and I hate that attitude.' Her problem was that she was now a mother and could not guarantee how her figure would return after she had given birth. Her transformation was remarkable and she emerged, if anything, slimmer than ever, so much so that everyone in the media was jumping up and down saying she was too skinny. David himself would later admit to being worried about how thin she was looking.

For her wedding, Victoria wore a Mr Pearl corset underneath her dress that further accentuated her waist, which would have been the envy of any self-respecting wasp. Even Kylie Minogue would have had to squeeze herself into it. She topped and tailed the outfit with a gold and diamond coronet designed by Slim Barrett and a pair of Vera's satin sandals. Her bouquet was a Sherwood mixture of ivy, red berries, other bits of greenery and a couple of plump red apples.

The three bridesmaids were Victoria's sister, Louise, who wore a dress by Chloë, which was then fronted by Stella McCartney, Louise's little girl, Liberty, aged thirteen months, and David's niece, Georgina, sixteen months. All the guests wore either black or white, which looked very stylish and elegant in the photographs. Fashion commentators had already noticed how much David and Victoria liked matching outfits. David's suit by English designer Timothy Evere might not have been an exact match but his cream three-piece morning dress perfectly complimented his bride's dress. Once again, he demonstrated how much he loved dressing up. He has been described as a dandy and certainly Beau Brummell would have been proud of his wedding day outfits, especially the white top hat, stripy waistcoat and white shoes. Five-month-old Brooklyn also wore a champagne and cream wedding outfit to compliment his mother and father. He was officially ring bearer for the ceremony.

The jewellery on show could have stocked a small shop in Hatton Garden. The wedding rings were made in London by Asprey and Garrard's. One of the published wedding pictures had the couple clutching hands so that the rings were shown to best effect. Victoria's was dominated by a huge diamond supported by a host of baguette diamonds set in 18-carat gold. David's was an eternity-style ring with twenty-four baguette diamonds and a further twenty-four smaller ones, again set in 18-carat gold. Asprey and Garrard derived considerable publicity from the event. The firm was also responsible for the couple's gifts to each other. David had chosen for his bride a pair of diamond earrings set in 18-carat gold to match her wedding ring. He also gave her an 18-carat gold waist chain with a diamond at one end. Victoria gave David a Breguet-designed steel watch. He also wore a diamond Cartier bracelet. Much more 'bling' was floating around on the day. The three bridesmaids were given £8,000 ($16,000) diamond necklaces from Tiffany. Best man Gary Neville's present was a £12,000 ($24,000) Cartier watch, while Victoria's brother, Christian, was not forgotten and received a £12,000 ($24,000) gold and silver Rolex watch for doing a spot of ushering.

Despite the extravagance, the wedding ceremony itself was sweet and simple. The Bishop of Cork, the Right Reverend Paul Colton, conducted the ceremony. He was a Manchester United fan and bore an uncanny resemblance to Friar Tuck from the Robin Hood stories. Victoria made her entrance on Tony's arm to Wagner's wedding march from the opera *Lohengrin*. Emma Bunton burst into tears. David and Victoria cried when they exchanged their vows. Victoria did not promise to 'obey' (how could Girl Power condone that?). The Bishop warned the couple about temptation, quoting an old Irish priest: 'The eyes that over cocktails seem so very sweet may not seem so amorous over Shredded Wheat.'

After the ceremony, the bride, groom and ring bearer disappeared to change into matching purple party clothes. They were designed by the then London-based Antonio Berardi, who had become one of the Beckhams' new circle of friends away from music and football. The outfits were very purple, down to David's purple suede Manolo Blahnik shoes and Brooklyn's cowboy hat. At least Brooklyn had the good grace to look pretty miserable in the reception shots. He was also sick down his father's suit, which added to the jollity.

Twenty-nine special guests had grown to 226 for the reception, which was surprisingly unstarry. Most of the Manchester United team were there, although not Sir Alex Ferguson, who sent a telegram because he was attending another wedding. The day was made for David's father, Ted, when he was introduced to his hero, Sir Bobby Charlton. The three other Spice Girls had brought their mothers. Mel B also brought her daughter, Phoenix, who was a month older than Brooklyn. She had been calling herself Mel G since her marriage the previous year to dancer Jimmy Gulzar. She would be back to calling herself Mel B before the year was out.

Geri Halliwell's absence was, according to Victoria, the saddest thing about the wedding. The two women had been so close. Victoria acknowledged that she could not invite her former bandmate because it was 'too public', which presumably meant that it would have attracted too much publicity and taken some of the attention away from the bride and groom. Geri sent her a handwritten poem. She had never met Brooklyn.

The speeches were charmingly old-fashioned. Tony Adams was bursting with pride and looking tanned, silver-haired and prosperous when he said he could not have wished for a better son-in-law. He also observed, 'It is very difficult for me to find anything to say that hasn't already been written by the *News of the World*, the *Sun*, the *Daily Mirror* . . . need I go on?' It was all very jolly. He recounted the story that David had been watching television when he had seen a certain member of a girl band and announced that she was the woman he was going to marry. 'Unfortunately,' he continued, 'he was talking about Louise from Eternal and Jamie Redknapp got there first.' David began his speech with 'My wife and I' to great cheering and Gary Neville told some risqué jokes in his best man's speech. He also wore a curtain as a sarong as a reminder of a famous Beckham fashion moment. It could have been any wedding on any given weekend but it was the best money could buy.

After the disco, the night ended with a five-minute firework display to the sound of the Björk hit 'It's Oh So Quiet'. The newlyweds had one other duty to perform before they could retire for their wedding night. They had to stifle their yawns to look over the photographs to approve those that could be published in *OK!*.

The honeymoon arrangements did not go as smoothly as the wedding ones. They were hoping to get away for ten days before David had to resume pre-season training. Unfortunately, Sir Alex took great exception to David's agent asking the United chairman for a couple of extra days' holiday for his client. David ended up with less than everyone else because the 'gaffer' thought he was going over his head. They would have only four days for the honeymoon. At the last minute, they were helped out by Andrew Lloyd Webber's wife, Madeleine, who said the Beckhams could stay at their villa in the south of France, which was not that much of a hardship. Victoria, who had been in total control of the big day, increasingly resented the control Ferguson had over her new husband. Something would have to change in the future.

Observers of Victoria and David's wedding tended to fall into two camps: those who loved it, finding it a stylish and opulent mix of Disney and Hollywood; and those who loathed it, claiming it was the last word in crass vulgarity. The reaction to the unusual invitations highlighted the carping. They were designed as if they were invitations to a castle in the time of Robin Hood. At the top was a mock heraldic crest that they used throughout the wedding paraphernalia, including on a large purple flag that flew above the castle throughout the day. The design included a swan, an age-old royal symbol. Needless to say, experts were found to rubbish it, in particular noting that the swan was pointing the wrong way. Victoria was not amused: 'So what if the poxy swan is the wrong way? Does anybody really give a s***?'

The wedding was planned as an entertainment and completely fulfilled its purpose. Copies of *OK!* flew off the shelves and no one suggested it was anything other than memorable. It launched a thousand conversations at the hairdresser's. That was exactly what Victoria wanted. There would be no ignoring Mr and Mrs Beckham.

'We're just going to go over the top and make it entertaining for everybody.'

15

A Game of Better Halves

Victoria does not have a love affair with football – far from it. After one match in which he had scored a goal from a sublime free kick, David rang home only to be told sternly that his roots needed doing. As far as Victoria was concerned, football was a commodity to be exploited. You did not have to go on a one hundred-date stadium tour to claim the spotlight. That was freely available to David Beckham every week just by running on to the pitch. Under sufferance, she put up with the Manchester United crowd serenading her with obscene chants every time she watched a match.

Even before the honeymoon fiasco, Victoria and Alex Ferguson had little time for one another. The famously fierce manager from a rough area of Glasgow did not appreciate anything that might upset his Old Trafford domain. Nobody was bigger than the club. The glitz and glamour of the Spice Girls threatened the very heart of that philosophy and turned a good-looking young footballer into the most famous sportsman in the country. When he met Victoria Adams, David Beckham was not really a celebrity; he was still a footballer.

When they became a couple, Victoria was a huge star with an estimated fortune in excess of £25 million ($50 million). David was a millionaire but probably worth no more than £7 million ($14 million). Their alliance and eventual marriage was the first step in building a joint brand. Andy Milligan, in his fascinating study *Brand It Like Beckham*, puts it simply, 'Think of Posh and you think of Becks. Think of Becks and you think of Posh.'

The most instant effect of their partnership was that it gave them huge media coverage. They attracted the tabloid press like moths to a candle. It was not just David who benefited. Until she met him, Victoria's coverage was as one of five Spice Girls. Her love affair separated her from the other girls and ultimately enabled her to eclipse them. The Beckhams could feed this coverage as much as they liked but buying each other expensive gifts was a good start. From the very beginning, they have expressed their love with extravagant gestures and presents. Victoria would buy David a car; he would respond with a £50,000 ($100,000) diamond ring as an anniversary present, a pair of earrings costing £30,000 ($60,000) for her birthday, or a £10,000 ($20,000) jewellery box in the shape of the Palace of Versailles to keep them in, which he gave her on Valentine's Day. He took her on a surprise second honeymoon to a beautiful Tuscan villa before they had been married a year. Behind the scenes, they send each other cards with little notes of love, David buys her flowers constantly – her favourites are lilies – and they speak all the time on their mobile phones even if they have only just said goodbye. Their obvious love and affection broadened their appeal by presenting a human face to the world. They like to hold hands, as if they were a pair of teenagers in love. Victoria observed, 'We're both very affectionate and I've never really been like that with any other boyfriends.'

David somehow appeared the softer of the two, as was the case in the way he obviously adored Brooklyn and seemed to spend every available moment of his wedding with his son in his arms. Victoria was still very much Posh Spice in the eyes of the public – the cool, pouty member of the Spice Girls – so, being happy and girly was never an image that would come easily to her.

Their marriage provided them with the opportunity to make one other very smart move. Victoria took the name Beckham. For the first twenty-four years of her life she had been Victoria Adams (except for her brief flirtation with Victoria Adams-Wood). She had achieved enormous fame as Victoria Adams but she was prepared to drop it immediately and take her husband's name. The name Victoria Beckham is so etched into the public consciousness that one can easily forget she has only had that name for one third of her life. The majority of stars keep their famous name in order to continue their brand – Britney Spears and Annie Lennox, for example. Other famous women fudge their name after marriage – Jennifer Aniston-Pitt, for instance, had to revert to her maiden name when she split from Brad Pitt. Victoria ditched any existing branding the moment she said, 'I do' at Luttrellstown Castle and became Victoria Beckham.

Victoria learned a lot watching Simon Fuller at work and took responsibility for marketing and promotion after he left. She had what Andy Milligan describes as 'savvy'. She probably inherited much of that from her father. Growing up, she recalls listening to him on the phone while he struck yet another hard bargain with a hapless customer. The Spice Girls would be a sobering example of how a brand can fall apart rapidly when it no longer has collective power. Fuller understood this but the ego-led music business often does not, which is why it is littered with the names of failed solo performers who thought they were bigger than the band. They did not realize that by leaving the band they were also leaving the brand.

Manchester United is a fine example of how to build and maintain a brand. The club always insisted that three players were present at any commercial opportunity so that the team as a whole would benefit and not just one individual. David Beckham, of course, while a money-making machine for United, threatened to become too big and subsequently obscure the club branding. At the height of his fame with the club, more than fifty per cent of its shirt sales worldwide were of Beckham's number seven.

Alex Ferguson hated the celebrity status Victoria brought to his star player and almost from day one it was a boxing match – Ferguson in one corner and the Beckhams in the other. His players called him 'the gaffer'. David explained, 'There's not one player at United who doesn't have some kind of fear of the gaffer, but it's not dread of him, more a respect for what he's done.' Ferguson was not at all happy that David had another gaffer at home organizing his life.

In the male-dominated world of sweat and embrocation, Ferguson had not been impressed that David would prefer to

Life as the Beckhams: The world's most glamorous couple arrive at the 2007 Sport Industry Awards at Old Billingsgate in Central London.

Her parents remain devoted to Victoria. Now working full time for the 'House Of Beckham', they join their daughter for the launch of a dVb collection in Toronto in February 2008.

Simon Fuller introduced Victoria to David when Manchester United played Chelsea in 1997. Ten years later they watched him play Chelsea once more – this time for his LA Galaxy team.

Victoria joins two of her favourite men, Sir Elton John and his partner David Furnish at an AIDS fundraiser. If only Elton had told her he was wearing pink . . .

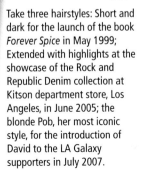

Take three hairstyles: Short and dark for the launch of the book *Forever Spice* in May 1999; Extended with highlights at the showcase of the Rock and Republic Denim collection at Kitson department store, Los Angeles, in June 2005; the blonde Pob, her most iconic style, for the introduction of David to the LA Galaxy supporters in July 2007.

Victoria has truly arrived in the world of fashion . . .

Arriving with Italian designer Roberto Cavalli at a show in aid of The Prince's Trust in Monaco in October 2005. Cavalli designed the costumes for the Spice Girls reunion tour.

Modelling for Roberto Cavalli on the runway in Milan in January 2006.

Posing with American designer Marc Jacobs at the Council of Fashion Designers of America annual awards in New York in June, 2008. Victoria was the face of his Spring 2008 collection.

Performing at the Victoria's Secret Fashion Show in Hollywood in November, 2007.

The beauty of wearing sunglasses to watch David play football is that nobody knows if you are paying attention: (*above*) At the World Cup in Germany, 2006, with Cheryl Cole, Coleen Mclaughlin (behind) and son Romeo; (*right*) Making sure son Cruz gets a good view when they join Tom Cruise and Katie Holmes to see Real Madrid capture the Spanish title in Madrid, 2007; (*below*) With son Brooklyn at Euro 2004 when daddy led England to a 3-0 win against Switzerland.

Victoria's three best girlfriends in Hollywood are Eva Longoria Parker, Kate Beckinsale and Katie Holmes. (*Top*) Eva was in Manchester to offer backstage support at The Return of the Spice Girls concert in January 2008; (*middle*) Kate chats at an LA Galaxy game in April 2008 while Tony Adams tries to watch the play; (*left*) Katie Holmes peers through the gloom of those shades at the Chanel Fashion Show in Paris in October 2006.

Hello, Goodbye! The Spice Girls perform at the O2 Arena, London, in December 2007. This time it really was Farewell.

Looking fabulous . . . a modern icon.

charter a plane to visit Victoria abroad rather than go home for a bit of telly and an early night. David spent many hours driving the 370-mile round trip between Hertfordshire and Manchester so that his manager would not know that he was visiting Victoria. He never dared catch a plane to or from Stansted airport because he was bound to be found out.

Victoria was exerting influence not just in David's private life. Not long after he was sent off against Argentina, she set up a company called Yandella Limited, a name bought off the shelf by her mother. She and Jackie became directors of what would soon be the Beckhams' family business. In March 1999, David became its third director. In theory, at least, it gave Victoria control over the commercial aspect of David's life. Technically, she and her mother, who was also the company secretary, could outvote David on any key decision. This was no hobby – the company was in place in time to bank an estimated £2.5 million ($5 million) in deals in the run-up to the couple's wedding.

As far as Victoria was concerned, the north began at Watford Gap services on the M1. She preferred life at The Old School House and celebrity nights out in London to dreary Alderley Edge. David liked that lifestyle as well. He chose to join his wife at a party for Jade Jagger in Covent Garden during London Fashion Week. Nobody forced him to turn up wearing a silk headscarf thereby guaranteeing that photos of him would appear everywhere. Ferguson was furious because the new season had only just started and he expected David to be in Manchester. He promptly fined him a record club fine of £50,000 ($100,000), the equivalent of two weeks' wages, and a huge sum to forfeit for a few air kisses and a glass of mineral water. David is a clothes horse who loves fashion, a weakness he and his wife have the money to indulge. Both of the Beckhams love shopping, not just Victoria, although she had the final word on styling her husband. As one insider remarked, 'David should have been a model from the start.'

Ferguson did not keep his opinion to himself: 'The showbiz element in his life, made inevitable by the pop star status of his wife, Victoria, has sometimes caused me to worry about a possible threat to his chances of giving maximum expression to his huge talent.'

Reading between the lines, the manager clearly wished the little woman would stay at home cooking a nice meal so that his player could be in peak condition for the big game.

The boss, however, was not alone in his concerns about David. The former Liverpool player and BBC commentator, Mark Lawrenson said, 'He has a pop star wife and lives a kind of pop star life. He is in the glare of the spotlight but I think he courts it sometimes. Jamie Redknapp is married to pop star Louise but you don't see them on every page, every day.'

Lawrenson rather missed the point of branding. The Redknapps do not have a brand to promote. If the Beckhams made the front page, it did not matter which one of them was being publicized because it was all oxygen for the brand. When Victoria talked about the sarong David famously wore while on holiday in the south of France, she knew her remarks would be picked up. She joked that underneath he was wearing her underwear and, sure enough, next day's front pages revealed that David liked to 'borrow her knickers'. Victoria is smart enough to know her one-liner would be news. In the short term it might promote a television programme she was making but in the long term they both would benefit. Even a sending-off was not the end of the world, as long as the brand was not threatened.

Victoria would have much preferred it if David had played for a London club so that they could have settled down in more familiar surroundings. In the short term, she persuaded him that they needed a home in the south and set about house-hunting. She did not need to look for long because she instantly fell in love with a 1930s mock-Georgian mansion at the end of a road marked 'Private Lane – No Unauthorized Persons'. Rowneybury, as it was called, was a large, Grade II-listed, seven-bedroom house set in seventeen acres just outside the small Hertfordshire commuter town of Sawbridgeworth and had previously been a home for disabled children. The property had become derelict but a local businessman stepped in with an extensive redevelopment scheme and subsequently sold it to the Beckhams for £2.5 million ($5 million) in October 1999. Victoria had such plans for the house that it would be nearly two years before the work was finished. Victoria has inherited a taste for interior design from her father and he was the first person she called when she needed help with her own 'Grand Design'.

The house is quite close to a main road but is completely hidden by a mini forest of mature trees. The only way for paparazzi to catch a glimpse of the home is round the back by the canal. Victoria and David were said to have spent a fortune putting their own stamp on the house. The garden, for instance, has three gazebos, each with a different theme – lakeside, romantic and ornamental. Each cost £10,000 ($20,000). In another part of the garden, they placed a 52-foot pavilion with a marble floor. They keep a four-foot barbecue, costing £70,000 ($140,000), in there, making it the perfect location for lavish parties.

Despite the opulence, the Beckhams wanted somewhere to call home. David explained, 'It was time to stretch out a little after a year and half of living in suitcases, stopping at Tony and Jackie's or the apartment in Cheshire.' Their careers meant they lived very itinerant lifestyles, travelling in trains and boats and planes – not forgetting high performance sports cars – all over the world. They wanted to put down roots. The challenge would be to turn Rowneybury into somewhere that Victoria could call home. As she herself said, 'I always called The Old School House home.'

The homely features she and her father added to Rowneybury included an indoor swimming pool, a recording studio, a snooker room, a gym and floodlit tennis courts. They spent £20,000 ($40,000) on hundreds of fibre-optic lights to create a night sky in Brooklyn's bedroom. Victoria also installed a bathroom devoted to Audrey Hepburn. The overall effect in the house is high camp, reflecting that both David and Victoria share good-natured, over-the-top taste. She revealed, 'There's a room like a tart's boudoir with leopard print everywhere and a mirrored ceiling. Then there's our bedroom which is quite virginal and white with a big four-poster old oak bed. The hall is completely camp, with bright red walls, a huge big tacky chandelier, and big, thick velvet curtains.'

The vast sitting room is a potpourri of ethnic flavours with full-sized Thai figurines and an African drum with a birdcage sitting on it. Upstairs, they installed a home cinema complete with popcorn machine. Part of Victoria's ongoing style is to mock her taste slightly, an approach that makes it more difficult for the snooty to pour scorn on nouveau riche taste. She had the money to do whatever she wanted to her house and is thought to have spent some £3 million ($6 million) designing what was almost a theme park within four walls. When they found out the extent of the upgrade, the media had fun changing the name of Rowneybury to Beckingham Palace.

The Sawbridgeworth shopkeepers saw endless opportunities to attract the Beckhams into their stores. The local dress shop, while not stocking Gucci, was more Bond Street than Bluewater. Victoria's sister, Louise, tried her hand at running a boutique when she opened a quaint shop called The Closet in Ware High Street but even her name above the door could not attract enough customers through it.

The best local story about the famous new residents, which may or may not have been true, was when they went for dinner at a fine dining restaurant five minutes' walk from the house. Victoria allegedly asked for a bottle of the much-derided wine Liebfraumilch. The restaurant did not stock it, so a minion was hastily dispatched from the kitchen to the local off-licence to purchase a bottle. The off-licence apparently confirmed that the sweet-tasting white was the wine of choice for the Beckhams.

Sawbridgeworth could not have been better placed. By car, it would take Victoria just twenty minutes to pop to her mum's for a cup of tea. David's parents were not much further away, the West End was an hour and Stansted airport was just ten minutes. If they left after breakfast, they could be at Elton John's house in the south of France for lunch. The only location it was not convenient for was Manchester.

Victoria might have had little interest in football but her reasons for disliking living in the north were more complex. Obviously, she missed her family and the familiar surroundings of Goff's Oak. She had few friends in Manchester and had little to say to the other wives and girlfriends on the odd occasions when she did take Brooklyn to a game. She preferred to play with her son in the players' crèche or chat to David's mother, Sandra, who was at every match. The principal source of her northern discomfort was that she did not feel safe. She worried constantly about her own security and, more importantly, that of her son.

They were not yet married when, for the first time, she was knocked sideways by a threat. One evening at David's flat in Manchester, she was rummaging around in a kitchen drawer when she came across two silver bullets. One had 'Posh' scratched on it, the other 'Becks'. David had been waiting for the right moment to tell her that he had received them in the post along with a sick note stating that they were 'both getting it'. Victoria was seriously shocked and, from that moment on, was deeply affected by any security scare. Much worse was in store.

In October 1999, while David was with the England team at a hotel preparing for an international at Wembley, the police contacted Victoria to tell her they had received a tip-off that an attempt would be made to kidnap Brooklyn the following day. Victoria went into meltdown. David, supported by the then England manager Kevin Keegan, sped to her side and it was decided she and Brooklyn should spend the night at the Burnham Beeches Hotel, where the squad were protected by twenty-four-hour security. All went well and David played in the game the next day when England thrashed Luxembourg. The damage was done to Victoria's peace of mind though and Brooklyn became the most protected little child in Britain.

Not long after this frightening incident, Brooklyn became ill and the north v. south divide came firmly into focus. David was at home at Rowneybury, preparing to drive to Manchester, but a nasty stomach bug gave Brooklyn a high temperature and made him feel very poorly. His doting father decided he wanted to be with his son and training would have to wait. His manager was not best pleased, a mood made even worse when pictures of Victoria out and about the next day made it appear that she had left David to babysit. As is often the way with youngsters' complaints, it quickly abated and Brooklyn was feeling much better the next day. The damage had been done, however, and Ferguson dropped David for the next game against Leeds, even declining to name him as a substitute. The *Daily Mail* said it was a triumph for discipline and integrity over celebrity and distraction.

The rift between David Beckham and Alex Ferguson was becoming too wide to mend. It was quite a difficult situation for Victoria. She did not want to damage her own standing by appearing to sabotage her husband's career, especially as her solo prospects were uncertain. She might have preferred it if he had played for Chelsea or Arsenal but she understood that she would be hated if he left Manchester United because of her.

She managed to deflect some of the attention away from football when she turned up at a birthday party, hosted by Elton John for his partner David Furnish, at the very fashionable Ivy restaurant wearing a tight, off-the-shoulder red leather mini dress. Her figure seemed even more slender while her breasts appeared distinctly pronounced, prompting a great deal of media comment. Former *Smash Hits* editor Emma Jones observes, 'When you see Victoria's figure you see this kind of slightly big, skeletal shaped head, a pert pair of bosoms and a seven-year-old girl's body.' Not for the last time would she deny having had an enlargement. In the television documentary *Being Victoria Beckham*, she explained that any woman could make her chest look bigger with the help of a 'bit of toupee tape, a nice basque, hold your stomach in, push your boobs up and a good bra.'

'I've got a big old pair of boobs.'

16

Not Forever

Victoria seemed very emotional. She was upset and on edge all evening. She called the other three girls together before they were due to go on to the stage at Earls Court and told them, 'I've had death threats,' and proceeded briefly to fill them in on how she had received bullets in the post and threatening letters and how she was worried that there were plans to kidnap Brooklyn. It should have been a great night for the Spice Girls, who received a lifetime achievement award at the Brits in February 2000 just four years after they felt like naughty schoolgirls playing truant at their first awards night. Mel B recalled that throughout the performance Victoria was as 'white as a sheet, her mind preoccupied by guns and kidnappers'.

The letter that had triggered her anguish had arrived two days earlier. Inside was a newspaper photograph of Victoria that had been tampered with to show blood spurting from a bullet hole in her head and the warning 'You are going to die', with the date 3 March 2000, the date of the Brits. She immediately called the police. Victoria did not know it at the time but Geri Halliwell had also received a chilling threat and she, too, was due to appear at that year's awards.

Victoria spent the day of the awards with a bodyguard by her side. The worst moment was when she came off stage following the afternoon rehearsal and saw a red laser light shining on her chest. It was like something from a Clint Eastwood movie. Victoria was terrified. Police dashed up to the gantry but whoever had been there had made their escape.

The evening took on a surreal quality. The Spice Girls were the last act to perform, so Victoria had hours to wait nervously. Geri performed her new single, 'Bag It Up', which would be her third solo number one, in an energetic, highly camp fashion. She had been asked to join the others on stage but declined, saying she did not want the first time she saw them in several years to be at such a public event. She left just before their opening song, 'Spice Up Your Life'. The girls had come down on to the stage, tastefully, from a giant egg.

They performed a medley of songs, including 'Say You'll Be There' and 'Holler', before finishing with their 1998 Christmas number one, 'Goodbye'. The audience thought it a symbolic choice, especially when Victoria appeared to be too upset to continue singing. In reality, she thought she had been shot. In her anxiety, she had mistaken the bursting of balloons for gunshots. She broke down in tears, which the world's media thought was because she was overcome with emotion. They were tears of joy that she was still alive.

Receiving the award was the culmination of the Spice Girls phenomenon. Seven years and more would pass before they were reunited on stage. Few knew at the time but the Outstanding Contribution Award that year was originally offered to Paul McCartney but was withdrawn when he would not agree to perform live. Four years of the Spice Girls could not match the achievements of the former Beatle over nearly forty years but the award acknowledged their place in pop history. In terms of exposure, money-making and commercial exploitation, nobody could equal the exponents of Girl Power. How much better it was that they should receive the award looking fantastic, while they were still young, their music fresh in the mind and their image not yet clouded by nostalgia. Nobody would want to see Spice Grannies coming on with dyed hair and wrinkles.

After her maternity leave, Victoria had resumed work on the Spice Girls' third album, the first without Geri. They had started writing for the album as long ago as November 1998, shortly after the end of the world tour, but babies and solo projects had slowed everything down. The other three girls, as well as Geri, had all released singles by the time of the Brit Awards and, more and more, the Spice Girls had to be fitted in around other commitments. Mel C, in particular, seemed to be moving away from the group. Her first solo album, *Northern Star*, was released in November 1999 and she appeared more interested in promoting that than concentrating on the Spice Girls. Eliot Kennedy, whom the girls spent time with while recording in Sheffield, noted that they were 'going through the motions'.

Three weeks after the Spice Girls walked off the stage at Earls Court, Geri reached the top of the charts with 'Bag It Up'. The following week Melanie C had a number one hit record with 'Never Be the Same Again' and, two weeks after that, Emma Bunton reached number one with 'What Took You So Long'. It was time that Victoria thought about life after Spice.

The principal concern on her birthday, however, was her missing luggage. British Airways had apparently mislaid some of her bags on a flight back from the US in April. Inside were designer clothes, her lyric book and a silver picture frame. Many of the items were discovered in a van belonging to a twenty-year-old binman called Mark Oliver. When he eventually stood trial in January 2001, Victoria had to give evidence and the media much enjoyed poking fun at the extravagant quantity of expensive clothes packed into her Louis Vuitton suitcases. She had given the police a list of more than a hundred items of designer clothing, which some commentators thought a 'criminal' case of over-packing. In all, they managed to recover £23,000 ($46,000) worth of lost items. Privately, she settled a complaint against British Airways for a reported £100,000 ($200,000). Oliver was sentenced to fifteen months in a young offenders' institution for handling stolen goods. Jackie Adams described the sentence as 'fantastic', although not many observers felt sorry for her daughter.

Victoria, meanwhile, had been working on some songs but progress was slow and her own solo album was not scheduled for release until well into the following year. She did not want to be away from the spotlight for so long that it would appear she was making a comeback before she had even started her solo career. She needed something to remind the public that she was still active. Out of the blue, Virgin were approached by Dane Bowers, who wanted to know if Victoria would guest on his next single. Dane had been a member of the boy band Another Level, which had enjoyed a string of hits during the last couple of years, including a number one with 'Freak Me'.

People assume that Victoria is too busy shopping to take much notice of other music but that could not be further from the truth. During her time in the Spice Girls, their PR, Muff Fitzgerald, thought she had the most contemporary taste, enjoying 'good garage and quality soul music'. In the early days, she would go dancing at clubs but her celebrity status had long consigned those pleasures to yesterday.

Mel B came closest to sharing Victoria's musical preferences. Mel B's solo career was more advanced than Victoria's, with an album soon to be released. The other Spice Mum and Victoria would never be best friends but they respected each other and would meet up from time to time with Phoenix and Brooklyn in tow to discuss the trials of being mothers. Mel B was able to pass on first-hand the difficulties of being a single parent. Being rich did not make it better and Victoria was well aware of how lucky she was to have such a strong family unit. It would take an atomic explosion to break up the Beckhams.

Victoria liked Another Level, whom she thought had produced some of the best British R & B of recent years, even though they were shoved on the post-Take That pile of boy bands topped first by Boyzone and then by Westlife. Another Level managed only two years before splitting up. Victoria also noted that each of the other three Spice Girls had collaborated with another artist on their first hit – Melanie C with Bryan Adams and Mel B with Missy Elliott; Emma had featured on a Tin Tin Out single. Unfortunately for Victoria, the media never treated hers as a joint record. As far as everyone was concerned, True Steppers and Dane Bowers featuring Victoria Beckham would be her first solo attempt. 'Out of Your Mind' was never anything other than 'her' record and success or failure would reflect totally on her.

True Steppers were two DJs, Jonny Linders and Andy Lysandrou, who specialized in garage music. They had already joined forces with Dane the previous year on a top ten hit called 'Buggin'. Victoria took a gamble that the public would buy into a more hip version of Posh Spice. The record itself may sound dated now but at the time True Steppers were cutting edge. Victoria clearly did not want to go down the flamboyant showgirl route chosen by Geri Halliwell. This was music she would listen to at home, when she could prise the sound system away from David, who was devoted to very loud rap music. She was much more likely to dance to True Steppers than she was to anything by the Spice Girls. The former was pleasure, the latter was work.

'Out of Your Mind' was an important step for Victoria because she was taking it as Victoria Beckham and not as Posh Spice. She was experiencing a routine strangely similar to the daily grind of Boyne Hill Road. A car would collect her and Brooklyn bright and early from The Old School House where they were staying. First stop was the dance studios in North London, where she rehearsed for their first live performance of the song at Party in the Park in Hyde Park, then on to a recording studio in Barnes to work on her first studio album, then back to Goff's Oak where David, if his footballing duties allowed, would have the supper ready. When he was away, her mother and father would look after her. Victoria loved to be busy and did not have time to mope around as she had done a few short months before. More than that, she was able to appreciate the mother and son things she did with Brooklyn and the rest of her family. Her sister, Louise, and niece, Liberty, were always on hand when there was a chance to go and feed the ducks.

Victoria was completely determined to do the best she possibly could for this record. The PR campaign became the stuff of legend. Party in the Park was just the start. Victoria, often with David beside her, went from store to store signing copies, smiling and giving everyone the superstar treatment, whether it was at a dance club in Ibiza, a Radio One Roadshow in Paignton or a personal appearance at Woolworths in Oldham to which 6,000 fans turned out. The *Sun* newspaper, unhelpfully, described her as 'desperate'. All she was doing was working furiously – as she always did – to maximize the result. She appeared at G.A.Y. and was enthusiastically received by a packed crowd who had always loved the high camp style of the Spice Girls, especially when Geri was in the line-up. They also revered David Beckham, perhaps the number one male gay icon in the country. In Cardiff she announced on local radio that she would kiss anyone who bought her record during a signing session. She travelled more than 8,000 miles and could not have done any more.

The problem for Victoria was that she had competition. 'Out of Your Mind' was scheduled for release the same day as 'Groovejet (If This Ain't Love)', which was proving to be a catchy and mellow summer tune. The set-up was very similar to Victoria's: a techno producer, Spiller (Cristiano Spiller), and a 'featured' female vocalist. The girl in question, Sophie Ellis-Bextor, was a tall and willowy brunette and the daughter of former *Blue Peter* presenter Janet Ellis. Sophie was privately educated and well-spoken, which was all the excuse the press needed for a few 'Posh v. Posh' headlines. The press had a rivalry story, which is always a lot of fun. Sophie fanned the flames by claiming that she, at least, was a real singer. Jackie Adams had to deny an accusation that she had gone into a local Woolworths and bought thirty-four copies of her daughter's record.

None of this mattered when 'Out of Your Mind' was number one in the mid-week chart, usually a solid indication of what would be number one on Sunday. On the Saturday, Ant and Dec's show, *CD-UK*, still had Victoria ahead. On the Sunday, however, she was second, outsold by 'Groovejet', almost at the last minute, by a little over 20,000 copies. It was disappointing but nobody died. Victoria's first week sales were 182,000, which was astonishing for August. She would have thrashed the previous week's number one, Melanie C with 'I Turn to You', or the following week's, Madonna's 'Music', which sold 40,000 fewer copies. It was just bad luck.

Victoria was shattered but did not consider it a failure. In commercial terms, 'Out of Your Mind' sold nearly 400,000 copies and was the bestselling number two of the year. It also spent longer in the charts (twenty weeks) than any other solo Spice Girl's record and that included Geri's. It was placed twenty-first in the bestseller charts of 2000. At least 'Groovejet' was not first in the list – that honour belonging to 'Bob the Builder'. In retrospect, the song has dated because music has moved on and the vocal sound effects, which Cher had popularized on 'Believe', are a gimmick of yesteryear. Many fans, however, consider it the best solo Spice single. 'Groovejet', which Victoria liked, has not aged much better.

The sad fact for Victoria is that, unjustly, any record that does not make number one is perceived as a failure. This was her best chance. The frantic schedule took its toll when she fell ill on a promotional trip to Germany and was diagnosed with viral meningitis, which required her to rest completely. Unsurprisingly, she did not want to stay at Alderley Edge but went to The Old School House, where Tony and Jackie fussed over her and looked after Brooklyn. 'She doesn't look like a pop star today, just my sick daughter,' said Jackie.

A sidebar to her work with Dane Bowers was a rather bitchy spat with busty celebrity Jordan. Dane and Jordan had been dating but suffered a messy break-up soon after 'Out of Your Mind', with the former model reportedly claiming his friendship with Victoria had changed him. It allegedly started a long-running feud between the two women, which had its brightest moment when Jordan started dating David's Manchester United teammate Dwight Yorke. When she made an appearance in the Players' Lounge, Victoria started singing the hit 'Who Let the Dogs Out.'

Before she could continue with her solo work, Victoria and the other three Spice Girls had to honour their group commitments. They adopted a more American sound for their third and final album, which was eventually called *Forever*. Absolute had started working with Geri, so they were not involved this time. The songs the girls collaborated on with Matt and Biff were not entirely successful, although the already released 'Goodbye' had made number one. The exciting aspect of this album was the involvement of Rodney Jerkins, one of the most lauded producer–songwriters in the world. He was already responsible for a string of hits for premier acts like Whitney Houston, Toni Braxton, Michael Jackson and Destiny's Child. The result was a more grown-up sound. The girls themselves had so many other commitments that they were less involved every step of the way. Victoria's lyric notebook was being used more to scribble down ideas for solo material than for Spice Girl songs.

The intense public focus on Victoria's first single revealed how post-Geri, she had become the focal point of interest in the Spice Girls. Her marriage and the birth of Brooklyn had dramatically increased her celebrity. Her first single is still perceived as a flop by many but compared to Mel B's solo efforts it was a triumph. Mel's single, 'Tell Me', a rant about Jimmy Gulzar, peaked at number four but her album, *Hot*, only made it to number twenty-eight when it was released two weeks later. That really was a disaster and made Victoria appear as successful as Madonna.

With hindsight, the end of the world tour in 1998 was the end of the road for the Spice Girls. The remaining four girls had coped with the departures of Simon Fuller and Geri Halliwell. They had bottled Victoria's old mantra 'I'll show you', and they had done it, but they did not have the desire to continue to show the world. The launch of their third and final album was a tepid affair. Both critics and the record-buying public were unimpressed.

They released a double A-sided single 'Holler'/'Let Love Lead the Way', which gave them their ninth number one. Two weeks later, the album limped in at number two, trounced by the new Westlife album, *Coast to Coast*, which was selling three times as many copies. The world generally seemed to have moved on in the short time the Spice Girls had been the biggest names in British music. Melanie C was not in a conciliatory mood: 'Westlife are a useless bunch of talentless tossers,' she said. Where was Geri when they needed her to maximize the publicity of any situation? Instead, they had Mel B at the album's party being loud and obnoxious. When the 3 a.m. girls who write the gossip column for the *Daily Mirror* walked in, she practically shouted, 'What the f*** are those sluts doing in here?' This did not guarantee favourable coverage. Victoria, as ever, did her best to calm things down but she was losing heart. She loved the album, believing it to be their best release, but none of them wanted to put in the intense effort needed to promote it.

The Jerkins posse, as they were known, were responsible for seven of the twelve tracks on the album. The Grammy-winning American producers Jimmy Jam and Terry Lewis wrote and produced two more. Matt and Biff ended up with just one track, 'Goodbye', which ironically was the biggest hit on the album. Even the cover image seemed strangely lacklustre, as they posed like a bunch of mature women at a wedding reception – no pigtails, no tracksuits and no exuberance. At least Victoria wore black, so that was comforting.

Entertainment Weekly observed, 'The music is so tasteful, restrained and assembly-line proficient that it makes early singles like "Say You'll Be There" sound like the rawest punk.' *Rolling Stone* damned it by saying it was 'OK'. Betty Clarke in the *Guardian* summed it up: '*Forever* is full of Americanisms, with "uh-uh"s and Chic basslines everywhere. But while each track is extremely polished, all that production has removed the enthusiasm that once characterized the Spice Girls – the fun factor replaced by a personally reassuring but professionally boring confidence.'

The sound might have been more current and less poppy, the vocals more soulful and mature but, unintentionally, they were dismantling the very Britishness of the Spice Girls. They had claimed our hearts by being girls you might meet in Tesco and this new, smoother sound did not reflect that. Betty Clarke added: 'Come back Baby, Ginger, Sporty, Scary and Posh. I miss you.' An unimpressed Eliot Kennedy, who contributed one track that he barely recognized when it appeared on the album, said, 'They were trying to make an American record with four very English girls. This was such a bad call.' America turned out to like it even less than the UK. *Forever* only reached number thirty-seven in the *Billboard* chart.

Forever sold about three million copies worldwide. *Spice* sold twenty-two million. *Spiceworld* sold nearly fourteen million. The sales were a disappointment whatever type of spin was applied. The album was beautifully produced but strangely uninvolving. It sounded more Backstreet Boys than Spice Girls, more glossy magazine than the fish and chip wrapping of 'Wannabe'. Everyone had a theory. LaShawn Daniels, one of the writers on the record, explained it to David Sinclair, 'I don't know if the public accepted they could really sing. I don't think the public accepted that they were really into the music and could really do it. I don't think the public was ready.'

Melanie C had seen enough and Victoria weighed up her options and decided this was the right time to move on. She might have been influenced by *Elle* magazine naming her 'Best Dressed Female' of 2000 at their style awards in November, the same time as *Forever* came out. There was life after Spice and she decided to devote herself to her own career. She might never be allowed to bin Posh Spice totally but that was her role within the group – 'the moody one with the pout'. She now wanted to create an image for Victoria Beckham.

Ironically, the sleeve notes for *Forever* ended with a mutual pat on the back: 'Even though we do each other's heads in, we stick together no matter what.' They stuck together until Christmas 2000, when they quietly agreed to call a halt. There was no announcement on *News at Ten*.

David was hugely encouraging of his wife. He kept telling her that she could do it. She seemed less sure that she would pull off her own record. She was the last of the Spice Girls to plan a solo career, which made it seem a little as if she had nothing better to do so she thought she might as well try it and see what happened. As a result, there was a certain amount of Spice Girl fatigue in the air by the time she was recording her debut.

She thought about moving into television and was offered the chance to be a stand-in presenter for *The Big Breakfast*, which had been a popular show when Chris Evans was the presenter. Wisely, she turned it down, sensing that she could do better. Instead, she produced her first documentary, entitled *Victoria's Secrets*, which was a celebrity soufflé but an enjoyable one. The biggest 'secret' was chatting to Guy Ritchie about his relationship with Madonna. She also went shopping for CDs with Sir Elton John, which was fun, and interviewed the famous fashion designer Valentino. The programme was well enough received and did not deter her from pursuing similar ventures in the future.

Victoria started going to acting classes in fashionable Primrose Hill and went up for the part of Alex in *Charlie's Angels* that was eventually played by Lucy Liu. The media liked to give the impression that she was floundering, especially when she was rumoured to have tried to secure the role as Lara Croft in *Tomb Raider*. The implication was that she was aiming out of her league if she thought she would be a match for Angelina Jolie. She enjoyed reading for roles but she was doing little more than dipping a toe in the water to see what might happen. She admitted that she wanted to do some acting but was nervous about making a bad choice that might do her more harm than good.

She had started working with a ghostwriter in 2000 on her autobiography, *Learning to Fly*, for which she was reportedly paid an advance of £1 million ($2 million). This was a very important strategy in transforming Posh Spice into Victoria Beckham. There had been Spice Girls books, of course, but they kept everybody to an image game plan. Here was a blank canvas on which Victoria could paint who she was when she shut the front door behind her. She makes too little of her own talents and dwells too much on her lack of confidence but she is also very funny and gloriously bitchy when laying in to a number of targets – people like Mark Wood and Geri Halliwell whom she considered at the time to have crossed her. The book became a huge bestseller, selling more than 400,000 copies and grossing a cool £4 million ($8 million). The critics loved it. The *Daily Mail* described it as 'like a rummage through a close friend's private diary.'

Among many stories is one in which she took Brooklyn to McDonald's for the first time and found she could laugh with the other mums when another little boy wandered over to play with her son: 'This was what being a mother was about. This was what being happy all was about.' The sentiment gave the cool, aloof Posh Spice a human side. She also said she wanted four children.

Both the book and the television work were essential marketing tools for the main business at hand – launching a proper solo career. She had been steadily working on her album but so many distractions had meant that progress had slowed. She went with Jackie up to Sheffield, where she spent some time working with

Eliot Kennedy, whom she had always liked. Nothing fell properly into place until she met some new people on a working trip to Los Angeles, which her record company, Virgin, and the most recent Spice Girls manager, Nancy Phillips, had set up.

She was introduced to Rhett Lawrence, who had produced the classic 'Vision of Love', the Grammy Award-winning debut number one for Mariah Carey. He had also written and produced the number one 'Never Be the Same Again' for Melanie C and Lisa 'Left Eye' Lopes, and had worked with Emma Bunton. He and Victoria agreed to write and work together on her next trip. She then met Steve Kipner who had been in the business for twenty-five years and written 'Genie in a Bottle', the breakthrough hit for Christina Aguilera. Through Steve, she met his long-term collaborator, London-based songwriter Andrew Frampton, who had been responsible for many of the hits of Steps and S Club 7. Between them these three would be largely responsible for the music that would feature on her first solo album.

Kipner and Frampton offered Victoria a song they had already written called 'Not Such an Innocent Girl' and, while she bridled against not having any input or credit, she thought the song so outstanding she decided to record it anyway. The title alone revealed the image she was trying to promote on this album – namely, look how sexy I am. The cover for the album was of a very slender Victoria, dressed in a black mini dress, looking sultry and catlike. Next to her, reinforcing the image, was a black panther wearing a diamond collar. While it was completely understandable that she wanted to move on from moody Posh Spice, the image was not entirely a successful one. More and more, Victoria was letting the world see her real personality – warm, witty and juggling a million things. The album image, however, was more like a poster for the movie *Cat Woman* and did not reflect how the public saw her. She was *Elle* magazine's 'Best Dressed Female', the wife of the England football captain and all-round hero, and the mother of a charming little boy. She was not some sexy bit of stuff.

Virgin scheduled the release of the single 'Not Such an Innocent Girl' for the last week in September 2001, with the album called, unoriginally, *Victoria Beckham*, to follow on 1 October. It was not the best timing. Kylie Minogue's new single and album were on exactly the same schedule and the much loved Australian singer was in the middle of a huge revival on the back of a pair of gold hot pants and some catchy retro disco music. Worse still for Victoria, Kylie's single 'Can't Get You Out of My Head' was an instant classic and destined to become her biggest ever hit. Rick Sky observes, 'Victoria's been very unlucky in her solo career to come up against two of the best pop songs written in the last ten years.' The media tried to whip up some rivalry, as they had done so successfully the previous year with Sophie Ellis-Bextor and Victoria, but this time there was no contest. Despite extensive airplay, Victoria's single came in at number six. One amazing statistic that Victoria's detractors seldom quote is the number of Spice Girls-related singles released since the beginning of 1999 – twenty-one. No wonder Spice Girl fatigue and apathy had settled in. Victoria was interesting as one half of the most talked about couple in Britain but less so as an ex-Spice Girl.

At least Victoria managed to have a laugh at the media's expense. In the run-up to the single's release, she appeared at the bank holiday Party in the Park in Birmingham sporting a ring through her bottom lip, which she claimed hurt like hell. She succeeded in claiming the front pages the next day, ahead of both Geri Halliwell and Ellis-Bextor who were on the same bill. It was a reflection of how the media have become progressively more obsessed with Victoria's looks and fashion. All sorts of 'experts' had their say about the pros and cons of such a fashion statement and the health risks if impressionable youngsters followed her example. It turned out to be an accessory that she binned five minutes after coming off stage.

The album only made number ten and then fell away quickly. BBC reviewer Jacqueline Hodges was unimpressed: 'A mish-mash affair of gushy sentiment and wishy-washy R & B.' She deemed it 'formulaic' and 'cringy'. At least it beat 'Bob the Builder' – just. Reviewers also remarked on the songs dedicated to husband, David, and son, Brooklyn, who is also heard on the record – such cuteness did not sit easily with the artist as a sex kitten. Can you be a mum and a vamp? As a solo artist, Victoria was finding it increasingly difficult to be taken seriously. *Victoria Beckham* was a very solid piece of work that perhaps suffered from being too safe and polished. The music resembled a Victoria Beckham outfit: well presented and promoting the chosen image. The nearest thing to a controversial track was one called 'Watcha Talkin' Bout', which seemed to accuse one of the Spice Girls of changing when fame came. Everybody immediately thought it was about Geri but it might just as easily have been a snipe at Melanie C. Renowned pop writer Rick Sky observes, 'I honestly don't think Victoria worked with the right people to help with her solo pop career. With her money and influence, they should have been at the top of the pile, not piss poor.'

'Everyone thinks of me as that moody cow.'

17

The Real Deal

The Beckhams had become the subject of the country's top soap opera, eclipsing the royal family. They were not *EastEnders*, of course, but characters in *Dynasty*, living lives of impossible glamour. Victoria was Joan Collins, a figure she much admired in real life. One can easily imagine Joan's character, Alexis, travelling with far too many pieces of Louis Vuitton. The public were fed episodes from their lives in instalments that featured every possible plot twist: kidnap threats, death threats, gold-diggers, theft, family dramas and soppiness. The soppy bits generally involved Brooklyn. He was apparently the first person Victoria told when she fell pregnant for the second time. On her instructions, her eldest son, aged three, raced over to his father and announced, 'Mummy is going to have a baby.' Right from the start Victoria wanted him to feel involved with his baby brother.

Sometimes there was unexpected humour, as when the Beckhams appeared in *Being Victoria Beckham*, a second television glimpse into her private world. 'I love being pregnant,' she announced. 'I like giving birth – oh, I love it.' 'You had a Caesarean,' said David. 'You didn't feel a thing.'

She had a second Caesarean on 1 September 2002. As he had done when Brooklyn was born, David popped out soon afterwards to tell the waiting media that they had a new son, Romeo. 'It's just a name we love,' he explained. Both sets of grandparents were on hand; David's mother and father had travelled to the hospital with Tony Adams.

One aspect of Victoria's domestic life that is often misrepresented is her relationship with David's parents. Ted and Sandra Beckham might have been much more interested in football than Victoria but they were also devoted to Brooklyn. Sandra shared the child-caring duties with Jackie when Victoria was recording her album and her daughter-in-law acknowledged that she could not have done it without the help of both grandmothers. Sandra looked after Brooklyn while his mother was in theatre having Romeo. David was devastated when his parents subsequently split up and divorced. David saw more of his mother after he bought a new house for her and his sister Joanne in Loughton, half an hour away.

When Romeo was born, Victoria had no manager, no record label and nothing much going on. She had parted company with Nancy Phillips after a disagreement over press coverage. Her split with Virgin was inevitable after the poor showing of her second single taken from the album. 'A Mind of Its Own', not an inspired choice for a single, had sold only 15,000 copies, peaking at number six in the charts. This sort of figure could not justify keeping anyone on, although Virgin maintained they were committed to releasing a third single, 'I Wish', from the album. That never materialized and the official announcement was made that her contract had 'come to a natural end' in June, when she was seven months pregnant. By then, only Melanie C of the original Spice Girls had not had their contract terminated but she, too, would be let go at the start of 2004. Virgin had parted company with all five girls just three years after their last record had been in the charts.

Even though she was experiencing a hiatus in her career, Victoria was by no means finished. She had been surprisingly slow to realize where her future might lie. She was voted the world's best dressed celebrity for the first of four years by *Prima* magazine the month before Romeo was born and fashion gradually began to take over her professional life. She was named the British ambassador for the prestigious Dolce & Gabbana line. Stefano Gabbana said, 'We want to become a bit more exclusive and not make clothes for every celebrity who asks.' Fashion designers were beginning to realize that an alliance with Victoria Beckham guaranteed publicity.

Both the Beckhams were going through a difficult period of transition. Victoria did not witness the flying boot first-hand but she was at Old Trafford in February 2003 when an angry Alex Ferguson let fly. David told her all about it after he had been to the treatment room and she was almost as mad as the manager had been. Sir Alex had apparently singled David out for criticism after the 2–0 FA Cup defeat by Arsenal and had kicked out at a boot lying on the floor. The boot flew up and caught David in the face, cutting him just above the left eye. David lost his temper and went for the man who had guided his footballing career for so many years. He described the 'flying boot incident' in his autobiography and admitted that he 'went for the gaffer'. He had to be held back by teammates.

Sir Alex observed, 'If I tried it a hundred times or a million times, it could not happen again. If it could, I would have carried on playing.' Clearly it was an accident but the manager did not seem to be taking it seriously enough and public sympathy lay with the England captain, who would need further treatment that evening to stop the bleeding. A month later, Victoria flew to Milan for the fashion shows, prompting speculation that she was laying the foundation for a big money move to Italy for her husband. The antagonism between David and Sir Alex had become irreparable and it was only a matter of time before Victoria would be house-hunting in another city well away from Manchester. She would have loved it to have been in Italy for the shopping and the fashion but, in the end, six months later it turned out to be in Spain.

The problem was that when David signed for Real Madrid for £25 million ($50 million) on 1 July 2003, Victoria had ideas for her future that were well advanced. The notion that she should drop everything and move to Madrid is a conveniently chauvinistic one. To begin with, she had breathed new life into her solo career by signing with the independent record label Telstar, negotiating a healthy £1.5 million ($3 million) advance with the help of her lawyer, Andrew Thompson, and her PR man, Alan Edwards, who had assumed some of the managerial responsibilities when Victoria split with Nancy Phillips. Victoria was the biggest name signed to Telstar, whose other artists included former *Brookside* actress Claire Sweeney and *Pop Idol* also-ran Rosie Ribbons. Telstar had been the company behind the Jive Bunny records, which sold three million copies in the eighties. In fairness, the company already had a toehold on the R & B market with Mis-Teeq and this was the direction Victoria saw for herself.

She had also noticed how well Emma Bunton had been doing since she went back to Simon Fuller's 19 group. Fuller had expanded from a single management company into 19 Entertainment with about twenty companies under his umbrella. He and Victoria were talking about a possible tie-up.

In the meantime, Victoria had joined forces with the black American producer and entrepreneur Damon Dash. The model Naomi Campbell furnished an introduction. David was a great fan of black music, especially the late Tupac, and he encouraged Victoria to pursue this new urban direction. Her alliance with Dash was completely misunderstood by the British media. The press described him as a minor record producer or hip hop artist. Tony Parsons, the novelist, described Dash in his *Daily Mirror* column as a 'little nobody'. He was, in fact, the multi-millionaire head of Roc-A-Fella records who had adopted a strategy of connected branding that would have delighted Fuller. He used his artists as a means of marketing his other brands, especially clothing, which is where Victoria came in. He wanted her to publicize his Rocawear clothing line and a sum of $1 million (£500,000) was mentioned. Victoria was becoming more aware of the commercial possibilities for her in fashion. In April 2003, she signed a £1 million ($2 million) deal to advertise handbags in Japan for the designer Samantha Thavasa. The Spice Girls were almost as big in Japan as in the UK and Victoria's face was already a familiar image there.

Dash was a streetwise businessman from Harlem who stayed in the background while his better known partner, Jay-Z, took the spotlight. Jay-Z, the boyfriend and now husband of Beyoncé, is one of the most successful artists in the American recording industry. Hip hop is a huge billion-dollar business in the US, moving far beyond its musical roots into lifestyle. That was the ambition of Dash and Jay-Z, one that echoed that of their rival entrepreneur Sean 'P Diddy' Coombs and his Bad Boy Entertainment group. Jay-Z was the public face of the Roc-A-Fella franchise but every artist they were involved with would wear the clothes, mention their brand of vodka in their lyrics or feature in one of the movies they were producing.

Figures can always be massaged to fit the purpose but one study put the number of hip hop consumers in the US between the ages of thirteen and thirty-four as forty-five million – and eighty per cent are white. That is the market that the ever ambitious Victoria is seeking to tap into. While David was signing for Real Madrid, Damon Dash was telling *Forbes* magazine that the turnover for Rocawear during the last year was $300 million (£150 million). Fashion, it seemed, could be linked to music and to personality to an extent not previously thought possible. It was no coincidence that the Rocawear label was launched during Jay-Z's *HardKnocklife* US tour in 1999. Dash explained, 'Every single thing is a commercial for the next thing. I can kill five birds with one stone – for the cost of one stone.' The commercial strategy was nothing new to Victoria, who had watched Simon Fuller build the Spice Girls brand layer by layer. It's not rocket science. If Victoria Beckham arrives for lunch wearing a pair of sunglasses, she will be photographed; they might as well be her own brand of sunglasses.

Dash explained his fashion alliance with Victoria: 'One reason I've got Victoria Beckham is because she's as non hip hop as you can get. She's not trying to be hip hop. She's recognizing the clothes for the quality. She would never affiliate herself with anything unless it was hot. People who didn't know about Rocawear before will at least be curious about it because of Victoria.'

Victoria found hip hop an exciting alternative to the pop world she was used to and infinitely preferred it to dull afternoons watching grown men chase a ball round the pitch. She travelled to New York for songwriting sessions with Dash and an album was more than taking shape by midsummer. Dash only realized how popular Victoria was when a group of photographers hung around all day hoping to get a picture of her in Harlem. He was impressed with her professionalism in coping with a world that must have seemed very strange to a girl from Goff's Oak.

In July 2003, after many months of negotiation, Victoria went back to Simon Fuller and his greatly expanded 19 Entertainment company. This time, however, she brought David and the Beckham brand with her. Fuller, who would be responsible for overseeing joint ventures revolving around the brand, knew exactly the way ahead: 'With the Beckham name so renowned the world over for music, fashion and football, there are no boundaries to what we can achieve together.'

Victoria was equally nice: 'I now have the time, energy, vigour and ambitions to continue to bring up my family while pursuing my career. Having stayed in touch with Simon over the years, I know there is no one better to help me achieve my dreams and I'm very much looking forward to the future.'

Simon's words are revealing – 'music, fashion and football'. This was the way ahead for the Beckham brand. Fuller's vision was to create a 'House of Beckham' through which the famous couple became a global illustration of a lifestyle which would appeal to everyone. Victoria recognized that the move to Real Madrid was a huge commercial opportunity for the family brand and it was no coincidence that Fuller was brought back on board the same month as her husband travelled to the Bernabéu stadium.

She had already made sure that David was by her side on a promotional tour – the Beckhams' first world tour – in the early summer. Anna Wintour, the hugely influential editor of US *Vogue*, threw a welcome dinner in New York for the Beckhams at which the couple were able to mingle with other A-listers, including David Bowie and Iman, Donna Karan and Calvin Klein. While the football-obsessed British media were focusing on Beckham's move to Madrid, Victoria was looking at the bigger picture and saw a future in the US even before her husband had signed for Real. Spain was just a stepping stone to bigger things.

Moving the brand forward involved the couple being seen together. Obviously, Victoria could not play football but she could be there when he signed. Her presence increased the power of the brand just as his had done in New York when he adopted a rap-friendly image, wearing ripped jeans, a white T-shirt and a back-to-front baseball cap. While she was in Madrid, Victoria was shown some potential houses for their Spanish base but nothing appealed. At this stage, David was still personally managed by the

SFX group and they appointed an assistant to look after the star during the first difficult months when he was settling in. Victoria met Rebecca Loos and saw no reason to veto the appointment. Rebecca, the daughter of a Dutch diplomat father and an Anglo-Spanish mother, was exotic, curvy and cosmopolitan. The world of music, fashion and celebrity inhabited by David and Victoria was full of the most striking young women in the world and Rebecca would not necessarily be seen as a threat, although it was rumoured that Victoria politely enquired if she had a boyfriend.

Meanwhile, Victoria was being seen everywhere dressed in Rocawear. Gone were the days of the little black Posh Spice dress and in its place were jeans, bomber jacket and baseball cap in Rocawear colours, usually white and red. A giant poster of Victoria went up in Times Square, New York, at the end of August 2003. She looked completely different from the familiar Posh or even the Natalie Imbruglio sex kitten look of her first solo album. First of all, she had so much hair. The hair extensions must have taken hours to prepare because she ended up with bushy, flowing locks that would have made Beyoncé proud. She was tanned and toned, wearing a brown one-piece with black trim that looked like something one might wear to a pool party. On her feet were a pair of flashy silver high-heeled shoes. Victoria popped over to New York to look at the giant billboard and thus grab another photo opportunity. She wore a green T-shirt, jeans, a baseball cap emblazoned with the logo 'American Hell' and a large pair of sunglasses that would become her trademark accessory.

These were golden opportunities to promote the Beckhams. If Victoria had sat at home making paella for David, the Beckham brand would have been operating at half power. David had been on tour with Real Madrid to the Far East and arrived back to score his first goal for his new club in September. Victoria travelled out to look at more houses and photographers captured her watching a game with David's personal assistant, Rebecca. A couple of weeks later, when she was back in London, pictures started appearing of David and Rebecca having a drink together in a club. They were apparently 'laughing and talking' at the popular Ananda Club.

Behind the scenes, it was later revealed that Victoria went mad when she heard about it and, it was claimed, she rang Rebecca and told her firmly, 'It is not your job to go clubbing with my husband, so back off.'

The Beckhams issued a statement that said: 'We are extremely happy together as a family. Since we first met, our careers have always meant that we've spent time apart. This is no reflection on the strength of our marriage and we are very much enjoying our new life in Spain.' Victoria had nothing else to say on the subject and, instead, was the star guest at the London launch party of Rocawear. Damon Dash was there and other guests included Jade Jagger, Jodie Kidd, Patrick Cox and Elton John's partner, David Furnish. Victoria looked sensational, poured into a zebra-style frock. David flew to London briefly in November to receive an OBE from the Queen – perhaps the first step on his path to a knighthood. Victoria joined him at Buckingham Palace and the two posed happily for photographs. David gave his wife an affectionate kiss on the nose.

The potential difficulty for almost every celebrity relationship is the amount of time the couple spend apart. It does not make the heart grow fonder. Instead, just saying hello in the wrong way on the telephone can cause problems. The problem for David and Victoria was that stories leaking out of Madrid planted the seed of doubt that all was not well with the best-known marriage in the country. David explained in his book, *My Side*, that they had intended to move together to Madrid but a combination of factors delayed them. They could not find a house they liked. They were concerned that Brooklyn would be harassed by the media when he went to school. In any case, he was settling in at a local school near Sawbridgeworth. One Spanish newspaper carried the headline: 'Beckham: The Madness Arrives'. They did not want that for their children. David did not mention that Victoria was working as hard as he was, but she was. Just before Christmas she was at Selfridges in London when Damon launched his own clothing line as part of the Rocawear collection in the store. Again her hair was Hollywood as she dressed down in a blue silk blouse and a pair of high-waisted jeans that made her waist almost non-existent.

Simon Fuller could have had no objection to the exposure

Victoria was getting in the fashion world. A ponytailed David was on the back pages while she was on the inside looking fit and fabulous. The only cloud on the horizon, as far as Fuller was concerned, was Damon Dash. They were not well matched. David Sinclair observed, 'On a gut level, Fuller regarded Dash as a rival rather than an ally.' Fuller had no presence in the world of hip hop and he did not want hip hop muscling in on his. Behind the scenes, he and Victoria engaged in a tug of war over her musical direction. He thought her image would be best served by being true to the pop roots of the Spice Girls. She thought hip hop – music she actually liked – would give her far more kudos. Damon Dash expected to sit down and talk tactics with Simon but he never even met him, prompting the hip hop mogul memorably to describe the pop tycoon as 'Simon Fullershit'.

A compromise was reached with the decision to put out a double A-sided single. One side was 'This Groove', a Damon Dash-produced track. On the other, was 'Let Your Head Go', a piece of Europop. Both sounded like different varieties of Kylie. The former began by Victoria talking on the phone, telling her man that he wouldn't believe what she was doing. It was an invitation for phone sex with a very catchy chorus. The accompanying video displayed Victoria writhing on a bed in a silk negligee while holding a phone, just in case there was any doubt what it was about. The overall effect was a very cool R & B sound. The Europop single seemed a little lightweight in comparison.

Victoria and Simon tried a neat marketing trick. Viewers of *Top of the Pops* were shown both videos and could then vote for the one they wanted released as a single. Proceeds from the phone vote would go to BBC's Children in Need. It was a win–win strategy. The public voted for 'This Groove', although 'Let Your Head Go' received more airtime. This time, Victoria stopped short of plugging the record by touring the nation's Woolworths stores but the promotional drive was aided by a well-timed documentary called *The 'Real' Beckhams*, which told the story of their Spanish adventure in a light manner. It was shown on Christmas Eve. Both tracks were released as a double A-side immediately after Christmas when traditionally the record market was dead and there was a better chance of reaching number one once the seasonal hits had finished for another year. Victoria managed number three which, not surprisingly, was made out to be a huge failure in the press. She was again in competition with her former nemesis Sophie Ellis-Bextor, who managed only number nine with 'I Won't Change You'.

We will never know what might have happened next in Victoria's solo career if two unconnected events had not occurred. The first was that Telstar plunged into financial difficulties leading to eventual bankruptcy. All the tracks for her new album that had been completed by Damon Dash reverted to Simon Fuller and 19 Recordings. They have still to be released. The second was that David left SFX and transferred overall responsibility for his management to Simon. He also appointed as his personal manager an old friend, Terry Byrne, who was working as Director of Football at Watford. As a consequence, Rebecca Loos lost her job.

On 4 April 2004, the front page of the *News of the World* screamed 'Beckham's Secret Affair' and then carried six pages detailing David's alleged adultery with Rebecca Loos. It was 'The Story You Thought You Would Never Read'. The story alleged four sexual encounters between David and his assistant – the first was the night of the Ananda Club visit and the last in December before she lost her job. David, it was claimed, also sent her some explicit text messages. Rebecca was said to be heartbroken that the story came out but, later, was reported to have been paid £500,000 ($1 million) in a deal arranged by kiss-and-tell broker Max Clifford.

The story alleged that David was lonely because Victoria had been ignoring him. The paper worked out that his wife was with him for thirty-five of his first eighty-nine days in Madrid. A 'family friend' helpfully pointed out that Beckham had been going 'weeks without sex'. Victoria, back at Rowneybury, was able to read a breathless account of her husband's sexual stamina. She would have to deal with the alleged infidelity under the full glare of the media spotlight. One thing was for sure: everyone would have an opinion.

David issued a statement: 'During the past few months I have become accustomed to reading more and more ludicrous stories about my private life. What appeared this morning is just one further example. The simple truth is that I am very happily married, have a wonderful wife and two very special kids. There is nothing that any third party can do to change these facts.'

Victoria immediately escaped from the UK and took Brooklyn and Romeo skiing at the fashionable resort of Courchevel in the French Alps. Her parents, Tony and Jackie, went along to support their daughter and take over some babysitting duties when David flew in from Madrid. The 'happy couple' posed for the posse of photographers who had followed them. David, in a sheepskin-trimmed jacket and hat, gave his wife a piggyback, and that picture appeared throughout the press the following day. They larked around and seemed completely at ease with one another, although it was pointed out that Victoria had a white baseball hat pulled down over her eyes so that it was impossible to see if she had been crying.

The Beckhams were able to see the story unfold while they played happy families in the snow. Curiously, none of the newspapers seemed to question the veracity of Rebecca's claims. Her brother said Rebecca had told him it was all true. Details of the text messages started to emerge and all sorts of 'friends' were giving quotes. Victoria told a 'family friend', 'There was no affair. She is a lying cow.' The story moved quickly on from what David allegedly did to question why he did it. Initially, at least, the general consensus was that it was all Victoria's fault for not being at her husband's side in Madrid. The impression was that anybody who had actually met Victoria had an entirely different view to those who had not. The anti-Victoria brigade were as one in believing that she had no career worth pursuing, choosing to ignore the fact that she had earned several million pounds in new commercial deals in 2003. The columnist Julie Burchill made a list of the reasons why she hated Posh, ending with the call for Victoria 'to give up your so-called work, Madam, and stand by your man'. Amanda Platell in the *Daily Mail* called Victoria 'greedy, grasping and graceless'. Tony Parsons observed, 'Victoria's casual attitude to her marriage is the reason this sad little episode has happened.'

The TV presenter Fiona Phillips, however, had an entirely

different view: 'I've met Victoria a number of times and she's funny, self-deprecating and appreciates the good fortune that's come her way. She's not one for showbiz parties, surrounding herself instead with close family. She's handled the events of this week amazingly well. He's the one who's been up to no good; she's the one who's had to drag herself out in the snow with a broken heart and a beaming smile.'

Victoria Newton, who, as the *Sun*'s pop columnist, had followed the Spice Girls, observed that Victoria is a loyal wife and a great mother. She added, 'Thousands of women every day hear stories about their partners committing infidelity, but to know that every little detail about these affairs is the talk of every pub and coffee shop up and down the country must cut deep.'

One of the most pertinent observations came from Damon Dash: 'She's a tough woman with a real gangsta attitude. My relationship with her makes me wonder "who is this person I keep reading about in the papers?" She's a person of substance with a pretty savvy attitude to life. I don't think she'll be humbled by all this. She's tougher than that. But their lives are like a reality show. Every second is covered. It's bugged. I couldn't live like that.'

Rebecca Loos continued with her revelations in the coming weeks and she was joined by another attractive woman, a Malaysian-born model, who alleged she had an affair with David while Victoria was pregnant with Romeo. Their trysts, she claimed, had begun when he was on tour in the Far East with Manchester United in July 2001. She also said they had met up again the following year at a hotel in Leeds. In some ways, the more women who came out of the woodwork with stories about David, the more the original revelations were diminished. One story alleged that David had slept with nine different women in Madrid. The *Daily Mirror* even said there were almost enough women to make up a football eleven and then proceeded to take a 'light-hearted' look at the team.

Once again, Victoria had to escape and flew with her family to Verbier, where she 'celebrated' her thirtieth birthday. The original plan had been to spend the day in Madrid with David but that all changed following the revelations. She was under constant scrutiny and there were reports of her three bodyguards getting into rows with photographers and her looking grumpy and spending most of the time on the phone. It was not the happiest of times and she was described as looking 'drawn and miserable'.

Two days after her birthday, she was back in London with David by her side when they attended a grand party at the Royal Albert Hall to celebrate the nineteenth anniversary of Simon Fuller's first company, 19 Management. The same evening Rebecca Loos was appearing on Sky Television. When Victoria walked in to the party, she was given an ovation that left nobody in any doubt that she was the star of the evening. Some two thousand guests cheered and clapped as she performed 'Let Your Head Go' in front of a throne. David gave a speech, 'I'm very proud to be part of the 19 party, but I'm even more proud of my beautiful and lovely wife, Victoria.' If the Beckhams were acting that night then they are in the wrong job and should be signed up by Spielberg immediately.

Victoria had two distinct situations to deal with: first, in private, the ghastliness of having to come to terms with the allegations against her husband; secondly, in public, determining the best way to proceed to protect their brand. She did consider a television interview with Michael Parkinson but decided against that course of action. Perhaps, behind closed doors, there were tears and tantrums but she said nothing on the matter until an eight-page interview appeared in *Marie Claire* magazine: 'I know for a fact David's been faithful to me and I know it in my heart. Every single Sunday, you pick up the papers and some footballer or other has allegedly done something with a Page Three Girl or wannabe this or that. It's happened for years. Obviously there's a market for it.' She also countered suggestions that her marriage was a business arrangement: 'I could not live like that. I couldn't live a lie and it would be unfair on our children.'

The upshot of a month of scandal was that Victoria decided to announce publicly that she was moving to Spain, politely describing Madrid as a 'fantastic city with wonderful people'. She knew that it would almost certainly curb her solo career but David's contract was for three years and the first was nearly up, so it would not be for ever. She could start making plans for their future right away. The Beckhams were hardly likely to settle happily in Madrid after what had happened but, for now, they had to make the best of it. Victoria watched every England game at Euro 2004 before travelling back to Madrid with David to continue the search for a suitable family home. In August, she announced that she was pregnant with their third child.

Unless there was a hidden video camera, nobody can know for sure what happened between Rebecca Loos and David Beckham. Despite all the thousands of words written about the alleged affair, it remains her word against his. Rebecca's account was given more credence in the media because she spoke nicely and was well educated. If she had been a long-haired lap dancer from Liverpool, she might have been laughed out of town. Victoria chose to believe her husband's version and preserve a close, strong and loving family unit. In his autobiography, David Beckham declined to mention Rebecca Loos and said it pained him to mention the 'whole sorry procession of spiteful stories'. He wrote, 'I hope they realize now that they misjudged my relationship with Victoria completely.'

> **'My Spanish is improving and I can now ask *Dónde Gucci*?" ("Where is Gucci?").'**

18

Hola, Adiós

Being pregnant in a foreign city, even one as sunny and sophisticated as Madrid, was not on Victoria's agenda. She had absolutely no choice but to make the best of it. Her motives were not ruled solely by public concerns over the state of her marriage and how that might affect the Beckham brand; she always put her family first, an instinct born out of the closeness of the Adams clan. She needed to get back to having a life and not a schedule, one in which her children saw their father in the evening before bed. She might have preferred to have been within 'popping in' distance of her mother and father and of Louise and Christian, who now had their own houses in the family plot back in Goff's Oak. For now, she would have to make do with visits.

The Beckhams rented a house in the residential area of La Moraleja, a leafy and upmarket suburb twenty minutes from the Bernabéu stadium. Security was always an issue wherever the family went. Brooklyn was enrolled in the exclusive, English-speaking Runnymede School, an event that proved to be the biggest in the school's forty-year history. On his first day, madness broke out as everyone tried to catch a glimpse or take a photograph of the family. Brooklyn and Romeo were as much a paparazzi target as their mother and father, stalked by photographers when they were doing no more than playing with friends. An armed security team were assigned to protect the family twenty-four hours a day following reports of kidnap threats by the Spanish capital's criminal gangs. The family have had to live with concerns over kidnapping plots for several years but now two burly bodyguards would squeeze themselves into the seats next to Brooklyn and Romeo when the boys went to the cinema.

They were not necessarily safer back home in Sawbridgeworth. Just a few weeks before she finally moved out to Madrid with the boys, an intruder, armed with a can of petrol, was found in the grounds of Rowneybury. He was discovered by a security patrol who called the police. A spokesman said, 'What was worrying is that we understand the man was carrying drugs and other items to attack the house and he clearly knew he was at the house of the Beckhams.' He would later be sentenced to seven months in jail.

Victoria now had three years to plan the next move both for herself and for the Beckham brand. Her husband's contract with Real Madrid ran out in 2007. Nobody realized it at the time but Los Angeles was already firmly established as the next step. Victoria and Simon Fuller both recognized that the next logical stage in the creation of the House of Beckham was to present the couple as international icons, both together and separately. Fuller himself was already tapping in to untold riches in the American media market with his *American Idol* show. He moved to California and sold 19 Entertainment in 2005 to the CKX corporation for $210 million (£105 million), although he remained at the helm of the business.

In the summer of 2004, the original plan was to go to Los Angeles for the launch of a David Beckham soccer school. The idea was postponed to a later date when it could be part of an orchestrated American offensive. Victoria's pregnancy and her move to Madrid meant the time wasn't right but it showed the 'American Dream' was firmly established for the Beckhams long before it became a reality. Instead, Victoria set about planning a grand christening party for her two children at Rowneybury. It would give her an excuse to go backwards and forwards to England without it appearing that she was deserting David or lending weight to the belief that she could not settle in Madrid.

She decided to hold the event at home because it would make security easier to control and would also be a more private family event. She would slip in and out of Gatwick, often travelling with Romeo, and would drive up the M11 to see how work was coming on. Her father had supervised almost all the redevelopment on the house over the years, including putting on an extra wing so they could have his and hers walk-in wardrobes. The plan for the christening was to build a chapel in the grounds where the service could take place. They wanted it to capture the mock ruins' atmosphere of Luttrellstown Castle, where they had married six years earlier. Victoria was thrilled when the Bishop of Cork, the Right Reverend Paul Colton, who had officiated at the wedding, agreed to fly over to conduct the baptism on 23 December.

On one trip Victoria was seen in the VIP lounge at the airport by the writer and agony aunt Dr Miriam Stoppard. The brief encounter provided a fascinating snapshot into the real Victoria, away from the cameras and the headline-chasing stories. Victoria walked in with Romeo in her arms. Miriam noticed he was quite a little lump for such a slight woman to carry and watched her while she sat down on a sofa. Victoria was by herself with no mother, nanny or minder in sight. She played with Romeo while she rang David on her mobile phone to tell him everything was OK. Miriam observed, 'She enquired about David in an affectionate way. She said she loved him and she was clearly sincere.' The conversation was, she thought, a kind and generous one between 'two loving people'. Miriam also described Victoria as an attentive mother looking after her son and as an elegant woman dying to join her husband. 'I was impressed,' she concluded.

The christening party, which cost an estimated £500,000 ($1 million), was full of glitz and glamour and a return to form for the Beckhams. Sir Elton John and David Furnish were there to act as godfathers to both children. At the beginning of the month, Sir Elton, always his own man, had been outspoken to *heat* magazine about the perceived problems that David and Victoria had endured since the footballer signed with Real Madrid: 'I think he missed her and the boys terribly. If you live six months in a hotel room in Madrid, or anywhere, it's going to drive you crazy. I think they should have gone as a family.' He thought the couple should have released a statement confirming their marital problems. 'But they just denied it and kept denying it and there were obviously problems . . . which now they seem to have sorted out.' Confirming that the couple were now back on track, Sir Elton concluded, 'They are two people who love each other very much.'

The quotes may or may not have been a surprise to Victoria. They seemed to do no harm whatsoever to her relationship with the singer and she and David would continue to be guests at his Venetian home in the future. The message to their fans was unofficial but clear: we had a problem but we are fine now. The christening party emphasized that.

Victoria was now more than six months pregnant and, perhaps understandably, suggested that female guests (attendants) might like to wear 'modest attire'. Liz Hurley mistook Hertfordshire for Hollywood and splendidly chose as her 'modest attire' an off-the-shoulder, low-cut ivory satin gown better suited to the red carpet on Oscars night. She topped it off with a white fur stole. Victoria might have been miffed but it was just the sort of stunt she could have pulled herself. A few years earlier, at footballer Phil Neville's wedding, she had famously upstaged the bride when she chose a strapless, low-cut coffee-coloured gown split daringly to the thigh. The bride, it was pointed out, happened to be Julie Killelea, one of David's old girlfriends.

The guests for Brooklyn and Romeo's big day were a mix of family, football and the famous. They included Wayne Rooney and Coleen McLoughlin, who had been adopted by the media as a favourite couple, Sven-Göran Eriksson and Nancy Dell'Olio, fashion designers Domenico Dolce and Stefano Gabbana and, from the fashionable art world, Sam Taylor-Wood and Jay Jopling. One of the less well-known guests was Maria-Louise Featherstone, who had been at Goff's Oak primary school with Victoria thirty years before and had been an unheralded yet constant presence in Victoria's team over the years. She was asked to be one of Brooklyn's godmothers.

After the service, everyone walked over to a 500-foot marquee for a six-course meal and a song or two from Sir Elton. The icing on the top of a perfect day was when David made a short, heartfelt speech thanking Victoria for making him so happy. By far the most interesting sidebar to the day was the inclusion of Simon Fuller and three of the four Spice Girls, Melanie C, Emma and Geri. Behind the scenes, Victoria had been agitating for a reunion, aware that it would be a priceless marketing tool. As long ago as February 2003, she had hosted an evening for all five girls at Rowneybury, which gave rise to rumours they would get back together, proof then that she was talking to Geri again. Simon Fuller was never keen for a reunion to happen before the tenth anniversary of 'Wannabe', which would have been in 2006 at the earliest. A music insider observed, 'Anything before then would have seemed desperate and quite frankly a missed business opportunity.' Keeping the possibility alive with some tantalizing gossip now and then made good sense. Mel B was expected but withdrew at the last minute, prompting speculation that she did not want to see Geri. Clearly Victoria had put her own feelings about Geri to one side.

Tom Cruise was rumoured to have been invited to the christening. He had met David and Victoria at a charity dinner in Los Angeles and had told the couple how much he enjoyed 'soccer'. A friend of the couple said, 'Tom told David he'd rather have been a famous footballer than an actor. He played for his college team and dreamed of making it as a professional but injured his knee and had to give up.' The Beckhams invited Tom to join them for a day out at Real Madrid while he was filming in Europe. He was subsequently spotted on various occasions in the VIP box at the Bernabéu. A friendship or just an alliance with arguably the biggest movie star in the world was a stepping stone to the Hollywood elite. For the moment, being on his Christmas card list was a good start.

Throughout her pregnancy, Victoria was given some respite by the media. As a mother of two young boys, it seemed she was fair game but an expectant woman was a step too far. Rebecca Loos et al. had their moment in the limelight but now the public were happy to move on. The Spanish rehabilitation continued to go well with the birth of another son on 20 February 2005. Tactfully, Victoria decided to have her third Caesarean at the Hospital Ruber International in Madrid. Going back to England to have the baby would have attracted all the wrong headlines. David, as had become the norm, trotted out to tell the media the child was called Cruz: 'He's gorgeous, healthy and his mum is good.' David had apparently signed an autograph for someone called Cruz and had liked the name. Meaning cross in Spanish, it is more familiar as a surname in Spain.

Quietly, over a period of six months, Victoria had built up the momentum for her new direction in life. She had announced that her solo singing career was over and she was devoting herself to fashion and to developing her own design label. She explained, 'I know that I could never become the best singer in the world but everything to do with fashion comes easily to me. I feel passionate about design and I don't think I'll ever feel that passion for music again.' The Beckhams signed a £5 million ($10 million) deal with the beauty giants Coty, with the intention of launching his and her fragrances in the autumn. The plans for the launch of David's soccer academy in Los Angeles were well advanced and a date was set for June, when he would be in the US promoting his alliance with Adidas, worth at the time an estimated £3 million ($6 million) a year. Victoria did her bit by signing a £500,000 ($1 million) deal with the California jeans company Rock and Republic. She did not have to increase the mortgage when she went shopping for David's thirtieth birthday present and came away with a ring from Madrid designers Suarez that was valued at £500,000 ($1 million).

The closed season for taking pot shots at Victoria lasted little more than a month after Cruz was born. She was photographed looking unnaturally skinny after a few weeks of being a new mum. She was wearing a pair of her tightest jeans and a fitted top when she went to watch David play at the Bernabéu stadium. Victoria was just pleased to be able to wear something that was not topped by one of her many ponchos. One beneficial thing about being pregnant was that she had been able to include fashion tips for the expectant mother in the book she was working on, her fashion bible, called *That Extra Half an Inch*. She would advise everyone that the essential item for a pregnant woman was a wrap.

Victoria was quite manic about getting back into shape after the birth of her children. She adopted the attitude 'If I don't do it now, I never will.' She later observed that her rigorous dieting had given her saggy skin and left her 'with no bum at all'. Among the most hurtful aspects of the whole Rebecca Loos saga was the snide suggestion that her husband had in some way preferred the more curvaceous charms of his personal assistant to those of his stick-thin wife. Rebecca claimed that David was always encouraging his wife to eat more.

Ever since her days at Laine Theatre Arts, Victoria had been obsessive about food, having lived most of her adult life on steamed vegetables. As a teenager, she was always under pressure to lose weight and that continued when she joined the group that would become the Spice Girls and Chic Murphy told her to lose a few pounds. She blamed Geri Halliwell, a self-confessed bulimic, for turning her into a chronic worrier about her appearance and what she was eating. In her autobiography, Victoria finally admitted that she had struggled with an eating disorder, at one stage she even stopped eating altogether. She confessed, 'When you have an eating disorder, you can fool people. Fooling people becomes part of the buzz.' Even later, when she felt like eating normally again, she never fancied a bowl of Frosties or a burger. Instead, vegetables, fruit and salad formed the basis of the diet that would eventually lead to her notoriously becoming a size zero. Liz Jones, the columnist and former editor of *Marie Claire*, observes, 'I think it's unfair for Victoria to say that she caught anorexia from Geri. I think Victoria had her own self-esteem issues very early on.' Victoria and Geri were not the only Spice Girls troubled by eating issues. Melanie C also admitted to chronic problems: 'I got so thin when I wasn't eating that my periods stopped and my bones became very fragile.'

Victoria was quite happy to talk about her obsession with food – or lack of it. She told the celebrated American interviewer Barbara Walters, 'It was awful. I could have told you the calorie and fat content in everything.' Even David admitted to being concerned after she wore a black leather mini to the Ivy restaurant after the birth of her first child. She was terrifyingly thin, prompting the newspapers memorably to christen her Skeletal Spice. She countered by laughingly pointing out that the same day the newspapers were accusing her of being a bad role model they carried advertisements for 'Lose a stone in a flash'. Emma Jones, former *Smash Hits* editor, observed, 'Unless you see Victoria in the flesh it's difficult to imagine just how thin she is.'

A trusted method of recognizing a celebrity with eating concerns is to monitor the number of times they mention what they are eating in interviews. Victoria talks a lot about food. Probably no celebrity has lost their baby weight as quickly or as successfully as she has. Pictures revealing her super-slim frame were, however, infinitely preferable to her children's nanny coming out of the woodwork to 'spill the beans' on the trials and tribulations of Victoria's pregnancy. The nanny in question, Abigail Gibson, had been Victoria's trusted companion for two years as she had struggled through a difficult period in her life. She had been dismissed after Victoria discovered she had been in touch with a beautician called Danielle Heath, yet another girl to allege sordid sexual shenanigans with David.

Gibson sold her story to the *News of the World* for a reported six-figure sum. Once again, Max Clifford was the go-between. The former nanny told of heated rows and of Victoria's insecurity about feeling fat during her pregnancy. Enough was enough and Victoria urged David to go to court to silence their former employee. They took immediate action and were able to prevent further 'revelations' from Gibson appearing the following week and at any time in the future.

Public opinion seemed to have moved on since the previous year's revelations about the Beckhams and even the media did not revel in more discomforts for Victoria. She was able to come out fighting like the old Victoria, inspired by a quote from the German philosopher Nietzsche, usually translated as: 'What doesn't kill you makes you stronger.'

The Beckhams seemed angrier at the 'betrayal' of the woman who had been looking after their children than any of the kiss-and-tell stories. David responded, 'I find it amazing, quite unbelievable. When you've let someone into your home to look after your children, which are Victoria and my most prized possessions, you begin to trust that person . . .' On another occasion he said, 'I'm sick and tired of everybody having a go at us just for being a normal couple. People can't seem to believe us when we say we're normal, but we are. Normal people have rows, normal people have good days and bad. We're happily married and are going to stay that way.'

His wife also went on the offensive: 'Yeah, we have our arguments, of course we do. But all couples row, don't they? So at least that makes us bloody normal. To be honest, I'm more sad that this happened now because me and David are really happy.' And that was the truth. The revelations of the former nanny, even if true in any way, were 'after the show' and, after the birth of Cruz, the Beckhams presented a much stronger, united front to the world.

It seemed they could trust no one. Victoria did, of course, trust her family and persuaded her father finally to give up his own company and work full time for the House of Beckham or, more precisely, her own Moody Productions. The ever shrewd Mr Adams would be able to sniff out anybody untrustworthy.

David and Victoria's 2005 grand summer tour of the US – New York and Los Angeles – was a resounding success. Americans had first come across David's name in the hit film *Bend it Like Beckham* which, three years earlier, had been popular in the US. Now they could see him in the flesh. His obvious good looks proved a hit on the *Today Show* and in LA he finally opened his soccer academy at the LA Galaxy ground, watched by a host of photographers and hundreds of would-be fans. The boss of the club, Tim Leiweke, met David and spoke warmly of the dream of getting David to play for his team. During the trip, the Beckhams rubbed shoulders with Hollywood A-listers and had dinner with their number one supporters, Tom Cruise and Katie Holmes. Victoria felt far more that she had arrived as Victoria Beckham than she ever did when she was one of five Spice Girls.

Despite her undervalued talents as a member of the Spice Girls, Victoria always gave the impression that she was swimming against the tide. In the world of fashion and design, she swam with the current. Her highly successful book *That Extra Half an Inch*, which sold more than a quarter of a million copies when it was published in 2006, revealed what she brought to the table. It was a book she might have bought herself when she was eighteen, obsessed by clothes but feeling a bit overawed in a department store. She did not talk down to her readership. It came across more as a cosy chat with a girlfriend. She told how, as a child, her most prized possession was a Gucci carrier bag that a friend of Jackie's had given her after buying some shoes there: 'I loved that bag and carried all my school books round in it for ages until the bottom of the bloody thing fell out completely.'

The clever aspect of this book was that Victoria gave a mention to practically every designer who had ever sewn a sequin – a wonderful advertisement for them and one guaranteeing Victoria's place at their table. Anyone in any doubt as to how her venture into the world of fashion would go could note that 3,000 people queued for up to twelve hours to attend the signing at Selfridges in October. The public fascination with Victoria Beckham showed no signs of diminishing.

Victoria and David continued their charm offensive about Spain, even buying their own £3 million ($6 million) Tuscan-style villa in 2006 as a signal that they were in Madrid for the duration. Melanie C went to visit Victoria for the day and was shocked at the life she was leading: 'I'd forgotten what it was like being stalked by the paparazzi and the state of your fringe being world headline news. I thought, "This would be fun for about a week." But it's exhausting. Of course she doesn't have to cook or clean or do a supermarket shop but it's like people living inside your head.'

Victoria continued her preparations for life after Spain, raising her own profile as much as possible. In late 2006, she went to hairdresser Ben Cooke's Chelsea salon and came out with the most iconic style since 'The Rachel' put Jennifer Aniston on the front cover of every glossy magazine. She was fed up with her hair extensions and wanted something much more manageable. The answer was a blonde bob with a twist, which was quickly nicknamed 'The Pob' (Posh bob). She sported a layered bob at the back of her head with sweeping textured length at the front that perfectly framed her accentuated bone structure. Almost immediately the style became a favourite among celebrities and on the high street – Paris Hilton, Sarah Harding and Eva Longoria were seen sporting their versions. Ben Cooke observed, 'It's flattering but I don't think any of the copies came close to the real Pob. Victoria always looks amazing.'

Victoria's heart had already left Madrid and was heading for Los Angeles. She started flying over to California for business meetings with Simon and to look quietly at property, although the moment she arrived the asking price always seem to increase by a million dollars.

With perfect timing, Victoria was named 'Woman of the Year' by *Glamour* magazine in June. The editor, Jo Elvin, said, 'For the past ten years, Victoria Beckham has been a figure of fascination. She has successfully reinvented herself from pop star to devoted wife and mother, to successful designer and business mogul. She is indicative of the modern woman, successfully juggling the work/home-life balance, and is a role model in terms of achieving it all.' She was just as pleased that they also named her 'Entrepreneur of the Year' for her development of the dVb brand of jeans, perfume and big sunglasses.

Further proof that Victoria's international stock was continuing to rise came when she attended the wedding of Tom Cruise and Katie Holmes at Castle Odescalchi in the picturesque Italian town of Bracciano, twenty-five miles north of Rome. David had time off for the pre-wedding party in the Italian capital but had to return to Madrid before the ceremony. So Victoria went alone and rubbed shoulders with Jennifer Lopez, Jim Carrey, Will Smith, Richard Gere and Brooke Shields – all important A-list celebrities in Hollywood. It was definitely the big time. Victoria joked, 'Despite what you might have read, I'm not the wedding planner.'

At last, it was announced that David, enjoying his best season with Real Madrid, would be joining LA Galaxy for a deal reported to be worth £128 million ($256 million). He would be leaving Spain in July 2007.

'I know I would sacrifice anything for my boys.'

19

Full Circle

The LA Galaxy football ground in Carson, California, is a world away from Beverly Hills. The Marc Jacobs boutique in ultra-fashionable Melrose Place is ten minutes from the front gates of the Beckhams' £11-million ($22-million) mansion. He does not have a branch in Artesia, the working-class area of south LA that Victoria has to drive through in the Bentley or the Porsche to watch her husband continue his footballing career in the US. There is no glamour here and little when you reach the Home Depot ground where Galaxy play their home games. It may not be Old Trafford or the Bernabéu but, ironically, David Beckham would be spending the next part of his footballing life in a second division setting located on Victoria Street.

The facilities are good and both the England team and Chelsea have trained at the ground in recent times, but there's no blood and guts. Even the club shop is very low key, barely acknowledging that one of the world's most famous footballers plays here. Victoria does not mind. She can sit in the VIP box with her three boys and enjoy a game in the sun as if she were watching a cricket match on a summer afternoon in a London park. Nobody can see what she's thinking behind her ubiquitous bug-eyed sunglasses. She does not have to shut her ears to the sounds of the Old Trafford chants questioning her sexual preferences. Instead, she can be content in the knowledge that she can be back by the pool in a couple of hours.

When Victoria and David officially arrived in Los Angeles in July

2007, Victoria had already made sure that a ticker-tape parade of celebrities would greet them. The Governor of California, Arnold Schwarzenegger, led the guest list at David's first game, an exhibition against Chelsea. Victoria and the children were joined by, among others: Eva Longoria, who would become her best friend in LA, Brooke Shields, Jennifer Love Hewitt, Alicia Silverstone and Mary-Kate Olsen. The game proved an anticlimax when David lasted only thirteen minutes before succumbing to an ankle injury and limping off. The pack of photographers and journalists seeking vantage points brought back memories of Princess Diana. Victoria managed to fit in a bit of business. She wore a fuchsia pink 'Moon Dress' designed by Roland Mouret. The dress could not have received better exposure and it was no coincidence that the designer's new company, 19 RM, was part of the Simon Fuller group. The Moon Dress became one of the most talked about and must-have items of the year. Victoria, as brand ambassador, also modelled another dress from the RM range when she appeared later on the *Tonight Show with Jay Leno*.

The next evening was more Victoria. All the careful cultivation of friendship with Tom Cruise and Katie Holmes paid off when the couple co-hosted a welcome party at the Museum of Contemporary Art with Will Smith and his wife, Jada Pinkett Smith. The celebrity count was high, including, again, Eva Longoria, as well as Demi Moore and Ashton Kutcher, Matthew Perry, Jim Carrey and Jenny McCarthy, and Bruce Willis. Tom had flown in specially from filming in Germany to attend.

The 'official' pictures reveal how snugly the Beckhams would fit into this glamorous world. David looked born to Hollywood in a pristine white shirt perfectly complimenting his gleaming pearly teeth. Only Victoria did not reveal a dazzling smile for the camera, preferring as ever to pout beneath her famous blonde Pob. She did, however, look a million dollars.

The only drawback as far as Victoria was concerned was that Jada was wearing a little black dress remarkably similar to her own. Victoria held centre stage, something which more and more people were observing. When she is in the room, she generates an aura that eclipses the others, including her husband. Alexandra

Shulman, the editor of British *Vogue*, observed, 'When they're in a room together, the one you notice – the one surrounded by the powerful force field – is Victoria.'

All in all it was a triumph for Victoria's tireless networking. Intriguingly, the alliance with Tom and Katie has always been seen as a one-way street – the famous Hollywood superstar and his wife being nice to the newcomers, showing them around the place and making sure they could get invitations to some of the smartest parties. Cynics were quick to point out that Tom was probably hoping to recruit the Beckhams to Scientology, the controversial religion that counts him as its most prominent member. Both Will Smith and Jim Carrey have denied being one. David and Victoria have been quick to refute the suggestion that the Cruises have ever tried to persuade them to join. 'We respect their religion,' said David, tactfully, while explaining that their friends have never shoved it down their throats.

Nothing is ever how it seems in this world of make-believe, however. The alliance between the two families was a massively important one for the Cruise brand. Combined, Tom and Katie were not nearly as globally famous as David and Victoria. By herself, Katie would have barely merited a paragraph in one of the glossy magazines before she became engaged to Cruise while they were in Paris in the summer of 2005. She was twenty-six and best known for her role as tomboy Joey Potter in the American teen soap, *Dawson's Creek*. She was nowhere near A-list. Cruise was forty-three and one of the richest movie stars in the world, regularly topping the list for the biggest box office draw, but as Los Angeles celebrity writer Cliff Renfrew observes, 'Tom Cruise's cool factor is zero.'

David Beckham has huge charisma and cool. Being next to David made Tom appear younger and more hip. Katie, however, stood to receive the most benefit from an alliance with the Beckhams. Victoria was one of the most recognized and photographed women in the world. Katie was guaranteed to have her picture in the paper every time she went out with Mrs Beckham. It was as simple as that. Yes, Victoria needed Katie for the introduction to Los Angeles society but Katie needed Victoria everywhere else.

The new best friends had seen plenty of one another on

Victoria's house-hunting trips prior to David leaving Madrid, dining at fashionable restaurants like Koi in Beverly Hills and attending private parties. They shared a love of designer shoes and shopped together on Rodeo Drive. The Neiman Marcus store stayed open late just so the two women could enjoy some privacy. Victoria encouraged Katie to buy towering heels, which was probably not too popular with the much shorter Tom Cruise. They were rumoured to spend $10,000 (£5,000) per shopping trip and eyewitnesses remarked on how much fun they seemed to be having.

Katie helped Victoria sort out possible schools for the boys while, in return, Victoria gave her advice on styling – much of which seemed to be connected to losing weight. Victoria said, 'Katie has helped me so much with the move. She's genuinely a nice girl.' One of Katie's friends observed, 'Victoria is the person who brought Katie out of her shell and taught her about fashion. She was as much a big sister as a best friend.'

The amusing aspect of Victoria and Katie's friendship was that the latter seemed to be turning into a taller version of the former. That impression was given credence when Katie unveiled her version of Victoria's Pob. Fashion pages were devoted to the two women's styles. One magazine uncovered seven occasions when Katie wore an outfit that was almost exactly similar to one Victoria had worn earlier. She was also said to be copying Victoria's method of eating – pushing your food around the plate to give the illusion of enjoying a hearty meal.

Ironically, after being established in the world's eye as best friends, the two women appeared to fall out when the Beckhams moved full time to Los Angeles. They barely spoke for months. Some suggested that Katie had taken exception to Victoria and Eva Longoria sending up Tom's energetic moves on the dance floor. Most Americans tend not to get British humour, especially sarcasm and irony. British friends, like Elton John, on the other hand, enjoy her humour, which is quite camp in its bitchiness. Eva is a rare example of an American who finds Victoria 'hilarious'. Victoria has a rapier tongue that would be too much for the average Hollywood body worshipper. She prefers to work out with a glass of white wine, a steamed carrot and her mobile phone.

Another possibility for the cooling of their friendship was that Katie found Victoria overwhelming and the attention she always attracted unsettling. Victoria barely had time to notice, however, as she continued building the House of Beckham. She used momentum from one event to promote something else. Her move to the US was the perfect time to launch the Intimately Beckham perfume range into American stores. She made a point of saying that she was involved in every step of the process that led to a product having her name on it. The following month, in September 2007, she launched a new range called Intimately Beckham Night, which featured fragrances for men and women, as well as flying to Tokyo to mark the start-up of her cosmetics line, V-Sculpt.

Her trip to Japan was cut short when Ted Beckham, David's father, suffered a heart attack. David immediately travelled to London and Victoria flew in from Japan to lend her support. Over the years, stories have often surfaced about tension between Ted and Victoria's family. Ted remained in the old family home in East London after his divorce from Sandra and saw much less of David and Victoria than he used to. Father and son were reported to have fallen out over a book Ted wrote in 2005 called *David Beckham: My Son*, allegedly because David's permission had not been sought. Any rift was quickly forgotten at a time of family crisis and it was a great relief to everybody when he was well enough to leave hospital.

The autumn of 2007 seemed like the perfect time to relaunch the Spice Girls. The group had been profoundly popular in the US and it made great sense for them to re-form. It also gave the Beckhams and the Cruises the opportunity to make contact again. David and Tom still enjoyed each other's company but their work commitments meant they rarely saw each other. Tom Cruise admires the work ethic of successful sportsmen. David found himself swept along by the movie star's famed energy and enthusiasm. They both had the problem, however, of getting their wives to speak to each other again. Katie eventually held out a small olive branch and rang Victoria, suggesting they could meet up while she rehearsed for the Spice Girls reunion tour. Victoria was pleased she rang. She said, 'Katie has told me before that she used to be a big Spice fan, so it was great for her to meet the other girls.' Tom and their daughter, Suri, went along too.

Each of the Spice Girls had different reasons for agreeing to the tour but they shared a common thread – publicity. Victoria stated that her reason was so that her three boys could see her perform and know that 'mummy was once a pop star'. Simon Fuller, who masterminded the reunion with Victoria, was more accurate when he revealed, 'Victoria's not really interested in making £2 million [$4 million] a night at the O2 Centre. What she's really interested in is whether Bergdorf Goodman have ordered her sunglasses.'

The money, however, was still an attractive proposition for everyone. The world tour would begin in December 2007 in Vancouver and end three months later in Toronto. It would include seventeen nights at the O2 Centre in London and eighteen in the US, including two in Los Angeles, now the home town of Mel B, Victoria and, from time to time, Geri. Tickets sales alone were worth £23 million ($46 million), merchandising the same; commercial deals like the Tesco ad campaign reportedly added £5 million ($10 million) to the purse and then there were record sales to come from the *Greatest Hits* album. One estimate put the money involved in the tour at £100 million ($200 million) but that figure is grossly inflated. Victoria might not have needed the money but it was very welcome for some of the others.

Victoria was the first to sign up officially to the tour with Simon. It was their joint brainchild, shuffled away as the ace in the House of Beckham pack for several years. The clinching factor in persuading all the girls to participate was that the tour was relatively short – forty-seven dates. This was no marathon 106-date world extravaganza like the one they had done ten years earlier. Some were more ready than others. Emma had given birth to her first baby, a boy called Beau, six weeks earlier and was dieting like mad to get in shape. Mel B had a personal trainer in Los Angeles and had lost three stone since the birth of her second child, Angel, in April 2007. She had worked on her fitness for her appearance on the US hit show *Dancing With the Stars*, in which, cheered on by

Victoria and the others, she eventually finished second. Geri had gone on a relentless diet and exercise regime and seemed in competition with Victoria to see who was the skinniest. Melanie C was reportedly in excellent shape after her eating problems and depression of a few years earlier. Even Victoria enrolled at upmarket LA gym The Sports Club, where, by all accounts, she was introduced to a personal trainer. Mothers everywhere would testify that looking after three boys was enough of a daily workout. She was rumoured to be on a diet to put weight on and was eating lots of spinach.

Stories abounded that the girls were not getting on. The dynamic of the group had changed in that, whatever the others might have thought, Victoria was the star now. She had the biggest entourage and the most media interest by a considerable margin. As ever, when it came down to business, the girls were prepared to drill themselves into a fighting unit. Nothing would have been worse than for the tour to start in December 2007 and for word to spread that they had lost it.

Victoria's principal concern was the fashion element. She enlisted the leading designer – and friend – Roberto Cavalli to design all the costumes. In the tour programme she took the trouble to thank him and his wife Eva. He was also given two pages in the programme, effectively a very nice plug. Melanie C had a page to publicize her albums; Geri had the same to promote her range of Ugenia Lavender children's books. The motives of the five girls were gradually becoming clearer. Victoria did not want to advertise dVb merchandise openly – that would have been tacky. It was far better to use Cavalli and a series of stunning costumes to suggest subtly that the Spice Girls had moved from sensational to sophisticated. Throw in the Tesco campaign and the genius of Victoria's branding and enduring popularity becomes much clearer – make the unattainable appear attainable. Her decision not to sing a solo but to emphasize her connection with fashion was a symbolic gesture.

The girls warmed up for the tour by performing at a show for the lingerie company Victoria's Secret in Los Angeles. The diamonds they wore were estimated to be worth more than £5 million ($10 million). The Cavalli outfits were said to have cost £20,000

($40,000) each. The next day they performed their new single 'Headlines (Friendship Never Ends)' by satellite for the BBC's Children in Need. Everything was in place for their tenth number one. The single, written in collaboration with their old friends Matt Rowe and Biff Stannard, was the first featuring all five girls for nine years; it was for charity; and they were riding the crest of a nostalgia wave. Despite that, the single completely flopped and was given the unwelcome accolade of being the worst-performing Children in Need song ever, selling less than 100,000 copies worldwide and peaking in the UK charts at number eleven. For the first time, the Spice Girls had failed to make the top ten. In fact, it was the first time they had failed to reach the top two. The critics described the song as 'dreary'. In the US, the track reached number ninety and that was that. Even the *Greatest Hits* album failed to make number one, outsold by the debut from *X Factor* winner Leona Lewis.

The result might have seemed disappointing in comparison to Take That, who topped the charts with both their comeback single and album, but the boy band had returned with fresh material and a new direction. The Spice Girls' reunion was all about the old tunes and for twenty-something women to remember when they were twelve and were given a Spice doll for Christmas. Nobody wanted new songs – they wanted 'Wannabe' and Victoria's favourite, 'Too Much'. As 'Headlines' crept into the charts, it was announced that 750,000 tickets had already been sold for the tour.

David Beckham flew in to snowy Vancouver to support his wife on the first night. He made a point of attending as many of the concerts as he could; all the family did, including his three sons. He spent £50,000 ($100,000) on diamond bracelets for each of the five girls. 'I met Vic when she was a pop star,' he recalled, 'and we can't wait for our boys to see her on stage.' The concert itself was a triumph of exuberance and professionalism. In little more than two months they had put together a show that Polly Hudson in the *Daily Mirror* described as camp, ridiculous, super-enthusiastic, beyond over the top and absolutely amazing. 'If you don't love every second of it,' she continued, 'check your pulse please because I think you might actually be dead.' She gave Victoria an A+ for her performance.

The reception in London was equally enthusiastic when they filled seventeen nights at the O2 Centre. The song 'Mama' stole the show when the girls brought on their children to much applause. It was gooey and sentimental and Victoria dressed her brood in black T-shirts with the word 'Posh' emblazoned across their chests. Victoria's outfits obviously attracted the most attention. It was even rumoured that she had reduced the size of her breast implants to enable her to fit into them better and be able to dance around the stage at the same time. She declined to comment on this, which was hardly surprising, considering she has never admitted to having a boob job in the first place.

'Mama' also brought the house down in New York when Cruz did some break dancing, including spinning on his head. 'He's the next Justin Timberlake,' said Victoria, proudly. The real bonus of the tour as far as her three sons were concerned was that they were taken out of school in Los Angeles and were 'home schooled' while they travelled with her.

Victoria loved being 'at home' in London. She and David could spend Christmas with the children at Rowneybury and all their friends could come to the concerts. It might have been the Spice Girls but in many ways it harked back to the nights at Broxbourne Civic Hall when all the family would cram into the front row to cheer her on. She invited Chris Herbert and his young family to the last show and for drinks afterwards. He recalls, 'We went on the Tuesday night and hooked up with the girls and Victoria said, "You've got to come back on the Friday because it's our last night and you'll have to bring your little boy, Southan. Come down early and he can play with the boys and he can meet David."' Needless to say, meeting David Beckham made little Southan's year.

Chris and his family sat with Victoria's parents. Chris chatted with Tony: 'Her father said to me, "All these years I've never really known what to say to you. I feel really awkward about it but it's nice that we've finally sort of sat down and had a conversation." Victoria impressed with the way 'she looked after us'. He observes, 'I thought she was incredibly down to earth; it was just like back in the day really. We had a really good laugh.'

The tour acted as closure for Victoria the pop star. Initially, there was talk that it would continue and take in other cities, including Buenos Aires, Cape Town and Beijing. Although the rumours were of rows and bitchiness getting out of hand, the more likely explanation is that it was not financially viable. A tour insider said, 'Simon Fuller is the business brain and he said no. Nobody was surprised. This was a very expensive show to take on the road and was much better suited to all those nights in London.' Tempers may well have been frayed on the road but, taking the renowned dedication of the Spice Girls into consideration, it seems very unlikely that they would not have stuck it out for a few more weeks if the money had added up. Victoria would have ploughed on even if she was homesick. They always did

The tour more than fulfilled its purpose for Victoria. On her return to Los Angeles, she was able to take stock and report, 'Some of the coolest stores are now taking dVb. A year ago they would have laughed. Maxfield, Fred Segal, Collette, Harvey Nichols . . . I've spent years banging these bloody doors down.' Job done. The chances of another reunion are Victoria's size – zero.

Victoria settled into her Hollywood mansion while David prepared for the new season with LA Galaxy. She has a beautiful home that was decorated with the help of Kelly Hoppen, the former partner of former England defender Sol Campbell. The two women had been determined to have a finished home ready for David when he jetted in from Spain. Victoria did not want a repeat of the wretched Madrid fiasco of making do with hotels for a while. Kelly explained, 'It was very important to her to have it perfect when they arrived – a proper home.' Incredibly, she revealed that David had not set eyes on his new house before he flew in for his LA debut. The Mediterranean-style 1920s house is in a popular area for stars, a millionaire's row, and completely hidden from the road by a huge ivy-clad wall. A one hundred-yard driveway is set behind it and from the terrace the view stretches down to the Pacific Ocean. No house in the neighbourhood would cost less than $5 million (£2.5 million). For the money, you can rub shoulders with Rod Stewart, who lives at the end of the street. His ex, Rachel Hunter, is also nearby. Seal and Heidi Klum live in the street and, at any time, you might see locals like Simon Cowell,

Madonna, Christina Aguilera, Jennifer Aniston, Courteney Cox and the Cruises.

In her present situation Victoria does not have to play 'Posh' every minute of the day. She never had time to develop friendships as a Spice Girl but now she has found real friends on the celebrity circuit. Her best pals are the stunning British actress Kate Beckinsale and Eva Longoria Parker, as she prefers to be called since her 2007 wedding. Eva is equally as slender as Victoria and one of the few with whom she could swap designer clothes. Eva is married to basketball star Tony Parker and understands the demands of being the wife of a famous sportsman. The two women think nothing of spending an hour on the phone to each other swapping designer tips and discussing the latest purchases for their homes. Eva is the person Victoria calls if she wants company at the nail salon or the hairdresser's. They live near each other and it's only ten minutes to Rodeo Drive. Eva calls her to invite her to lunch at the restaurant, Beso, she has opened in Hollywood. She finds Victoria a breath of fresh air in stuffy Beverly Hills: 'She just has the British sense of humour. She's so frickin' funny.' The only thing Victoria has to be careful of is blurting out a future storyline from *Desperate Housewives* when she is having her hair done. *American Idol* host Ryan Seacrest, who knows both women, observes, 'The thing nobody realizes about Victoria and Eva is that they are both homebodies at heart.'

Kate Beckinsale is Victoria's 'mum pal'. The daughter of the late comedy actor Richard Beckinsale is the same age as Victoria and has lived in Los Angeles for many years. She also has a nine-year-old daughter, Lily, who is the same age as Brooklyn. Both Kate and Eva happily hang out at the Beckhams' house in the evening, sipping wine, smoking and swapping stories. Victoria tends not to eat after 6 p.m. but will happily open a bottle of Californian white and smoke a cigarette or two while watching the sun go down.

When she was thirty-four in April 2008, she had two celebrations: the day before, she went with her sons to order chicken fajitas at a local Pink Taco Mexican restaurant; on the day itself she went to the fashionable Vio Veneto restaurant in Malibu with a host of A-list friends, including Elton John, Will Smith, Seal and

Heidi Klum, and Kate and Eva, of course. She was delighted that Katie Holmes also stopped by to wish her a happy birthday. The two women, however, are no longer joined at the hip. The very next day Victoria was not among the guests at Suri's second birthday party at a private house on Mulholland Drive. A paparazzi photographer in a helicopter did a sweep of the Beckhams' home and saw Victoria playing with her sons by the pool.

Six weeks later, Tom and Katie held a housewarming at their new $20 million (£10 million) Beverly Hills mansion and, again, there was no sign of David and Victoria. Cliff Renfrew observes, 'If both Victoria and David have learned anything from their time in LA LA Land, it's this – even your best celebrity friends can be extremely fickle.'

Victoria was delighted, therefore, to bump into a familiar face from home – Paul Sculfor, who used to go out with her stylist and school friend Maria-Louise Featherstone. Paul, originally from Essex, briefly hit the headlines in the UK when he dated Jennifer Aniston and, subsequently, Cameron Diaz. Victoria had not seen him for ten years and was amazed when he turned up in LA. Hollywood is actually quite a small village, not much bigger than Goff's Oak for gossip and seeing people you know.

Some acting work helped to increase her profile. She appeared in an episode of the top rated show *Ugly Betty*, in which she sent herself up as the maid of honour to the show's villainess, Wilhelmina Slater. The art of not taking yourself too seriously was neatly illustrated when Wilhelmina (Vanessa Williams) is seeking a bridesmaid: 'I have hundreds of back-stabbing, two-faced, superficial friends that are pouring in from all over the globe to be part of the wedding. Any of them would be thrilled to be my maid of honour.' She then dials a number and announces, 'Victoria Beckham, please. Yes, I'll hold.' Wilhelmina's gay assistant Mark says, 'The Beckhams have conquered America. Accept it. They're our leaders now.'

Victoria cannot take acting too seriously because she is working seven days a week on the Beckham brand. She is more likely to be responsible for costume and fashion on a film than to act in it. Victoria made a breathtaking fashion breakthrough when she was chosen as the face of the spring collection of Marc Jacobs, one of the world's leading designers. This is the equivalent of having a solo album topping the charts on both sides of the Atlantic and was guaranteed to put a few noses out of joint in the notoriously bitchy world of fashion. One young designer said, 'How could he choose *her*!' Victoria topped up that success by appearing as the cover girl for the April 2008 edition of UK *Vogue*. Sales of the magazine went up by ten per cent.

Now that she was into her stride in Los Angeles nothing, it seemed, could interfere with a near perfect world. Her family was settled and happy and, for the most part, Los Angeles suited her much better than Madrid ever did. Just occasionally the downside of fame resurfaced. When Victoria was watching a Galaxy game in June 2008, a man ran out on to the pitch towards David. He turned out to be a fan who had eluded stewards and had to be tackled by one of the family's own bodyguards. Victoria, fleetingly, stood up, her hands held to her face as her security fears came flashing back.

That was a small bump in Victoria's smooth progress in the California sunshine. A much larger one presented itself unexpectedly. Just when everybody thought David was winding down his footballing career, he found a new lease of life. He may have passed thirty and be deemed a senior statesman in playing terms, but the desire to compete at the highest level continued to burn brightly. Having achieved his one hundredth cap against France in March 2008, he set himself the goal of playing for England in the 2010 World Cup finals in South Africa. To achieve that, he would need to be playing regularly in more auspicious surroundings than the Home Depot ground.

Rumours began to circulate that he would return to Europe and it was no surprise when it was announced in the autumn of 2008 that he would be joining AC Milan for a three-month loan period starting in January 2009. What would that mean for Victoria – another move to a European city where she did not speak the language? In the short term, Victoria was preparing for the all-important launch of her first 'Victoria Beckham Collection' at the New York Fashion Week in September 2008. To gather as much publicity as possible, she unveiled a dramatic new hairstyle and hogged the headlines at the event. Polly Hudson of the *Daily Mirror* was stunned at the new pixie cut: 'Blimey, this is a bit dramatic, isn't it?' The celebrity hairstylist Nicky Clarke said, 'It's brave but it suits her petite features.' Victoria called it a 'gamine crop'.

Her first collection was a range of ten posh frocks which unashamedly chased the money. The majority cost a four-figure sum. When she launched the designs in London in December 2008, the fashion critic Amber Moralis commented, 'If only they were at a price real women could afford.' Not everyone was impressed with the range itself. Cheryl Cole thought the dresses were suited to older women and not something Girls Aloud would wear. That was probably true enough, but not exactly the sort of publicity Victoria needed.

Just as David began his Milan adventure after the New Year, Victoria and the children headed back to LA so that the boys could be home for the start of the new school term. It was the first time she and David had been apart for an extended period since the Madrid debacle in 2003. Victoria did not want to disrupt the children's settled school life. They attended the exclusive Curtis School on Mulholland Drive, on the hill not far from their house. 'The other mothers were amazed to see Victoria turn up to collect the kids,' observes Cliff Renfrew. 'She is happy to chat away like any other mum. Other stars don't do that and they like her for it.' Victoria finds time to go on school trips and pops in to lend a hand with dinners if it's her turn.

Victoria was anxious to let the world know her family's situation. She told *Reveal* magazine that their home was in Los Angeles: 'I love living in LA. I've had amazing career opportunities and it's a great place to bring up kids. We're very happy there.'

If David's strategy worked and he made the World Cup finals, then it would almost certainly be his last hurrah. Victoria realized she would have to make the best of it in LA until then, especially when the three-month loan period became six months – and would be the same again next season. She broke the habit of a lifetime and started going to the gym. This was not any old fitness centre but the Sports Club LA, a place where the stars go to work out and where your sweaty clothes are laundered in time for your next visit. Several days a week, Victoria can be seen doing cardio exercise on the treadmill before taking her regular Pilates class.

David was stuck in Milan and missed her thirty-fifth birthday in April 2009. She spent the day at home and celebrated quietly with the boys and her family from Goff's Oak who were visiting. She did go out the previous evening when she was joined by the 'girls', her best friends in LA including Kate Beckinsale, Eva Longoria Parker and Katie Holmes, who seems to flit in and out of Victoria's circle.

Her new career in fashion is thriving. Her second 'Victoria Beckham Collection' was unveiled in New York in February 2009. The critics loved it. The 23 pieces for Autumn/Winter 2009 were universally acclaimed. Natalie Theo in the *Daily Mail* said the collection 'wowed the catwalk, the crowds . . . and me.' She enthused, 'Posh has taken her collection to a new level, with a far more youthful air, featuring bright colours, glittering embellishments and lashings of legs.' The comments were just reward for Victoria's commitment – she never gives less than one hundred per cent. The biggest boost to date came when Madonna started favouring her designs. She wore a tight-fitting black dress with white trim for a magazine photo shoot. You could easily imagine Audrey Hepburn wearing it in *Breakfast at Tiffany's*. Then, Madonna wore another, a black, slinky evening gown, to the high-profile *Vanity Fair* Oscars party. Victoria was understandably thrilled: 'For her to wear one of my designs – wow. She looked so amazing in it. I was overwhelmed.' Other celebrities including Heidi Klum, Elle Macpherson and Brooke Shields followed suit and wore a Victoria Beckham dress. Perhaps Victoria is at last getting some of the recognition her talents deserve.

'It's exhausting being fabulous.'

Last Thoughts

July 2009

My favourite recent picture of Victoria Beckham was taken last summer on a lovely June day in LA. She and David took their boys to Disneyland and, afterwards, they were pictured looking happy, relaxed and a little tired. David pushed a sleeping Cruz along in his pushchair while Victoria ambled alongside clutching Romeo's hand. I have never seen Victoria looking so casual. She was wearing a black T-shirt, baggy blue jeans and flat sandals. It looked for all the world as if she had raided her husband's wardrobe. My first thought was that she had left Posh Spice at home.

Being 'Posh' has been a goldmine for Victoria. It gave her an easily defined image that she could adopt every time she left home – pouting and posing in ridiculous heels. That's not the real person, of course. It's the role she plays as a star. The biggest celebrities have a persona that they slip on like an overcoat hanging by the door. Rob Williams, a working-class lad from Stoke-on-Trent becomes Robbie Williams; Kylie Minogue, a suburban miss from Melbourne becomes Kylie Showgirl; Britney Spears, a sweet churchgoing girl from the Deep South becomes Britney, the sex vamp, and so on. Victoria Adams, an unworldly girl from the Hertfordshire commuter belt becomes Posh Spice. Perhaps that is changing for her. As Victoria Beckham she is developing her fashion and design interests with flair and confidence.

Hopefully, we will see more of Victoria *not* playing Posh Spice. The best description of her true nature was given to me by her former press officer and friend Muff Fitzgerald: 'Despite the exhaustion, the jet-lag and then the paparazzi intrusions on her life, Victoria always maintained a very positive outlook. She was emotionally buoyant, when other band members were not. She would raise their spirits.

'She was also very down to earth, had a playful nature and a terrific sense of humour. She would always exude a positive demeanour, was considerate and demonstrated an awareness of the people around her, the other Spice Girls and the team who worked with them.

'It's true that she would light up a room, and when she and the other girls left, for instance, a photo shoot, as we cleared up, there was always that little sense of loss, until we reconvened at the next shoot, public appearance, or performance. I have fond memories of the time I spent working with her and, yes, remember her as "a little darling!"'

It might seem strange to describe Victoria Beckham as a 'little darling' but time and time again I was struck by how much people's warm recollections of her differ from the picture painted in the media. Those who know her think she is treated very poorly by the press. Here are just three of the comments made to me: 'I'm very unhappy about everybody slagging her off.' 'I think some of the press have been quite beastly to her.' 'Having worked with her, I'm always amazed by the rubbish the newspapers write about her. Their mendacious stories could not be further from the truth, from the woman she really is.' Music journalist Rick Sky made this observation to me: 'The media are very cut off from what ordinary kids think. They always have been and they always will be.'

Others will point to the fact that, long ago, Victoria entered into a Faustian pact with the press and anybody who sells their wedding for £1 million ($2 million) has to accept the unfavourable attention. Victoria, herself, is well aware that she will attract good and bad press. As photographer Geoff Marchant commented to me: 'I think she would be gutted if one day she woke up and no one was writing about her.'

Vogue said of Victoria: 'Love her or hate her, you'd be hard pushed to ignore her.' A classic example of this is the national debate over Victoria's breasts and whether or not she has had a boob job. Let's face it, most people think she has. Her former boyfriend, Mark Wood, said in a television interview, 'Believe me, the boobs she's got now are not the boobs she had when I went out with her.' Victoria engaged in some light-hearted banter with DJ Chris Moyles, who tried to coax her into admitting she had 'fakies' as he called them. She said her breasts were two big Christmas presents for David but declined to answer Moyles with anything specific. As long as Victoria stays firm in her denials, an element of doubt and mystery will remain and that is the point.

In my introduction to this book, I wrote down three questions I wanted to answer: What motivates Victoria, what talents does she actually have and why is she so popular? Victoria is a very driven woman. During the first year of the Spice Girls, she worked 363 days out of 365 – two days off. She grew up in a house of hard work and ambition. Her father transformed his family's fortunes by his tenacity and application – two traits Victoria has inherited in bundles. Success in her world is measured by fame, money and possessions. You can never have enough of any of these.

Victoria is also spurred on by an 'I'll show you' mentality. In her autobiography, *Learning to Fly*, she proudly states that she is the most successful person ever to come out of Laine Theatre Arts despite, she felt, being unappreciated while she was there. She showed them.

Talent can take many forms. Her role as Posh Spice directly led to the assumption that Victoria can neither sing nor dance. In order to make the image work, she needed to define the contrast or difference between herself and the other Spice Girls. She had to look bored, pose, be aloof and totter about in high heels. As Posh, she sometimes appeared to lack rhythm. Perhaps she played the part too well. She has always been a very accomplished dancer, spending ten years at the Jason Theatre School, where she won numerous trophies, before winning a scholarship for a full-time *Fame* course at Laine's.

The myth that she can't sing sprang from the unfortunate circumstance of her not having a solo line on the first Spice Girls hit 'Wannabe'. Chris Herbert, her first manager, told me she was a good singer and she certainly had no trouble belting out songs in her younger days. She won a part in a stage musical when she was still at college and you don't get hired if it's all an illusion. I have not come across any criticism whatsoever of Victoria as a performer from those who worked with her. She is a thorough professional in a notoriously tough business. To say she has no talent is ridiculous.

Personally, I think Victoria's biggest talent is as an entrepreneur. She exploits and promotes Victoria Beckham in a creative and lucrative manner. If she were in advertising, she would be hailed as one of the best in the business.

As I wrote in my introduction, Victoria is transparently the most popular of the Spice Girls. Those who loathe Victoria will never give her credit for anything. They don't understand that she makes a connection with the public. That connection is the secret of her popularity. In April 2008, she was the cover girl for *Vogue* magazine. In June, she was voted 'Best Dressed British Celeb' in the *Sunday Mirror*'s High Street Fashion Awards 2008.

Those two events really tell you all you need to know about her appeal. Ordinary girls and young women look at Victoria and want to be her and believe that they can be. All over the country she is a (very slim) figure of fascination and inspiration. She is still only thirty-five but has been married nearly ten years, has three children and is one of the most famous women in the world. She also has the common touch by being self-deprecating and very funny in a rather bitchy and camp way. My favourite Victoria response occurred when the former *EastEnders* actress Tamzin Outhwaite spoke of her fantasy of a one-night stand with David Beckham. Victoria came back with the classic, 'Firstly I wouldn't say that about a married man, and second, as if, love.'

It's a bit of a class thing where her critics are concerned. They sneer at her, mainly through ignorance of her strengths and achievements, for what they see as vulgarity – her accent, her spending and, really, everything about her. I have never come across as much bias against an iconic figure as I have with Victoria Beckham. The critics don't get her and they never will.

Life and Times

17 April 1974 Victoria Caroline Adams is born at the Princess Alexandra Hospital in Harlow, Essex. Her parents, Tony and Jackie Adams, are living in the first family home, a modest house in Caxton Road, Hoddesdon.

Nov 1977 Her sister Louise is born. Her parents had just moved to The Old School House in Goff's Oak and set about turning their new home into the grandest in the village. Attends the local junior school.

Aug 1979 Her brother Christian is born.

April 1982 Persuades Jackie to enrol her at the Jason Theatre School in Broxbourne. The registration fee is £2.50 ($5). She is inspired by The Kids from *Fame* and loves dancing so much she stays at the school for eight years.

Sept 1985 Begins at St Mary's High School, Cheshunt. Victoria says she was bullied there. Her father drops her off in his Rolls-Royce.

Feb 1990 Goes on her first date with an American boy who enrolled at St Mary's when his father became the local vicar.

May 1990 Meets her first steady boyfriend, Mark Wood, when he comes to her parents' house to fit a burglar alarm.

Sept 1990 After gaining five GCSE passes at St Mary's, she is accepted at Laine's Theatre Arts in Epsom, where she receives a scholarship from her local council.

Jan 1992 Has her first set of professional photographs taken by Geoff Marchant. Returns with Mark in September for more shots.

April 1992 For her eighteenth birthday, her parents arrange for Victoria and Mark to go to Paris on Eurostar.

July 1992 Performs 'Mein Herr' at an audition for a new musical, *Bertie*. Wins the role and immediately gets engaged to Mark.

Sept 1992 Makes her professional debut in *Bertie* at the Alexandra Theatre, Birmingham. Earns £250 ($500) a week for the six-week run but the show never opens in London.

Aug 1993 Applies to be the lead singer in a new band called Persuasion. Sends in a picture of herself dressed in black, imitating her idol, Audrey Hepburn. Sings 'Mein Herr' at audition and is hired.

March 1994 Sees advertisement in the *Stage* newspaper asking for girls who are 'streetwise, outgoing, ambitious, dedicated' for a new all-female pop act. The ad is placed by Bob and Chris Herbert's father and son management team.

April 1994 Attends audition at the Dance Works Studio off Oxford Street, wears black and sings 'Mein Herr'. Chris Herbert believes she has the classy looks that might appeal to a slightly more mature man. Uses the professional name of Victoria Adams-Wood.

May 1994 Moves into a house in Boyne Hill Road, Maidenhead, with the four other selected girls: Geri Halliwell, Melanie Brown, Melanie Chisholm and Michelle Stephenson. When Michelle leaves soon afterwards, she is replaced by Emma Bunton. The group is called Touch.

Nov 1994 Now known as Spice, the five girls perform their first showcase at the Nomis Studios in Shepherd's Bush. They sing and dance the same four songs repeatedly throughout the day and everyone agrees it is a big success. They are finally offered a management contract by Bob and Chris Herbert but decide not to sign it.

April 1995 Breaks up with Mark a few days after her twenty-first birthday. Spends a whirlwind week with Hollywood star Corey Haim, who is visiting London.

May 1995 The girls slip away from Boyne Hill Road and turn up in Sheffield at the recording studio of songwriter Eliot Kennedy. They never return to the Herberts. Meet Simon Fuller for the first time and decide to appoint him manager. Victoria starts dating florist Stuart Bilton, whom she met in a bar near her parents' home.

July 1995 Spice sign a deal with Virgin Records for a reputed £1 million ($2 million). Victoria celebrates by becoming very drunk and having her knickers thrown out of a taxi by the other girls.

Feb 1996 Now called the Spice Girls, they try to create an impression at the Brit Awards, mingling with, among others, Lenny Kravitz and Take That, whom they idolized.

July 1996 *Top of the Pops* magazine calls Victoria 'Posh Spice' for the first time. The first single, 'Wannabe', is finally released and knocks Gary Barlow off the top spot. Victoria's parents celebrate at home while she is alone in a hotel room in Japan.

Oct 1996 The Spice Girls' second single, 'Say You'll Be There', goes to the top of the charts, proving they are not a one-hit wonder. A few weeks later, David Beckham sees the video while sitting in a hotel room in Tbilisi and, pointing to Victoria, tells Gary Neville, 'That's the girl for me'.

Nov 1996 The Spice Girls turn on the Christmas lights in Oxford Street. Their first album, *Spice*, goes to number one.

Dec 1996 The Spice Girls are interviewed for the *Spectator* magazine. Victoria famously says, 'John Major is a boring pillock.' Simon Fuller gives each of the girls a cheque for £200,000 ($400,000) at his office Christmas party. '2 Becomes 1' becomes their first Christmas number one.

Jan 1997 'Wannabe' becomes number one in the American charts. *Spice* follows suit and will be the bestselling album of the year in the US with 5.3 million copies.

Feb 1997 Performs at the Brit Awards for the first time. The Spice Girls win Best Single for 'Wannabe' and Best Video for 'Say You'll Be There'. Victoria meets David Beckham when Manchester United play Chelsea at Stamford Bridge.

March 1997 Travels to Old Trafford to watch Manchester United play Sheffield Wednesday. Tells David, 'If you don't ring me, I'm going to kick you in the bollocks the next time I see you.' Informs boyfriend Stuart that it's all over between them. Double A-side 'Mama'/'Who Do You Think You Are' becomes the fourth number one for the Spice Girls. The girls are paid a reported £500,000 ($1 million) to launch Channel Five.

April 1997 Mark Wood's kiss and tell account of their relationship appears in the *Sun*. Four days later the newspaper reveals she is dating Becks. The Spice Girls give their first live performance when they appear on the cult US show, *Saturday Night Live*.

May 1997 Meets Prince Charles at the Prince's Trust Concert in Manchester. Spends the night with David Beckham for the first time. 'Wannabe' named Hit of the Year and Bestselling British Single at the Ivor Novello Awards.

June 1997 Filming begins in London on the feature film *Spice World* .

Oct 1997 First live Spice Girls concert takes place in Istanbul. The *Guardian* says, 'In terms of pure spectacle, you'd be hard pressed to find anything better.' Fifth single, 'Spice Up Your Life', enters the chart at number one.

Nov 1997 Prince Charles is there again when the Spice Girls meet Nelson Mandela, who declares it to be one of the greatest days of his life. They sack Simon Fuller as manager while he is recovering from an operation on his back. Second album, *Spiceworld*, goes to number one, selling 191,000 copies in the first week.

Dec 1997 'Too Much' becomes the second Christmas number one for the Spice Girls. *Spice World* is released and takes more than £5 million ($10 million) in the UK in its first week.

Jan 1998 Victoria and David announce their engagement at the Rookery Hall Hotel in Nantwich, Cheshire. In the US, the girls promote *Spice World* by appearing on *Oprah*. They feature in Mr Blackwell's notorious 'Worst Dressed List' for the year. They win three American Music Awards for Best Pop/Rock Album for *Spice*, Best New Pop/Rock Act, and Best Pop/Rock Act.

Feb 1998 Tells *Top of the Pops* magazine that the last time she had sex in a public place was 'recently and it was in a car'. The 106-date world tour begins at The Point in Dublin. The girls close with 'We Are Family'.

March 1998 After six consecutive number ones, 'Stop' reaches only number two, kept off the top by 'It's Like That' by US rap group Run-DMC.

April 1998 David and Victoria move into a new three-bedroom penthouse flat in the village of Alderley Edge near Manchester. The £300,000 ($600,000) apartment has a private lift.

May 1998 Geri leaves the band. Victoria says she is 'really upset and gutted'.

June 1998 While touring the US, Victoria tells David on the phone that she is pregnant. He flies to New York to see her after being sent off in the World Cup match against Argentina.

Aug 1998 Normal service is resumed when 'Viva Forever' becomes the group's seventh number one. Mel B joins Victoria in announcing her pregnancy. Victoria spends much of the latter part of the tour throwing up.

Oct 1998 Allegations in the *News of the World* that David had a liaison with a lap dancer are met with a swift legal response. The newspaper settles out of court for a substantial sum, which David and Victoria give to charity. David is pictured kissing her bump during a holiday in Marbella.

Dec 1998 'Goodbye' is the Spice Girls' third consecutive Christmas number one, mirroring the achievement of the Beatles. The heavily pregnant Mel B and Victoria are cheered when the Spice Girls appear at the Royal Variety Show.

March 1999 The Beckhams' first son, Brooklyn Joseph, is born by Caesarean section in the Portland Hospital, London. He weighs seven pounds. Victoria says, 'He has my nose and David's thighs.' The Spice Girls collectively win the Golden Raspberry, the 'Razzie', for Worst Actress for their performances in *Spice World*.

July 1999 The wedding of the decade: Victoria and David marry at Luttrellstown Castle near Dublin. *OK!* magazine pays an estimated £1 million ($2 million) for the exclusive picture rights. Victoria wears a champagne-coloured Vera Wang-designed wedding dress. A planned honeymoon in the Far East is cancelled when Sir Alex Ferguson refuses to extend David's summer break.

Oct 1999 David and Victoria buy Rowneybury, a mansion in Sawbridgeworth, twenty minutes from Goff's Oak. The media name the £2.5 million ($5 million) property Beckingham Palace. It includes a snooker room, a gym, floodlit tennis courts and an indoor swimming pool. The police tell the Beckhams they have received information about a plot to kidnap Brooklyn.

Feb 2000 Makes her catwalk debut for friend Maria Grachvogel as part of London Fashion Week. Looks exceedingly slim in a pair of lime-green hot pants and matching tight top. 'I was absolutely terrified,' she says.

March 2000 The Spice Girls are presented with a lifetime achievement award at the Brits and are compared to the Beatles. The evening is marred for Victoria by a death threat she has received. She briefly thinks she has been shot when some balloons burst.

Aug 2000 Despite a huge publicity drive, Victoria's first non-Spice Girls' record, 'Out of Your Mind' (with True Steppers and Dane Bowers), reaches only number two, pipped by Spiller's 'Groovejet', featuring Sophie Ellis-Bextor. Tells listeners of G-A-Y radio that David is an 'animal in bed'.

Nov 2000 Another double A-side, 'Holler'/'Let Love Lead the Way', becomes the Spice Girls' ninth and final number one record to date. Their third album, *Forever*, disappointingly manages only number two. Victoria is named 'Best Dressed Female' by *Elle* magazine.

Dec 2000 The Spice Girls call it a day.

Jan 2001 A binman is found guilty of handling stolen property, namely Victoria's luggage, which had gone missing on a British Airways flight. The media marvel at how many designer clothes she packs into her Louis Vuitton suitcases.

Sept 2001 Victoria's autobiography, *Learning to Fly,* is published and sells more than 400,000 copies. She is paid a reported £1 million ($2 million) for the book. Her solo single, 'Not Such an Innocent Girl', peaks at number six in the singles chart. Tells television interviewer Michael Parkinson that her nickname for David is 'Goldenballs'.

Oct 2001 Solo album, *Victoria Beckham,* presenting a new sexy image, reaches number ten in the charts, selling 50,000 copies.

Feb 2002 Second single from the album, 'A Mind of Its Own', sells only 15,000 copies.

May 2002 Victoria and David host a £350,000 ($700,000) Japanese-themed party at Rowneybury to launch England's bid for the World Cup. A charity auction raises close to £1 million ($2 million) for the NSPCC.

June 2002 Announces that her contract with Virgin Records had 'come to a natural end'. Begins negotiations for a £1.5 million ($3 million) deal with Telstar Records.

Sept 2002 Second son, Romeo James, is born at the Portland Hospital. Named 'Best Dressed Woman of 2002' by *Prima* magazine.

Feb 2003 Hosts a private dinner at Rowneybury for the other four Spice Girls at which it is rumoured they discuss re-forming for the first time.

July 2003 David joins Real Madrid in a deal worth £25 million ($50 million). He signs the contract using a pen given to him by Victoria. She returns to Simon Fuller's 19 Entertainment company.

Aug 2003 A giant billboard of Victoria advertising Rocawear goes up in Times Square, New York. She is wearing a brown one-piece with black trim and silver high-heeled shoes.

Sept 2003 David is pictured at a Madrid club with his personal assistant, Rebecca Loos, prompting speculation about the Beckhams' marriage. They issue a statement denying a crisis and saying, 'We are extremely happy together as a family.' Victoria wins 'Most Stylish Female in Music' at the British Style Awards.

Nov 2003 Joins David at Buckingham Palace, where he receives an OBE from the Queen. They finally move into a property in Madrid.

Jan 2004 Victoria's double A-side single, 'This Groove'/'Let Your Head Go', reaches number three in the charts.

April 2004 Rebecca Loos claims in the *News of the World* that she and David had an affair. He says, 'I am very happily married'. Further allegations follow, including one from a Malaysian-born model. Victoria spends her thirtieth birthday with her family in the resort of Verbier. David is in Madrid but is rumoured to have bought her a diamond ring costing £1 million ($2 million). At a party hosted by Simon Fuller, he announces he is proud of his 'beautiful and lovely wife'.

May 2004 Tells *Marie Claire* magazine that David has always been faithful and that 'our marriage is absolutely not a business arrangement'. Prepares to move to Madrid full time with the children.

Nov 2004 Signs up with Rock and Republic to promote a premium line of denim called VB Rocks.

Dec 2004 The Beckhams throw a lavish christening party, reportedly costing £500,000 ($1 million), for Brooklyn and Romeo at Rowneybury. Sir Elton John is one of the godfathers. Victoria is seven months pregnant. Liz Hurley steals the show in an off-the-shoulder, low-cut ivory satin gown.

Feb 2005 Gives birth to a third son, Cruz David, at the Hospital Ruber International in Madrid, again by Caesarean section.

Dec 2005 Attends the party celebrating the civil partnership between Elton John and David Furnish at the pop knight's country home near Windsor.

Jan 2006 Appears on the catwalk at Milan Fashion Week promoting the Roberto Cavalli collection.

Oct 2006 Unveils a new hairstyle, the Pob, which becomes the most iconic cut of the decade. More than 3,000 people queue at Selfridges in London to witness Victoria signing copies of her new style book, *That Extra Half an Inch*, which subsequently sells over 250,000 copies. Enjoys Paris fashion shows with Katie Holmes.

Nov 2006 Attends the celebrity-packed wedding of Tom Cruise and Katie Holmes at Castle Odescalchi near Rome.

March 2007 Acts as guest fashion editor on *Harper's Bazaar* magazine and styles her friend Katie Holmes for her first photo shoot since her marriage.

June 2007 Wins two awards from *Glamour* magazine, one for 'Woman of the Year' and another for 'Entrepreneur of the Year', recognizing her achievements in promoting her fashion brand. Launches dVb denim collection and sunglasses at Saks Fifth Avenue in New York. The Spice Girls reunion tour is announced.

July 2007 David joins LA Galaxy in a deal rumoured to be worth £128 million ($256 million). The Governor of California, Arnold Schwarzenegger, heads the welcoming party at an opening friendly against Chelsea. Victoria wears a fuchsia pink 'Moon Dress' designed by Roland Mouret. The next evening the Beckhams pose at a party with Tom Cruise, Katie Holmes, Will Smith and Jada Pinkett Smith. They have arrived in Hollywood. Move in to a $22-million (£11-million) Beverly Hills mansion. Her arrival in LA is featured in a documentary entitled *Coming to America*.

Sept 2007 Rushes to London from Tokyo, where she is launching the V-sculpt cosmetics line, to be with David when his father, Ted, suffers a heart attack.

Nov 2007 Announced as the new face of Marc Jacobs' 2008 spring collections and says she is 'over the moon' at the prospect. Plays herself on the hit television show *Ugly Betty*, reportedly earning $140,000 (£70,000) for her cameo performance.

Dec 2007 The Spice Girls reunion tour begins in Vancouver. They begin seventeen nights at the O2 Centre in London.

Jan 2008 Tops Mr Blackwell's forty-eighth annual 'Worst Dressed List' with the citation: 'In one skinny mini monstrosity after another, pouty Posh can really wreck 'em.'

Feb 2008 The Spice Girls cut short their reunion tour, cancelling proposed gigs in the Far East and Australia. Victoria says that from now on her business is fashion.

April 2008 Makes her debut as cover girl for the April issue of UK *Vogue*, which devotes twelve pages to her, with stunning pictures by Nick Knight. In an interview with editor-in-chief Alexandra Shulman, she says, 'It's exhausting being fabulous.' David buys her a vineyard in the Napa Valley for her thirty-fourth birthday. The *Sunday Times* Rich List estimates the

Beckhams' fortune at £125 million ($250 million) and ranks Victoria as the fifty-second wealthiest woman in the UK.

May 2008 Launches dVb jeans and sunglasses at Harrods during a promotional visit to the UK. Intends to sell off her recent Spice Girls costumes to raise £1 million ($2 million) for a children's charity.

Sept 2008 Reveals dramatic new pixie hair cut at the New York Fashion Week where she also debuts her first Victoria Beckham fashion collection of twenty exclusive dresses.

Jan 2009 David joins her at Milan Fashion Week before beginning his loan spell with AC Milan. Victoria returns to LA to supervise her children going back to school.

Feb 2009 The critics love the second Victoria Beckham collection unveiled at the Waldorf Towers in New York. Madonna wears one of the dresses to the *Vanity Fair* Oscars party. Victoria says, 'It's phenomenal.'

April 2009 Celebrates her thirty-fifth birthday at Cecconi's restaurant in Beverley Hills. Eva Longoria Parker, Kate Beckinsale, Katie Holmes, Jennifer Lopez and Nicole Ritchie sing 'happy birthday' to Victoria. The girls eat swordfish and drink champagne. David is in Milan.

May 2009 Reportedly paid £15 million to be the new face – and body – of Emporio Armani's raunchy underwear campaign. Pictures of David and Victoria wearing not much appear round the world.

Acknowledgements

Luckily for me, the Beckhams moved to Los Angeles in 2007. It gave me the excuse to cross the Atlantic and visit one of my favourite cities. My thanks to Cliff Renfrew for being my host and sharing his knowledge of LA Galaxy. He is a great fan of Glasgow Rangers, who visited California in May 2007 and beat the Galaxy 1–0 in a friendly. David Beckham, of course, had yet to make his debut.

Victoria and David live in a star-studded part of Beverly Hills, where the homes routinely cost in excess of $10 million (£5 million) and Rod Stewart and Tom Cruise live down the road. It's all a bit different from Victoria's start in life in a small house on an estate in the Hertfordshire town of Hoddesdon. I am grateful for everyone who shared their thoughts and memories of Victoria Adams as she travelled her eventful journey through life. Some wished to remain anonymous because of the very small-world nature of the music business and the rich and powerful circles that now surround Mr and Mrs Beckham. I have probably come across more people asking me not to use their name than in any other book I have written. I have respected their wishes and I hope they enjoy the book. Others included Rory Blain, Mandy Block, Steve Chapman, Kelly Fordham, Jenny Gould, Chris Herbert, Angela Leah, Geoff Marchant, Ruth Moor, Sonia Poulton, Kate Randall, Rick Sky, Joy Spriggs and Greg Stewart.

There have been quite a few books featuring Victoria over the years and I list those that have been of help in the bibliography. Victoria, Geri Halliwell and Mel Brown have all written very entertaining autobiographies and I hope, at some stage, that Melanie Chisholm and Emma Bunton will also share their stories. David Sinclair's biography of the Spice Girls, *Spice Girls Revisited*, is a superb history of the group. I also loved Muff Fitzgerald's *Spiced Up*, an account of his helter-skelter year as the girls' press officer. Victoria seems to produce a documentary about her life almost annually and these make great viewing.

At Simon & Schuster, my thanks to Jonathan Atkins for his commitment to this project, Jo Edgecombe for overseeing production, Lizzie Gardiner for her stunning cover design, Rob Cox and Emma Harrow for looking after marketing and publicity respectively. I am grateful to my editor, Angela Herlihy, for bringing a much needed cool head to proceedings and to Rory Scarfe for expertly taking over the reins when Angela began her maternity leave. Arianne Burnette did a superb job copy-editing my original manuscript. Caroline Turner has been enormously helpful in sorting out my profile on the Simon & Schuster website. My thanks also to Sally Partington for overseeing this new paperback edition.

My agent, Gordon Wise at Curtis Brown, has offered good advice and great enthusiasm. Adele's Typing Works has been supremely efficient in transcribing all my tapes. Adele has also managed to bring me into the twenty-first century with digital technology. The incomparable Madeleine Moore has once again produced a memorable birth chart. I never look at the chart until I have finished the book and am always astonished at how many of her observations match my own research and interpretation. Finally, I am grateful to Jo Westaway for her research, her patient support and encouragement.

Select Bibliography

David Beckham with Tom Watt, *My Side* (Collins Willow, 2003)

Victoria Beckham, *Learning to Fly* (Michael Joseph, 2001)

Victoria Beckham, *That Extra Half an Inch* (Michael Joseph, 2005)

Melanie B, *Catch a Fire* (Headline, 2002)

Muff Fitzgerald, *Spiced Up* (Hodder & Stoughton, 1998)

Geri Halliwell, *If Only* (Bantam, 1999)

Andy Milligan, *Brand It Like Beckham* (Cyan Books, 2004)

David Sinclair, *Spice Girls Revisited* (Omnibus Press, 2007)

Spice Girls, *Forever Spice* (Little, Brown, 1999)

Spice Girls, *Real Life, Real Spice* (Andre Deutsch, 1997)

Picture Credits

Index